HAPPY LIVING!

A Guidebook for Brides

by Evelyn Enright
and Ann Seranne

American Bride Publications
Los Angeles, California

Designed by Sheila Lynch

Manufactured in U.S.A. by
R.R. Donnelley & Sons Company
The Lakeside Press, Chicago, Illinois

Contents

(Continued)

Introduction

THE BEAUTY OF YOUR WEDDING DAY can last a lifetime if you are as anxious to become a good homemaker as you are to be a lovely bride.

This book—a primer on all phases of homemaking is written especially to supply you, the bride, with the guidance you need to build a firm foundation for your domestic future. Here you will find the basic information you should have in order to furnish your first home and cook your first meals.

No doubt you have qualms about your ability to choose china, silver, glassware, linens and kitchen equipment. Then there is the even more overwhelming task of coordinating dozens of separate elements—furniture, fabrics, floorcoverings and accessories—into a harmonious whole. In the first sections of this book, you will find reassuring answers to all your questions about what to buy and how to buy it, from a lowly can opener to a majestic seven-foot sofa. You'll also find expert advice on decorating and color-coordinating from several famous interior designers. Finally, there is a chapter on keeping your home neat, clean and attractive despite a busy schedule of outside activities.

Truly a boon to brides is the cookbook section, written with a sympathetic understanding of the beginner's dilemma. This cookbook really begins at the beginning, leaving no questions unanswered for those of you taking your first timid steps into the culinary world. Here you'll find breakfasts to please a hearty male appetite, yet get you to the office on time. Then you'll progress to simple, appetizing luncheon and dinner menus, taking heart from the fact that even with limited skills, you'll be able to master a wide variety of tempting recipes. As a further boost to your self-confidence, there is a chapter on entertaining your first guests with all the graciousness and charm of the experienced hostesses you've envied.

While you may be dismayed by the stores of knowledge you have yet to acquire about homemaking, remember that as a woman, you are endowed with an instinct for domesticity. There is nothing in life more gratifying than the ability to create and maintain a warm, livable home for someone you love. Now is the time to accept the challenge and begin to reap the rewards of a satisfying new career.

11

Decide on Your Needs

FURNISHING YOUR FIRST HOME is a once-in-a-lifetime experience that rivals the wedding itself as a source of excitement and happy memories. Long after those gay kitchen curtains have outlived their usefulness, you will recall the red letter shopping day when you discovered them after giving up hope of finding exactly what you wanted.

Starting from scratch to make a home for two may seem overwhelming at first, but actually, you are in an enviable position. Except for a chest of drawers and a chair or two you may have inherited from the family attic, you are making a fresh beginning, unencumbered by mistakes of the past and with only the future to consider. This gives you an advantage over someone who already owns a great many household possessions and must find a way to include them in a redecorating project.

To make the most of this wonderful opportunity to get off to the right start, it is necessary to have a complete plan before you buy anything. All the things you need—china, glass, silver, linens, kitchen equipment, furniture, floor coverings, curtains, draperies and accessories—may serve different purposes, but each should be related to the other if your home is to be attractive, well organized and properly budgeted.

Well Begun Is Half Done

"Where do I start?" is the question that comes to mind when facing any sizable project. In this case, the logical way to start is by resisting the urge to buy so much as an ash tray without first having some notion of what kind of table you will place it on—a large, heavy piece of Mexican pottery may be fine in a contemporary setting, but all wrong for the delicacy of Louis XV. How much money you can spend for either the ashtray or the table also depends on the overall plan.

Do all the window shopping you like. An afternoon spent wandering through a department store, where you can see everything all at once, is invaluable in

13

deciding what you want and need, and in determining what styles and colors you really like. But before committing yourself to any purchases, you and your fiancé should take these steps:

1. Work out a budget for now. Few people ever have as much money as they would like to spend, but by using some common sense, you can get the maximum benefit out of what funds you have. Starting with the total figure, decide how much you are going to allow for each room. Then, using the check lists at the end of this chapter, break this figure down, allotting a reasonable amount for each item you plan to buy. Although you may wish to keep these average figures in mind—55 per cent for furniture, 20 per cent for floor coverings, 7 per cent for curtains and draperies, 18 per cent for lamps, linens and accessories; and china, glass, silver and other basics to come primarily from wedding gifts—be very flexible about following this or any other rule of thumb. Include only the essentials in the initial budget. You are going to be married a long time, and it isn't necessary, and often not even desirable, to begin with a completely furnished apartment. In the decorating section of this book, you will find ideas for making the sparsely-furnished home livable while you wait.

2. Work out a budget for the future. During the first few years of marriage you can gradually add the important secondary items that will make your home more comfortable and luxurious—extra chairs, tables, storage pieces and accessories; and the additional china, glass, silver and kitchen equipment necessary for more elaborate entertaining. Estimate the cost of these additions and work out a five-year plan for future buying.

3. Overcome the temptation to lower your standards. You can rush out and buy a whole room full of furniture for no more than it takes to acquire a few good pieces. But in a few years, you'll have nothing but sagging springs and warped wood to call your own, and it will be time to throw everything out and start all over again. When you put your money into quality, you have the nucleus for building something worthwhile. As a general rule, buy the best you can afford in any item that will see heavy service—particularly mattresses, towels, sheets, dishes, flatware and kitchen equipment. Better merchandise gives your home a luxurious tone and is usually cheaper in the long run because it lasts so long. When buying anything for temporary use, of course, it makes good sense to consider price rather than quality.

4. Know your merchandise. You aren't going to become an expert overnight in appraising the value of home furnishings merchandise—there is just too much to know. However, you can learn some basic facts that will enable you to detect signs of quality in materials and workmanship and increase your understanding of why two articles that appear much the same on the surface may differ vastly in price. The remaining chapters in this section are devoted to helping you become a smart shopper.

5. *Decide on a decorating theme.* Your home, like your wardrobe, should be tailored to the way you live and the style you like—formal or informal, contemporary or traditional, or a combination of these elements to suit personalities of many facets. Although for practical purposes a bride should choose her china, glass and silver patterns, linens and kitchen equipment first so she can receive them for shower and wedding gifts, all the categories of home furnishings are inseparable. As soon as possible, you should have a mental picture of the trend your home will take so you can choose everything accordingly. Even the pattern you select in bath towels may differ, depending on whether you plan casual Early American interiors or lean toward the latest in contemporary design.

6. *Seek help if you need it.* The department store bridal registry is a tremendous asset in enabling you to obtain many of the things you need as wedding gifts, thereby striking them from your budget list. In addition, you may want to consult a member of the store decorating staff for advice on some of your problems. Remember, decorators only suggest, they don't try to influence you or change your taste, and their superior knowledge of the field may help you to avoid expensive mistakes.

7. *Plan everything, then tackle one project at a time.* If you were knitting a sweater for the first time, you'd read the instructions through to find out what's involved, then come back and proceed one step at a time. A home should be furnished in the same way. Never take the first step until you know what else is entailed, or you may wind up with beautiful bedroom furniture, but no money to buy a decent mattress set.

Use the check lists that follow to formulate a plan for your new home. Once you know exactly what you need to set up housekeeping, it is much easier to work out a sensible budget. If you don't know what things cost in the style and quality you want, take some shopping trips, read advertisements, and discuss home furnishings with your mother or married friends.

LIVING ROOM	BUY NOW	PROBABLE COST	BUY LATER	PROBABLE COST
Sofa				
Chairs				
End tables				
Cocktail table				
Nest of tables				
Desk				
Desk chair				
Hi-fi cabinets				
Cabinets				
Book shelves				
Rug or carpet				
Window coverings				
Slipcovers				
Lamps				
Accessories:				
TOTAL COST:				

DINING AREA	BUY NOW	PROBABLE COST	BUY LATER	PROBABLE COST
Table				
Chairs				
Buffet				
Hutch				
Tea cart				
Rug or carpet				
Window coverings				
Light fixtures				
Accessories:				
TOTAL COST:				

BEDROOM	BUY NOW	PROBABLE COST	BUY LATER	PROBABLE COST
Mattress set				
Headboard				
Bed frame				
Dresser				
Chest				
Blanket chest				
Night tables				
Chair				
Lamps				
Desk				
Vanity				
Mirror				
Bedspread				
Rug or Carpet				
Window coverings				
Accessories:				
TOTAL COST:				

FLATWARE	MFR.	QTY.	RECD.
PATTERN			
PLACE SETTINGS			
Place knives			
Place forks			
Place or soup spoons			
Salad forks			
Teaspoons			
Butter spreaders			
OTHER USEFUL PLACE PIECES			
Cocktail or oyster forks			
Additional teaspoons			
Iced beverage spoons			
Coffee or cocktail spoons			
Steak knives			
IMPORTANT SERVING PIECES			
Table serving spoons			
Gravy ladle			
Sugar spoon			
Butter serving knife			
Tomato or flat server			
Jelly server			
Pie or cake server			
Salad set			
Cold meat or buffet fork			
Carving set			
Cream or sauce ladle			
INFORMAL FLATWARE PATTERN			
Service for			

GLASSWARE	MFR.	QTY.	RECD.
PATTERN			
Water goblet			
Champagne			
Wine			
Sherbet			
Iced tea			
Tumbler			
Juice			
Sherry			
Liqueur			
Brandy			
Beer			
Pitchers			
Dessert plates			
Ashtrays and urns			
Punch bowl set			
Cruets			
Relish dish			
Decanters			
BAR ACCESSORIES			
Old Fashioned			
Highball			
Martini			
Whiskey sour			
Measuring glass			
Cocktail shaker			
Ice bucket			

HOLLOW WARE	MFR.	PTRN.	RECD.
Well and tree platter			
Vegetable dishes			
Serving trays			
Buffet dishes			
Gravy boat			
Bread tray			
Bowls			
Salts and peppers			
Pitchers			
Tea service			
Coffee service			
Sugar and creamer			
Candlesticks			
Candelabra			
Ashtrays			

DINNERWARE	MFR.	QTY.	RECD.
PATTERN			
PLACE SETTINGS			
Cereal saucers			
Soup plates			
Meat platter			
Salad bowl			
Vegetable dishes			
Cream soups			
Fruit bowls			
Demitasse cups			
Gravy boat			
Chop plate			
Soup tureen			
Coffeepot			
Teapot			
Sugar and creamer			
Set of informal or			
melamine dinnerware			

LINENS	MFR.	CLR.	QTY.	RECD.
TABLE LINENS				
Dinner cloth and napkins				
Extra dinner napkins				
Luncheon cloth and napkins				
Tea cloth and napkins				
Formal mat sets				
Informal mat sets				
Bridge table cloth				
Cocktail napkins				
BATH LINENS				
Bath towels				
Hand towels				
Washcloths				
Fingertip towels				
Guest towels				
Bath mat				
Rug and lid set				
Shower curtain				
BED LINENS				
Flat sheets				
Fitted sheets				
Pillowcases				
Pillows				
Winter-weight blankets				
Summer-weight blankets				
Comforters				
Automatic blankets				
Mattress pads				
Blanket covers				
Pillow covers				
Bedspreads				
Dust ruffles				
KITCHEN LINENS				
Dish towels				
Glass towels				
Dish cloths				
Pot holders				
Appliance covers				
Aprons				

KITCHEN	SIZE	MFR.	RECD.
COLOR SCHEME			
Coffee maker			
Tea kettle			
Covered saucepans (1, 2 and 4 qts.)			
Double boiler			
Small and large skillets			
Egg poacher			
Dutch oven			
Casseroles			
Pressure cooker			
Roasting pan and rack			
Cake pans			
Muffin tins			
Cookie sheets			
Pie pans			
Colander			
Molds			
Mixing bowls			
Canisters			
Measuring spoons, cups			
Wooden spoon			
Utensil set (spoon, fork, ladle, turner, slotted spoon, spatula)			
Carving knife set			
Paring knives			
Bread knife			
Salt and pepper set			
Can opener			
Food chopper			
Cutting board			
Funnel			
Egg beater			
Meat thermometer			
Timer			
Baster			
Pastry brush			
Grater			
Juicer			
Strainer			
Vegetable peeler			
Corkscrew			

KITCHEN ELECTRICS	SIZE	MFR.	RECD.
Toaster			
Coffee maker			
Mixer			
Fry pan			
Blender			
Sandwich and waffle grill			
Deep fryer			
Rotisserie-Broiler			
Knife sharpener-Can opener			
Hot tray			

MAINTENANCE	QTY.	MFR.	RECD.
Vacuum cleaner			
Floor polisher			
Carpet sweeper			
Brooms			
Wet and dry mops			
Dustpan and brush			
Dusters			
Pails			
Steam iron			
Ironing board			

Your Silver, China and Glass

RANKING HIGH ON THE LIST of very important occasions will be the first time you set a table for two, the night the whole family comes for dinner and the first party you give in your new home. Every day of your married life, in fact, will bring opportunities to invite admiration from your husband, family and friends for your ability to set an attractive table and make even the simplest meal a pleasant interlude rather than a routine occurrence.

Few things say as much about you as the china, glass, silver and other table accessories in your trousseau and the manner in which you use them. These are personal possessions to enjoy for many years to come, so make your selections with great care. Although almost all china, silver and fine glassware patterns are pretty to behold, certain designs are much more appropriate for your own taste than others. It's a wise bride who does her shopping early when she is unhurried and free from the pressures of last-minute wedding planning.

The Bridal Registry

Like anything worth having, complete services of fine china, sterling and glass are worth waiting for. Gradually adding to your service through the years, in fact—a set of goblets on your anniversary, a china vegetable dish for Christmas and another sterling place setting for your birthday—keeps the excitement and fun of trousseau building with you long after your wedding gown has been packed away. But for now, you'll want to have enough of the basic pieces so you can start setting pretty tables right away, and if you take full advantage of the bridal gift registry service, you can make sure of getting what you need.

The department store gift registry consultant is a staunch ally. With your cooperation, she can see to it that there are no disappointments beneath those yards of white ribbon and tissue paper. As soon as possible after the engagement is official, you should spend some time with her and have your gift preferences in tablewares, linens and other household items recorded on a card to be kept in her file. When friends and relatives begin calling the store to find out what you would like to have, she offers suggestions and then checks off the items they purchase for you.

You and your mother, of course, are responsible for spreading the word to as many people as you possibly can that they can learn what you want by contacting the registry. If gifts you have checked on the preference card arrive from other sources, you should alert the consultant so she can keep her records straight and see that you get a balanced selection of gifts. If you already have four place settings of your china pattern but only one in sterling, for example, she'll inform people of this fact and try to build up your silver service.

Since silver, china and glassware are the traditional favorite categories of wedding gifts—and the ones you are probably most anxious to receive—it's best to make these choices the starting point for your household trousseau shopping. But stop before you shop. In making any important purchase, the first step is to find out all you can about how to recognize quality and appreciate the beauty of what you are buying.

SELECTING YOUR SILVER

The day when a dowry came with every bride has long since passed, but the delightful custom of receiving silver as a gift from one's family lingers on. In the past, fathers actually had the bride's dowry of silver and gold currency melted down, then crafted into household objects. The motive was purely practical—stolen money was hard to recover, while utensils were often found and returned to the owner. Today, parents give silver for a different reason—they want to give their daughters a good start toward assembling complete flatware and hollow ware services. Usually, the parents give several place settings, then let friends and relatives fill in with additional place settings and serving pieces.

The basic setting of six pieces, designed to suit average needs, includes a knife, fork, salad/dessert fork, teaspoon, place spoon (soup/cereal/dessert) and butter spreader.

Sterling Flatware

Sterling silver, a precious metal that has enduring value, is required by law to contain 92.5 per cent pure silver, with some copper added to harden and increase its wearing qualities. It comes in two finishes—a bright, high polish that is most often used, and a duller surface known as a butler finish. Terms you will hear that pertain to the beauty of silver are oxidizing, which means the darkening process applied to the design to give it rich contrasts; and patina, or the interesting surface silver acquires after is has been in use.

When buying sterling flatware, check the feel and balance of each piece in your hand as though you were actually using it. Be sure the shanks are strong and the fork tines smooth.

Monogrammed Silver

Because silver is so rich in tradition and sentiment, many brides like to add the very personal touch of a monogram. The type of monogram that is appropriate depends on the pattern itself. A single letter—your married or maiden name initial—may be best if the pattern is ornate. If you prefer three initials, these variations are correct—M E S for Mary Ellen Smith, bride of John Doe; M S D for Mary Smith Doe; or an M and J with a D centered underneath for Mary and John Doe.

Letters may be the same size, or one large and two smaller letters. In the latter case, the large initial is always in the middle and it stands for the surname —small M, large D, small S in that order reads Mary Smith Doe.

Silver Plate

Plated silver is similar in appearance to sterling but without its lasting qualities. It is made by coating a base metal, usually a nickel alloy, with pure silver by the process of electroplating. The base metal may be thinly or thickly coated with silver, depending on how long the piece is submerged in the silver and how often the process is repeated. The thicker the coating, naturally, the longer the wear. Silver plated flatware may last anywhere from a few years to a life-

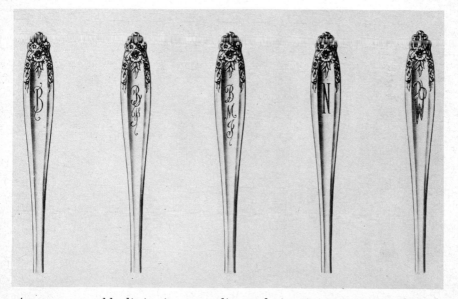

A monogram adds distinction to sterling and gives it a more personal touch. You may have either one, two or three initials. If the pattern is very ornate, it is best to omit monogramming or place it on the back.

When and How to Use Your Flatware

THE BASIC PLACE SETTING

THE REGULAR TEASPOON
—perfect for fruits, some vegetables, desserts, fruit cocktails, coffee, tea, cereals, and bouillon.

PLACE FORK
—for all but formal meals; for fish course in formal dinner. (Luncheon fork, smaller than place size, available in some patterns.)

PLACE KNIFE
—for all but formal meals; for fish course in formal dinner. (Luncheon knife, smaller than place size, available in some patterns.)

SPREADERS
—or *Individual Butter Knife* (Hollow or Flat Handle) for butter, on the sandwich tray, for cheeses, relishes, jams and jellies, for hors d'oeuvres, on cheese trays.

INDIVIDUAL SALAD OR PASTRY FORK
—salad, fish, pies, pastries, cold meats.

PLACE SPOON
—for soup, cereal, dessert, and for use as a small serving piece.

OTHER PLACE PIECES

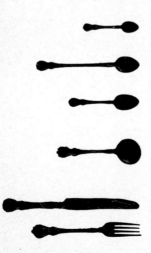

COCKTAIL OR OYSTER FORK
—seafood cocktail, fruit cocktail, lobster.

COFFEE OR COCKTAIL SPOON
—after-dinner coffee, baby's feeding spoon, blender for Old Fashioneds.

ICED BEVERAGE SPOON
—iced coffee, iced tea, fruit drinks, milk shakes, highball mixer, and parfait.

SMALL TEASPOON
—for fruit cocktails, sherbets, sugar spoon for a small sugar bowl, junior spoon.

CREAM SOUP SPOON
—soups in dishes or bowls, for serving sauces.

DINNER KNIFE AND FORK
—essential to the formal dinner and whenever more than one knife and fork are needed. The fork also acts as a serving fork—companion to the tablespoon.
(Many people prefer eight-piece place settings since formal entertaining demands the larger knife and fork.)

time and can vary greatly in price. The best you can afford is the most sensible choice.

Better qualities of plate are reinforced at points of greatest wear. Insist on this when you buy, since it is very important to the life of your flatware. Reinforcing may be done by an inlaid process—an extra block of silver is inlaid at wear points—or by an overlaid process, in which wear points are given an extra coating of silver over the plating. Other guides to quality are fine design, smooth edges, good balance and an even application of the silver.

Stainless Steel

As a second set of flatware for everyday use, stainless steel has great popularity. Patterns are becoming increasingly varied, and you will find many handsome traditional designs as well as the justly popular contemporary styles. Since grades of stainless range from poor to excellent, look carefully for evidence of quality. Check rims of spoon bowls and tips of fork tines for smoothness, and see that all surfaces are free of pit marks. Because of its great strength, stainless steel flatware need not be as heavy as silver, but neither should it be tinny, and backs should be finished with the same care as the fronts. You have a choice of two finishes—a mirror effect and a satin finish.

Hollow ware Selections

Hollow ware, as opposed to flatware, is just what the word implies—tableware that is hollow inside, such as a coffee pot or bowl. You may choose hollow ware in sterling, silver plate, pewter, stainless steel and other metals. Silver plate is extremely popular because it goes well with your sterling flatware and is much less costly than sterling. For serving and entertaining you will need

CARVING PIECES

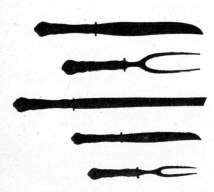

ROAST CARVING KNIFE
—for large roasts, fowl, and ham.

ROAST CARVING FORK
—to hold roasts and fowl skillfully.

SLICER
—sharp and slim and long, essential for thin-slicing roasts.

STEAK CARVING KNIFE
—for steaks and small roasts, fowl, and other meats such as sliced ham.

STEAK CARVING FORK
—for use with either Carving Knife as a server when roasts or fowl have been sliced or carved.

SERVING PIECES

TABLE OR SERVING SPOON
—serves salads, vegetables, berries, fruits, and desserts.

PIERCED TABLE OR SERVING SPOON
—for vegetables or fruits served in their juices.

GRAVY LADLE
—serves sauces, gravies, or dressings from either boat-shaped dishes or round bowls.

COLD MEAT OR BUFFET FORK
—serves cold meats, chops, and food served on toast, or a variety of platter salads.

TOMATO OR FLAT SERVER
—can be used for tomatoes, cucumbers, eggs, asparagus on toast, or for platter salads.

SALAD OR SERVING SPOON
—for fruits, berries, desserts, salads, vegetables. It can be used as a spare serving spoon.

BUTTER SERVING KNIFE
—for use on the butter plate in informal dining and on the cheese tray; for serving certain jams.

SUGAR SPOON
—for the sugar bowl and for small bowls of mayonnaise or sauce.

CREAM OR SAUCE LADLE
—ladles gravy, stews, liquid dishes, and dressings, along with cream sauces.

JELLY SERVER
—serves cream cheese, preserves, jam, relishes, jellies, and marmalades.

LEMON FORK
—serves lemon slices.

BON BON OR NUT SPOON
—for nuts, candies and some canapés.

OLIVE OR PICKLE FORK
—in addition to serving olives and pickles, it doubles as a lemon fork and butter pick.

SALAD-BOWL SERVERS
—for graceful efficient service of tossed salads. (Note: the Cold Meat Fork and the Salad Spoon make a small salad set.)

CHEESE SERVING KNIFE
—serves brick cheese, and cheese or similar spreads, and can be used for molded jellies.

PIE OR CAKE SERVING KNIFE
—essential for cutting and serving pies and cakes, and for aspics and frozen desserts.

RELISH OR JAM SPOON
—for relishes, jams, jellies, preserves, and useful as a spoon for serving mayonnaise.

SUGAR TONGS
—for use in the sugar bowl or on the candy dish.

certain basic pieces, depending on what china and crystal hollow ware items you have. Workmanship and quality are important—be sure to check for smooth, evenly-rounded edges, balance and substantial non-tilt bases.

CHOOSING YOUR CHINA

The word "china" in current use loosely includes all categories of dinnerware such as porcelain, bone china, stoneware, earthenware, pottery, ceramic and glass compositions and many others. The qualities of each vary greatly, depending on the raw material used and the degree of firing.

This festive board achieves a picnic table look indoors. The melamine dinnerware features plates with flowered borders and plain cups and bowls.

Most brides plan on having two sets of dinnerware—fine china for occasions that demand the best, and either earthenware, pottery or molded plastic for informal use.

China Or Porcelain

The finest dinnerware you can buy is china or porcelain. Both are made of highly refined clays and minerals which are fired at such an intense heat that the components melt and fuse into a strong translucent body. This process is called vitrification, and the color may vary depending on the clay used. English bone china, because of its bone ash content, is characterized by a pure white translucency. American china is famous for an ivory body achieved by a special hardening agent.

Despite its fragile appearance, genuine china is tougher and more resistant to chipping and breaking than other ceramics. The glaze will not crackle, and even if it does chip, its nonporous body will not absorb food stains.

When you shop, you will naturally be influenced most by pattern and color, but be sure to keep these points in mind when buying fine china:

1. Hold a plate in front of the light. You should be able to see your hand through it.

2. Balance a plate on three fingers and tap with a pencil. Listen for a bell-like ring.

3. Run a finger around the rim of a cup to be sure it is perfectly smooth. Test the rim underneath a plate or cup in the same way to see if it is smooth and glazed.

5. Examine the cup handle. Is it balanced from top to bottom and easy to grasp in the hand?

6. Look at the color. Good china is clear and gleaming without a suggestion of muddiness.

7. Take a critical look at the pattern. If the workmanship is good, the design will be neatly executed without flaws or breaks.

8. Examine the saucer. The depression should hold the cup securely.

9. Lift the plate. It should feel light enough to grace a formal table yet have a feeling of strength at the same time.

China is usually purchased in five-piece place settings—dinner, salad and butter plates; cup and saucer. Eight place settings will fill your basic requirements, plus four additional dinner plates which come in handy when you are having buffet-style meals. It's also a good idea to have some extra cups.

Exotic is the word for this color-rich table setting. The china, glass and silver patterns are the essence of tasteful simplicity, providing the perfect foil for imaginative backgrounds of your own creation.

You will also want some lovely and practical serving pieces—covered vegetable dishes, platters, bowls, sugar and creamer sets, tea or coffee pots. These may be selected to match your place settings or add a note of contrast with a different pattern.

Earthenware

Earthenware is opaque, porous, fully glazed and in its finer forms closely resembles china. The clay used is less refined and fired at a lower temperature, resulting in a softer ware not as durable as china but stronger than pottery. Patterns are characterized by brighter colors and applied with a heavier hand than is typical of their china counterparts. Thus dinnerware made of earthenware is more informal in appearance. Crazing and discoloration can be caused by extremes in temperature, and chipping is far more frequent than in china.

Pottery

The heaviest of the three principal types of dinnerware is pottery, and like earthenware, it is opaque and porous. It may be glazed or unglazed and is sometimes uneven in shape and texture. Unrefined clays and low firing, combined with freehand designs applied in bright colors, give it a very informal and at times even primitive appearance. It is not very durable, but attractively low prices make it quite suitable for informal use.

Molded Plastic

Plastic dinnerware, because of its practical qualities, has become extremely popular for casual use. Dishes made of melamine, a molded plastic, are virtually unbreakable, can be placed in the dishwasher without deterioration and are resistant to cracking and chipping. Quality varies considerably, depending on weight and the care used in finishing. Some of the better lines offer such advantages as stain-resistant cups.

BUYING GLASSWARE

One of the most ancient artistic materials known to man is glass—a mixture of silica-sand, lime and other substances heated to a fluid state, then blown, pressed or drawn to obtain the desired shape. Blown glass can be made by hand, meaning someone actually breathes air into it; or by machine, in which the

Contemporary classics, these china and silver patterns are versatile enough to suit a variety of moods. For festive occasions, a touch of whimsy is in order—tiny orange candles, flowers tucked in a napkin ring and a butterfly nestled on the napkin.

Fine, hand-blown stemware is often at its prettiest when no decoration is added. The beauty of this pattern is in the shape of the glass itself.

liquid is shaped by compressed air. Pressed glass is put in a mold and forced into shape by a plunger. Drawing is the process of wrapping the molten glass around a core that is later removed.

While these are the basic methods and materials, glassmakers employ so many variations that a lifetime could be devoted to the study of their art. By changing the mixture of raw materials, the shape and the means of applying decorating, creators of fine glassware have kept this ancient craft constantly new, exciting and fascinating to follow.

When glass is made from a mixture that contains a substantial amount of lead, the resultant product is called crystal. Lead imparts a clear, brilliant sparkle. Crystal can be pressed or drawn as well as blown—the ingredients, not the method of manufacture, are the determining factor. The word crystal is also used to distinguish between glass that is clear as opposed to glass that is tinted in various colors, so that a sales person may describe a certain pattern as available in red, blue, amethyst and crystal.

Start with The Basics

You will no doubt want to own fine stemware, plus additional less expensive glasses to go with your casual dinnerware. Glasses may be purchased in complete sets of one item—eight goblets, for example—or in place settings.

For a minimum basic place setting, you might want to have the goblet, medium wine and sherbet. The wine glass can double for juice and the sherbet for champagne. Later, you can gradually build up your service to include other frequently used glasses. On the opposite page is a complete service that will equip you for every occasion, from formal to casual.

GOBLET
Water

SHERBET
Appetizers,
desserts,
champagne

ICED TEA
Iced tea,
milk,
water

COCKTAIL
Cocktails,
desserts

CORDIAL
Liqueurs

JUICE
Appetizer,
fruit juice,
whiskey sour

9-OUNCE
TUMBLER
Water,
milk

WINE

12-OUNCE
TUMBLER
Water,
iced tea

PLATE
Desserts,
salads

DESSERT BOWL
Appetizers,
desserts,
salads,
finger bowls

Look for Quality

Much of our fine stemware is blown crystal—thin, clear and elegant in appearance—and it is usually blown by hand. To be sure you are getting the best, look for these signs of quality:

1. *Examine the shape.* There should be a pleasing symmetry between bowl and stem. Ornamentation, if any, should be subtle—the glass itself and the beauty of its shape must not be overshadowed.

2. *Look for clarity and luster.* Good glass sparkles. You will find tiny bubbles in any glass, but in fine crystal these marks are relatively few.

3. Check the edges for smoothness. Run your finger along bowl and base. Inferior glass may have scratches, beads or other irregularities.

4. Listen to the ring. Blown crystal resounds with a clear, bell-like tone when tapped with a pencil.

Many lovely stemware patterns are made of pressed glass, the best of which are done by hand. Pressed glass, too, should have a balanced shape, luster and smoothness. In addition, inspect the finish to be sure there are no prominent mold marks or ridges—these are removed from better glassware by reheating after the mold has been removed. Test the weight of the glass. It should feel strong and substantial.

Two patterned and one plain is the rule followed in this elegant setting—ornate sterling, a classic geometric-patterned china and simple stemware.

COORDINATING PATTERNS

Your china, glass and silver will spend the rest of their days in each other's company, so be sure all three patterns are compatible before you play the matchmaker.

Bringing the right designs together really isn't difficult at all if you follow a few simple rules of good taste. Keep uppermost in your mind the fact that over-decoration is never desirable. You wouldn't wear a floral print dress, matching fabric handbag and big flowered hat. Neither should you choose elaborate floral china, glass and silver patterns and pride yourself on the fact that everything matches.

Instead, strive for a balance between decoration and simplicity—either two decorated patterns and one plain, or one decorated and two plain. Consider, too, what kind of linens and accessories you may be using. Centerpieces and interestingly textured or patterned cloths are added attention-getters and you don't want the overall effect to be too busy.

Contrast provides a change of pace that is pleasing to the eye. Let that ornate china pattern show off to advantage against simple flatware and conservative stemware.

When choosing two patterns, look for some kinship between them, but not an exact match. Instead of a rose etched on a glass to go with your rose-strewn china, pick up just the leaf in the pattern, or a swirl motif reminiscent of curving flower stems. Try to catch the spirit, not the letter, of the design. Examine the shape and flow of decoration on a plate, then look for a similar feeling in silver or glass.

The Shopping Trip

There is only one way to buy china, glass and silver, and that is by seeing them next to each other. The sales person in any of these departments will be glad to arrange the pieces in model place settings once you have some idea of what you want. She may even offer suggestions on patterns that coordinate especially well, but you must make the final decisions. Since most of us learn best by example, spend some time studying photographs, windows and in-store displays that feature table settings. When you see patterns that strike you as particularly appealing, analyze them to find out why.

HOW TO SET A TABLE

Once you experience the thrill of owning silver, china and glassware, you'll want to be sure of using them correctly. It's easy to master the established rules of etiquette because they are nothing more than common sense—everything is put in place for maximum convenience.

The diagrams shown, illustrating service for a typical dinner menu, may be adapted to breakfast, luncheon or dinner for all but strictly formal occasions.

MENU: Shrimp Cocktail
Soup
Main Course
Salad
Dessert and Coffee

Beginning
of
Meal

Ready
for
Main
Course

Ready
for
Dessert
and
Beverage

The place plate—or service plate, if you are using one—goes in the center, butter plate to the left and water goblet to the right. If wine is being served, place the wine glass to the right of the goblet. Flatware is then arranged in order of use, starting from the outside. All forks go on the left except the cocktail or oyster fork. Spoons and knives line up on the right. The napkin is placed to the left of the forks and may be folded in an oblong, square or triangle. The butter spreader belongs on the butter plate, either across the top as shown or at the right side, but never centered on the plate. Steak knives, when included, are always in addition to place knives and not a substitute for them. Both belong on the table, with the steak knife to the right of the other.

Before the guests sit down, you may have the first course—in this case, shrimp cocktail—on the table. Have a saucer under it and set it on the service plate. Leave the service plates on the table for the soup course, then pick them up with the soup bowls or cups and bring in the dinner plates for the main course.

Salad may be served next as a separate course, although some hostesses prefer to combine it with the main course. In serving dessert, you may bring the silver in on the dessert plate after the main course is cleared away, or place it above the center at the beginning of the meal.

The Formal Dinner

Aside from the fact that more pieces generally go into the setting because more courses and wines are served, there are certain variations in custom for formal service. The butter plate and spreader are not used, since butter is not served. The napkin usually goes in the center of the plate and dessert silver is always brought in on the dessert plate. Wine glasses, like flatware, are placed in order of use. A dinner cloth, usually white, is always used whereas place mats are a popular alternative at informal meals.

Buffet Style

Serving meals buffet style is particularly popular with newlyweds who have many social obligations to repay and often lack the facilities for inviting several guests to a sit-down dinner. There are no set rules for arranging the table except that logic should prevail, with artistic effect a close second. Before the guests arrive, do a trial run to be sure you have made it as simple as possible for diners to make their way from one end of the table to the other, first picking up their plates and then helping themselves to whatever they wish. Then appraise the table to be sure it looks attractive. Since food contributes a good deal of color and interest, distribute it rather than bunch it at one end. Never stack flatware—place the pieces parallel to each other.

Your Trousseau of
Table, Bed and Bath Linens

Y OU ARE TWICE BLESSED when you own things that are as beautiful as they are useful. Since table, bed and bath linens belong in this category, they are an important part of your household trousseau.

Linens are on display so much of the time that it's a good idea to consider them decorative accessories. From the table cloths brought out only on special occasions to the towels you use every day, think as much about color, pattern and texture as you do about thread count, washability and wearing qualities.

A single visit to the linen department, where color spills forth from shelves and counters like jewels overflowing from a pirate's chest, is enough to convince anyone that a towel has a contribution to make beyond its original purpose of absorbing moisture, and a linen cloth does more than protect the table it covers.

Table Linens

To a homemaker who thinks of serving meals as a creative part of her household routine, a good selection of handsome table linens is essential. Linens are the all-important variables that enable you to achieve dozens of different effects even though you are using the same one or two sets of china, glass and silver every time. Just as you would change the mood of your living room by painting the walls a different color, so can you change the table cloth as the basis for varying the theme at mealtime. Your choice of a cloth is important in determining the degree of formality or informality of the occasion and the colors to be used in centerpieces or other accessories.

On the most formal occasions, white linen damask with napkins to match is the traditional favorite of long standing, with lace or combinations of linen and lace ranking next in popularity. For correct size, measure the table and allow an equal drop on all four sides of from fifteen to eighteen inches. A short overhang—from eight to twelve inches—is considered luncheon size. The cloth you select should have a French hem and be luxurious to the touch so that it is a fitting companion for your best table accessories.

For informal use, the cloth may be of any suitable fabric or color. In linens alone, the variety of weaves is inspiring to the imagination and ranges from the finer weaves that look best in delicate pastels to the heavier textures seen in bright solids or gay prints. Cotton, rayon and organdy are also fresh and pretty. Delightful, too, are the unconventional ideas you may devise, like the occasional use of felt or drapery fabrics rather than the usual table coverings.

Entertaining at a Swiss fondue is the kind of fun that calls for a lighthearted background—like pine cones and felt bows tied on the chandelier and oranges as candle holders. The tablecloth is a printed drapery fabric.

In lieu of a regular cloth, place mats are preferred by many people for casual settings. Today, place mats are correct around the clock and offer the advantages of being colorful, inexpensive and easy to launder. There are sets tailored to every use from breakfast to dinner, in materials ranging from the informality of straw or burlap to the more conventional linens, organdies and other fabrics.

What To Buy

Personal preference and household routine differ so much that it's best to make up your own list of required linens rather than be guided by what others have done. Many homemakers like to have several table cloths in both dinner and luncheon sizes, while others find it desirable to make place mats the mainstay of their linen supply. The following represents a basic supply for daily use and a moderate amount of entertaining.

> 1 good dinner cloth with 12 large napkins
>
> 2 luncheon cloths with napkins
>
> 2 easily laundered breakfast cloths or place mat sets with napkins
>
> 2 extra place mat sets appropriate for luncheon or dinner
>
> 1 bridge table cloth
>
> 12 pretty cocktail napkins

BED LINENS

In shopping for bed linens, you must first decide on the bed size—twin, standard double or extra width. Sheets and blankets are available for all these sizes, but more limited as to color and pattern in the extra widths.

For a combination of excellent wear and luxuriousness, most brides prefer sheets and pillowcases made of percale, meaning they are woven of combed cotton yarns. The finer the weave, the softer and more luxurious the sheet. This is where the term "count" comes from—counting the number of yarns per square inch. Thus a 220-count percale sheet will be more finely woven and softer than a 180-count. Especially fine is pima, an extra-long staple cotton which has extraordinary wearing qualities, making high-count percales more durable than ever before.

Also popular and very durable are muslin sheets, more loosely woven and of heavier cotton threads than percale, and with a correspondingly lower thread count. They are coarser to the touch and naturally less expensive.

To judge quality, hold the sheet up to a light and look for uneven yarns, knots and bunches. These are weak spots and indicate that the sheet will not be able to withstand heavy wear. If you choose a reputable brand name and refuse to be led astray by questionable "bargains," it is really not necessary to examine the merchandise.

Contour sheets are a good investment, since they cut down on bedmaking time and don't really have to be ironed. Be sure to have the exact measurements of your mattress so they will fit properly.

In selecting patterned sheets, don't go overboard on demure prints without consulting your fiancé—your he-man may not share your enthusiasm for those rosebuds. In any case, include some co-ordinating stripes or solids and a number of plain white sheets and pillowcases as well.

Buying Blankets

Blanket warmth comes from the thickness of the fabric and the height of the nap. The nap is formed by thousands of little curls which make air pockets —these are the real secret of keeping the warmth in. Your blankets will keep you warm just so long as the nap wears, so quality is the best investment. Remember, it's air, not weight, that creates warmth, so don't be mislead into thinking a very heavy blanket is best. Two lighter blankets are better than one heavy covering because there will be a layer of air between them.

The best blankets you can buy are wool, synthetics such as Orlon and Acrilan, or a mixture of wool and synthetics. The synthetics launder especially well and are strong and durable. A new process for wool, called Dylanizing, has likewise made it machine washable and dryable.

When you buy a blanket, look for close weave and deep nap. Check the binding for evenly matched stitching. A nylon binding will give you the most wear resistance. Blankets without bindings, although less decorative, are also practical because bindings often show wear first.

Automatic blankets can be judged in the same way as others except for the mechanism, and for that a reputable brand name is your protection. Although seemingly expensive, electric blankets are a good buy—one of these provides all the warmth you need for normal conditions.

TOWEL TIPS

The best towels are made from fine-yarn terry cloth, and here again the count—number of threads per inch—is indicative of wearing qualities. Loops are the important factor in absorbency, for they act as tiny sponges that soak up moisture and also help to stimulate circulation.

Towels in the $4 to $5 price range for bath size are the best buy for your money in terms of wear, absorbency and luxury. These better grades also offer a plus factor in size that is important to your husband—men like extra-large, extra-absorbent bath towels.

AVERAGE LINEN REQUIREMENTS

In selecting the linens you will need for bed and bath, bear in mind that you will require no less than one set in use, one in the laundry and a spare on hand in the linen closet. Aim for this as a basic supply:

6 sheets for each bed (3 white and/or pastel fitted sheets)
    (3 printed or plain top sheets)
6 pillow cases
2 winterweight blankets
       or
1 automatic blanket
       or
1 winterweight blanket plus 1 comforter
2 summerweight blankets
2 mattress pads
2 pillow covers
12 bath towels (6 each of two harmonizing colors or
    4 printed towels and 4 each in two harmonizing colors)
12 hand towels
16 washcloths
12 fingertip or fancy guest towels
2 bath mats
1 shower curtain
2 rugs

Equipping the Kitchen

THANKS TO GLEAMING GADGETS and efficient electric servants, today's bride comes closer to being a queen than a slave in her kitchen. But meal preparation is still far removed from the push-button stage. To get the most out of time and labor-saving devices, you have to equip your kitchen according to the amount of space available, the type of meals you'll be making and the demands made on your time by other activities.

How much cooking are you really going to do the first year or two of marriage? Will you have time for such frills as home-baked rolls and pastry? If you plan to continue working, the chances are you'll adhere to simple menus, relying on prepared foods as shortcuts. This means your equipment need not be elaborate. If cooking is a labor of love, on the other hand, you'll want all the intriguing tools you can get your hands on.

On the next few pages, you'll find two lists—the first containing items considered essential for most people, and the second adding useful extras that are nice to have. Adapt these lists to your own requirements by going over them and deciding which items you would find most useful.

When buying kitchen equipment or listing your wedding gift preferences, think about style as well as utility. More and more, cookware and utensils are being given the glamour treatment in color and design so that it's easy to make your kitchen a cheerful, pleasant place in which to work. There are dual-purpose advantages to pretty kitchen wares, too—some pots and pans are so attractive you can bring them right to the table and serve from them, and others are perfect for displaying as decorative accessories when not in use.

HOW TO BUY POTS AND PANS

Aluminum, stainless steel, copper and cast iron are the metals most widely used in the manufacture of pots and pans. In addition, oven-to-tableware made of various other materials is becoming increasingly popular. Here are some facts you should know about each.

Aluminum. A durable, lightweight metal, aluminum heats quickly and evenly, with no hot spots to cause burning or sticking of foods to the pan. Therefore, it is a good choice for both baking and top-of-the-stove cooking. If your pots and pans are of fairly heavy gauge aluminum, they will resist warping and denting and give years of service. Extra-thick aluminum pots with tight-fitting covers give the nutritional advantages of waterless cooking, in which more vitamins and minerals are preserved. Aluminum does become discolored from certain minerals in food and water, particularly in areas where water is hard, but these stains may be removed easily.

Stainless Steel. Pots and pans of stainless steel are more expensive, but practically indestructible, extremely light in weight and easy to clean. This metal performs best when used to cook foods in water or other liquids. It is less effective for frying because steel can develop hot spots that cause food to brown unevenly. By using steel with another metal—copper or aluminum bottoms, most generally—many manufacturers have combined the best features of two materials.

Copper. Because this is such an attractive metal, homemakers who plan to display pots and pans invariably choose copper, or stainless steel with copper bottoms. Copper is expensive but extremely durable. It heats evenly and conducts heat faster than other metals. Although it does require special care after each use to retain its beauty, there are cleansers which keep copper bright with little effort.

Cast Iron. The slow, even heat provided by cast iron makes this a material gourmet cooks insist upon for certain dishes. Cast iron is inexpensive and durable, but requires care to retard rust spots. Many cookware lines now feature cast iron coated with colorful enamel finishes that are a bright addition to the kitchen and may be brought right to the table for serving.

Ceramics. Porcelain, glass, pottery and other materials offer the advantage of being able to cook, serve and sometimes even freeze food in the same attractive pot. New colors and designs are constantly being added to an already impressive selection. Some cook-and-serve ware may be used for top-of-the-range cooking, while other types are meant to be used only in the less intense heat of the oven. To derive the maximum benefit from owning this kind of cookware, it is important to know what temperature extremes it will withstand.

Kitchen Cutlery

One of the most important tools of all is the kitchen knife, which is wielded on an average of thirty-two times a day for slicing, paring, trimming, coring and spreading. Good stainless steel cutlery can last a lifetime if treated with care.

Any knife will stay sharp longer if a cutting board is used—hard porcelain

BASIC KITCHEN EQUIPMENT

1. Canister Set
2. 4½-qt. Dutch Oven
3. 10″ Fry Pan with Cover
4. 6-8 Cup Coffee Maker
5. Tea Kettle
6. Combination Cooker
7. 3-Quart Covered Sauce Pan
8. 2-Quart Covered Sauce Pan
9. 1-Quart Covered Sauce Pan
10. 10½″ Chicken Fryer
11. 8″ Fry Pan
12. Automatic Toaster

13. Portable Mixer
14. Broiler Fry Pan
15. 3-qt. Colander
16. Measuring Spoons
17. Ladle, Pierced Spoon, Pancake Turner, Spatula, Potato Masher, Fork
18. Strainers
19. Juicer
20. Vegetable Scraper
21. Parer
22. Kitchen Scissors

23. Rubber Scraper
24. Measuring Cups
25. Beater
26. Can Opener
27. Wooden Spoons
28. Cookie Sheet
29. Cutlery Set
30. Mixing Bowls
31. 9″ Pie Pan
32. Measuring Cup
33. Square Baking Pan
34. Roasting Pan

enamel, glass, china or metal surfaces are damaging. Never use a knife for opening bottles, cutting string or other purposes for which it was not intended. For sharpening, a rough-textured sharpening stone is recommended.

These knives will prove most useful in your kitchen:

1. *Paring knives* with short blades, 2½" to 3½" long, and sharp and tapered points. Use the tapered point for peeling and slicing lemons; the sharp point for preparing salad garnishes and many other uses.

2. *A utility knife* with slender blade, 5" to 7" long, necessary when the paring knife is too small. Use for halving and trimming fruits and vegetables, cutting sandwiches, boning meats, dicing vegetables.

3. *A French knife* or chef's knife, with an angled blade 8" to 10" long, is perfect for carving hot roasts or mincing small quantities of onions.

4. *A narrow slicer* with a flexible 7" to 12" blade is best for slicing bread, serving poultry or cutting melon rings.

5. *A carving knife* with stiff blade, 9" or longer, for carving roasts or fowl.

6. *A boning knife*, 6" long, for boning ham, leg of lamb and other cutting operations.

7. *A light cleaver*, 6" to 7" long, for cutting joints, lobsters and poultry and for mincing.

8. *A serrated edge bread knife* for bread, cakes and pastries.

9. *A frozen food cutter* with deeply serrated edge for cutting while food is still frozen.

Small Appliances

Putting electricity to work is the next best thing to having a full-time maid in the kitchen, and since most of us react to mechanical gadgets like small boys do to new trains, shopping for appliances is a delightful pastime.

If you were hiring a maid, you'd find out what she is capable of doing and then decide whether or not she is the best person for the job. Select appliances in the same way, starting with those that can save you the most time and effort, then adding the luxuries you might use less frequently but would still like to have. Bear in mind that any appliance is much more useful when you can keep it handy rather than having to store it away on a top shelf.

To help you decide, here are some facts about small appliances most popular with brides:

Coffee Maker: It shuts off automatically when the brew is just right, thus putting an end to boil-overs and other catastrophes of coffee making. Size is a major consideration—a 14-cup or larger pot is fine if you want it mostly for entertaining, but the smaller sizes are best for daily use.

Toaster: New models incorporate special features, such as a thermostatic control for reheating cold toast. Designs are so compact that four-slice toasters now take up little more room than two-slice models.

NICE-TO-HAVE KITCHEN EQUIPMENT

35. Square Baking Pan
36. Automatic Sandwich Toaster and Waffle Maker
37. Fry Pan with Broiler Cover
38. 11" Fry Pan
39. Wire Lettuce Basket
40. Cake Rack
41. Blender
42. French Whisk
43. Pastry Brush

44. Meat Thermometer
45. Rolling Pin
46. 3½-Cup Mold
47. Garlic Press
48. Flour Sifter
49. 8-Hole Cupcake Pan
50. 6-Hole Cupcake Pan
51. Automatic 10-Cup Coffee Maker
52. Teapot

53. Spice Rack
54. Wall Can Opener
55. Extra Cookie Sheet
56. Extra 9" Pie Pan
57. Pepper Mill
58. Cookbook
59. Covered Roaster
60. Electric Pressure Cooker
61. Wooden Cutting Board
62. Electric Mixer

Sandwich and Waffle Grill: This dual-purpose appliance has round-the-clock usefulness in busy households, providing the means for quick, hot suppers or late snacks.

Mixer (Standard or Portable) : Indispensable to any woman who plans to do a lot of baking, it beats, whips and mixes. The many attachments on the standard model enable economies on your food budget. You can grind leftover meat into croquettes, shred and slice vegetables for salads, grind coffee and spices and accomplish dozens of other tasks. If your kitchen facilities are limited, you may find a small portable mixer adequate.

Frying Pan: This is a boon to inexperienced cooks because you can set it to the exact temperature needed for frying, stewing or braising. There is a setting for keeping foods hot, so this doubles as a chafing dish.

Deep Fryer: Fryer is a misnomer for this appliance which cooks everything from soup to dessert. Settings start at simmer—a low heat that's difficult to achieve on a range—and go up to the high heat needed for deep-fat frying.

Saucepans: These come in various sizes and provide controlled cooking for vegetables, soups and stews. You can deep-fry, steam, roast and bake in them.

Grill: An excellent auxiliary cooking tool, the grill provides ample surface for cooking bacon and eggs, pancakes, hamburgers and other main courses en masse. It's handy for patio parties.

Rotisserie, Broiler and Dutch Oven: Owning one of these is a necessity if you have limited cooking facilities, for any of the three acts as an auxiliary oven. They are especially useful for patio barbecues or for indoor cooking when it's too hot to use the range oven.

Warming Tray: This is the answer to the problem of keeping foods hot during serving and eating. Some models have a drawer for warming plates or keeping rolls, pies and hot hors d'oeuvres.

Blender: This handy appliance takes up little space and performs a variety of services. It chops, blends, purees fruits and vegetables, makes milk shakes and other drinks. For entertaining, you will also want the ice crusher attachment.

Juice Extractor: You'll find this economical as well as convenient because it extracts the last drop of juice from fresh fruits. In addition to daily use at breakfast, it's a real timesaver in preparing desserts and beverages calling for fruit juice.

Knife Sharpener: If you are getting an expensive carving set for a wedding gift, this is a wise investment. With an automatic device, you can't ruin a knife by oversharpening or uneven sharpening. If you sew, choose one that sharpens scissors, too.

Knife: For a perfect carving job, an electric knife does the trick. The blades are detachable for easy cleaning.

Can Opener: Make sure the one you select opens all types of cans you are likely to use frequently—round, oval, square and extra-large.

How to Buy
Furniture and Bedding

EVEN THOUGH you've never shopped for furniture, you can invest your money wisely just by using good judgment and looking for the telltale clues that indicate quality.

Before you start, determine the role of furniture in your home. It will be a tangible reflection of both your personalities, so don't be misled into buying pieces that may clash with your way of life. Have you discussed plans for entertaining—will you invite small groups or wipe out obligations with occasional crowded buffet affairs? Will you dress and entertain casually? If so, furnishings with a formal air will be dampening to the real spirit of your home.

If you love music and games or simply listening to the radio or watching television, mentally allow room for these hobbies. Never fear the open space left by lack of furniture pieces. It's better to use floor plants to soften these wall areas than it is to buy unneeded pieces in a hurry. Choose only furniture that is pleasing to you two—and do take his size into consideration and buy a comfortable sofa and chairs. You're creating a home, not a showroom.

To help decide on the type of furnishings you want, look at the styles on display in the furniture department. It isn't necessary to be an expert on names, dates and places of origin associated with Early American or French Provincial in order to know whether or not you like it, but it is helpful to have a general idea of what is available.

The Furniture Styles

In the home furnishings industry today, a general four-way classification of furniture styles has been agreed upon—traditional, provincial, Early American and contemporary. Traditional has a regal air, since it embraces reproductions of actual court furniture. Occasionally named for the original designer, such as Sheraton, it is more often identified by the reigning monarch of periods when these designs were created, literally, to the king's or queen's taste. Decoration is generous in traditional pieces, and ornate signatures include gilt, paint, carvings, fretwork, claw-and-ball feet and extravagant fabrics. Curved or straight-backed chairs, tables, lowboys, desks and other pieces often feature the cabriole leg—a gracefully curved knee that is one of the most familiar trademarks of traditional furniture.

Provincial furniture—French, Italian and the others—is the result of the frank envy of the outlying provinces where craftsmen tried to duplicate the designs of the court in local and less expensive woods. Provincial inherits the grace, charm and form of court pieces, but eliminates the lavish decoration, thereby achieving a timelessness of design which makes it ideal for today's homes.

Early American traces its origin and practicality to our colonial artisans who shrugged off the idea of decoration and built furniture for practical use by hardy pioneers. This once rugged, now refined, style is currently being translated into casual furniture at home in any room in the house.

Contemporary furniture is current design and is a classification that refers to the simplicity of line and modern functional qualities found in today's furniture. These designs offer a charm dependent upon grace of line, and decoration is usually inherent in the piece—a beautiful wood grain or inlay, perhaps, rather than something added on for purely decorative value. Actually, modern furniture dates back to the designs of 1925—a period of experimentation from which evolved a whole new school of thought. You may buy a beautiful piece advertised as "Danish modern," but do drop the modern and call it contemporary instead.

After style, the next most important factor is the type of wood your furniture is made from.

Choosing Furniture Woods

Hardwoods, which come from leaf-bearing trees, are best for furniture construction. You will find six fine hardwoods prominent in the styles popular today. Although many woods may be stained or bleached to any color tone, the natural blondes are fine-grained birch and maple. Birch—strong, sleek and generally blonde, but sometimes finished in soft brown for contemporary pieces—is moderately priced and a favorite with young couples. Maple is white to pinkish brown naturally, but best known for the reddish finish created for Early American furniture. In the browner tones, too, maple is beginning to develop as a popular contemporary design wood.

Mahogany and walnut are the aristocrats of woods and hence the most widely imitated. True mahogany, a rich brown wood imported from Africa, Central America and the West Indies, offers the very finest wood figures. So-called "Philippine mahogany," on the other hand, is not mahogany at all, but a term applied to a whole group of woods imported from the Philippine islands.

Walnut, the cabinetmaker's ideal, is used for every type of furniture except Early American. It is not heavy, but extremely strong, and its natural brown color may be bleached or finished to any tone.

A Guide to Period Furniture

American ladder-back
chair with rush seat

Queen Anne chair,
curved splat back

Louis XV fauteuil
with painted frame

Italian Empire chair
with wood frame

American bow-back
Windsor chair

American Chippendale
armchair

Hepplewhite chair
with shield back

American wing chair
with wide flare

English Regency
open armchair

American Sheraton-
type armchair

Duncan-Phyfe
lyre-back chair

Hitchcock chair
with stencilled back

Connecticut
ladder-back

Cherry has become increasingly popular in the past several years for both provincial and traditional furniture. Characterized by a rich and vibrant reddish brown color and an interesting soft grain pattern, this hardwood is the only true fruitwood now in general production, although you may see an occasional piece with pearwood accents.

Making a comeback in the fashion world of woods is oak—coarsely grained in appearance and sturdy in performance. Practically indestructible, oak is excellent for ranch-style furniture.

While these are the woods you will see most often when shopping for furniture, there are, of course, many other varieties, such as rich and exotic teak that is favored by so many contemporary designers.

Furniture Finishes

In finishing, the natural wood tone is either carefully maintained, deepened to a darker hue or lightened to achieve a new effect. This treatment enhances the natural grain and gives more lasting beauty to hardwoods. A final coat of lacquer, rubbed again and again, covers the surface to bond in the color and protect the wood. Lacquered furniture needs only a semi-annual paste waxing to keep it lovely. Some pieces are finished with pure linseed oil, and in this case an occasional oiling will enrich the wood's appearance.

The Shopping Trip

Armed with basic information on furniture styles and woods, you should also know the terminology of the trade before you shop.

You will find furniture woods referred to as solid, veneer and genuine. Most hardwood furniture you see will be veneered, simply because the lavish grains and figures of these woods are prohibitively expensive in solid form. Veneers make woods even stronger than they are naturally and permit the use of costly woods for general manufacture—a surface layer of a rare hardwood may be attached to a less expensive base wood.

Solid pieces are often made of maple and less frequently of other woods, since a solid piece might be extraordinarily heavy as well as costly. The label genuine indicates the use of the hardwood, such as "genuine mahogany," for veneers on surfaces and in solid form for structural parts—legs and stretchers, primarily. Be sure to look for tags identifying woods and know what you are buying.

Don't confuse "wood" with "finish." When a piece of furniture is identified as "walnut finish," this usually means a less expensive wood has been colored to resemble walnut, just as the costume jewelry you buy in "silver" or "gold" is merely another metal finished to resemble silver or gold.

Just as important as good materials is good workmanship. When buying a chair, table, chest or similar piece, rock it to test its steadiness. Inferior furniture may be made of unseasoned wood and loaded with glue in the joints, and

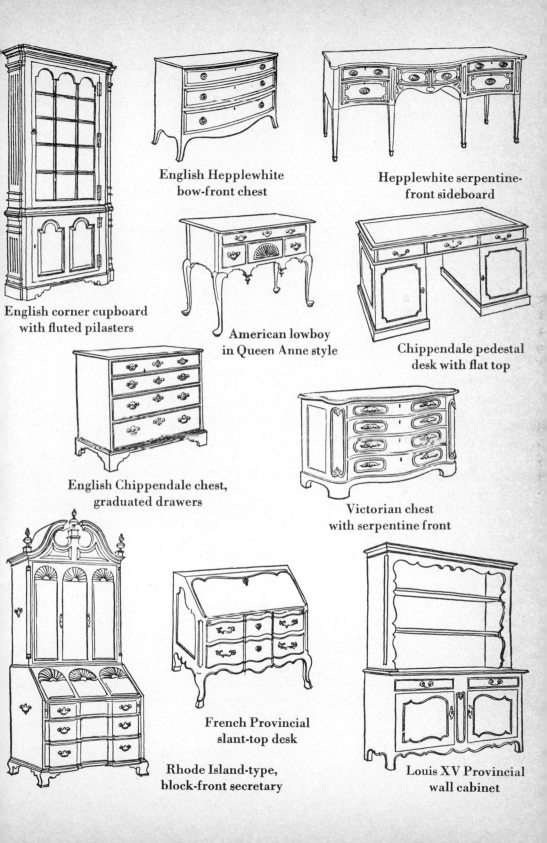

English Hepplewhite
bow-front chest

Hepplewhite serpentine-
front sideboard

English corner cupboard
with fluted pilasters

American lowboy
in Queen Anne style

Chippendale pedestal
desk with flat top

English Chippendale chest,
graduated drawers

Victorian chest
with serpentine front

French Provincial
slant-top desk

Rhode Island-type,
block-front secretary

Louis XV Provincial
wall cabinet

you can detect this by its wobbly action. Check drawers for free and easy motion, and look for dovetailed joints at front and sides. Ask to be shown the guides and corner glue blocks at the bottom corners of each drawer. Turn a chest or dresser around to check the back. The back panel should be recessed into grooves in the upright posts, not simply nailed flush to the back.

Well-made furniture has proper reinforcement at places of strain, so have the salesman turn over the table or chair you are considering to assure yourself of this safeguard. Blocks will be screwed and glued into corners if the furniture is sturdily constructed.

If you are splurging on one or two fine pieces, look for indications of superior workmanship. Drawer tops and insides of drawers should be hand-finished and show the same veneers as exposed areas. Backs should be finished the same as sides and fronts, and back legs of chairs should be as carefully made as front legs. Finishes should be creamy smooth to the touch, and in these expensive pieces you will see the most impressive examples of veneer magic—luxurious figures and skillfully matched wood grains.

ALL ABOUT UPHOLSTERY

There's a lot more to an upholstered chair or sofa than meets the eye. The most important features of construction—the frame, webbing, springs and filling material—are carefully hidden behind a fabric cover.

When buying any item with hidden quality features, it's important that you shop in a reliable store. Few people are gullible enough to buy a television set in a store that may be a fly-by-night operation, yet many will take their chances with furniture merchants whose sensational "bargains" are of mysterious or unknown origin. Before you grasp the alluring price tag that reads "far below original wholesale," let your common sense assert itself.

You Get What You Pay For

First of all, the making of upholstered furniture represents an amazing paradox in this age of mechanization. Although new filling materials, springing techniques and other advancements have brought about revolutionary changes in style, much of the work is still being done by hand. Today, skilled workmanship is one commodity that is never sold at cut-rate prices. A well-made sofa is an object of pride and able to command a fair price in a competitive market. If the workmanship is there, you have to pay for it, and if it isn't there, you shouldn't buy it.

Learning something about the various steps in construction will enable you to detect certain evidences of quality and to ask the salesman intelligent questions about parts you can't see or touch. First, let's deal with these hidden construction features.

1. The Frame. Upholstered furniture is usually built around a wood frame.

American tilt-top
side table

English gate-leg table

Duncan Phyfe pedestal
dining table

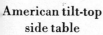

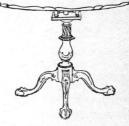

English Sheraton
drum table

French Empire table,
sphinx-head supports

Piecrust table
with tripod base

French Provincial
table, curved legs

Pembroke drop-leaf
table, Sheraton-type

American butterfly
drop-leaf table

Sheraton-type card
table, inlaid top

Queen Anne Colonial-
type tea table

To be strong, the wood should be of fairly substantial lumber that has been kiln-dried (seasoned to prevent warping). It should be put together with dowels and reinforced with corner blocks. In assembling the frame, enough glue must be used so it won't come apart.

2. *Webbing.* You've seen outdoor chairs made by fastening strips of webbing material to a simple frame. This webbing technique is also used to form the base for upholstered furniture. The strips are made of some strong fiber, like jute, and often they are interlaced for greater strength. The closer the strips, the sturdier the finished product.

3. *Springs.* Most furniture is constructed with springs and stuffing in the seat, and sometimes there are springs in the back as well. Good springing lends both comfort and wearability. Contrary to what you may have heard, no one spring construction is superior to all others. Most manufacturers, in fact, use several different methods because the same type spring is not suitable for all furniture styles. The same construction used in a well-padded traditional sofa can't be duplicated in a streamlined contemporary model. In general, the closer together and deeper the springs, the better—an inexpensive chair will have four to six rows of springs; a higher priced chair will have more. Springs should be tied to each other so they will not come apart. Sometimes, springs are found in loose cushions as well as the body of the chair, but today, springless cushions are by far the most popular. A layer of burlap is used to cover the springs, and then the filling materials are added. Some manufacturers have perfected techniques for eliminating springs from seats as well, thanks to tough, bouncy modern fillings that have built-in comfort and durability.

4. *Filling materials.* Both the quality of the filling and the amount used are important to the comfort and wearability of the furniture. Almost every state has a law requiring that stuffing and cushioning materials be described on a tag attached to upholstered furniture or bedding. Look for this tag and read it carefully. Among the materials you'll see mentioned most often are hair, foam rubber, polyurethane, down, Dacron, Fortrel and Kodel.

Hair, or combinations of hair with other materials, varies in quality. Curled or rubberized hair from animals is the best kind. Horse and cattle hair are better than hog hair as they are longer and more resilient. Hair is normally used with a top layer of cotton to prevent prickling. Less expensive are moss; cotton, which is not as resilient as hair and should be used in combination with hair; sisal, a tough grass; and excelsior, the cheapest filling. The better the filling, the less tendency it will have to mat down and make the furniture lumpy, uncomfortable and misshapen.

Foam rubber is one of the most widely used cushioning materials. Although associated with contemporary furniture because it permits slim styling and crisp lines, foam is also extremely prevalent in traditional upholstery. It is long wearing, comfortable and has excellent resiliency—the seat bounces back after you get up and it's never necessary to plump up the cushions.

Queen Anne settee
with cabriole legs

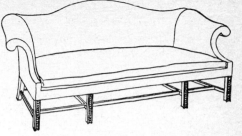

English Chippendale sofa
with straight legs

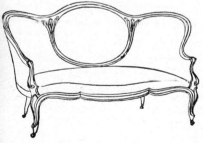

English Sheraton sofa
with spindle arm

Duncan Phyfe sofa with scroll
arms and reeded base

American Victorian sofa
with oval-panel inset

Adam gilt mirror

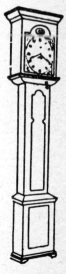

Early
American-
grandfather
clock

ransitional American
irror, Empire columns

Federal convex mirror,
gilt frame

Directoire
cross-legged banquette

A more recent development is polyurethane foam, which in characteristics and appearance is similar to foam rubber. Polyurethane is lighter in weight and somewhat lower in cost.

Down, very definitely in the luxury class, is wonderful to sit upon and gives a soft look to furniture. While some women object to the fact that down cushions become rumpled and have to be fluffed up, this is the basis of their charm to others. Not everyone admires the type of cushions that never look as if anyone sat on them.

Dacron, Fortrel and Kodel fiberfill are man-made materials that have a soft look and feel somewhat like down, and they spring back without plumping. They are often used in combination with another core material—as a wrapping around foam rubber or polyfoam, usually, to give a softer line.

What You Can See for Yourself

So much for what's underneath. But except for the filling materials that must be labeled, what's the good of knowing all this if you can't see it anyway?

First of all, some manufacturers voluntarily attach tags to their furniture describing features of the frame, springs, webbing and other construction details. If there is no tag, ask the salesman to point out these facts to you.

Now for the features you can see, touch or test for yourself. Women, many salesmen claim, often overlook the most obvious way of judging quality—that is, by sitting on the furniture to see how it feels. Good springs and quality filling materials give a chair comfort. Next, take off the seat cushion and touch the furniture. If a chair is not well padded, you can feel the springs. Then push down the border of the seat and see if it gives—this will tell you if it has spring-edge construction, a comfort and quality feature. Hard-edge construction, which has no give, is a cheaper technique, although perfectly satisfactory. As for springs and webbing, you could ask the salesman to turn a chair over so you can look at the under side, but the chances are the burlap or cambric dust protector tacked to the bottom will be too heavy to see through. You will have to assume that if the sofa meets other tests, the manufacturer has not stinted on quality inside.

Take a good look at tailoring and other details, just as you would when buying a coat or dress. Does the fabric fit neatly, and if patterned, has it been carefully matched? Do loose seat and back cushions zip off for cleaning? Is the welting trim and even? Ask if the fabrics are cut on the bias, as this is a technique used by manufacturers to keep cushion covers from twisting.

Finally, consider the fabric. Although looks and color are important, you should give some thought to wearability, since re-covering furniture is expensive. Usually, you are given a choice of several grades of fabric. It's wise to buy the best grade you can afford, but price alone is not a barometer of quality—some of the silks are expensive but not meant for long, hard wear. Some of the synthetics, like nylon, have remarkable durability. Often, upholstery fabrics are blends of two or more fibers. Many fabrics at modest price levels feature a cotton warp, which is very sturdy, and a rayon or nylon filling. Don't use thinness or bulk as a criterion—a thin fabric may be firmer and stronger than a heavier one. Closely woven fabrics wear better than loose weaves. Fabrics that pull if something catches on them are not practical.

Be sure to ask questions about care—your covers will look fresh and new much longer if you remove spots immediately and follow any other recommendations on upkeep.

THE BEST IN BEDDING

There are hundreds of tips and gimmicks and gadgets that are supposed to induce sleep. But for most of us, nothing succeeds like good bedding. Here are some pointers to insure you the best value for your money.

Buying the bed itself is a matter of choosing the furniture style you like, but do select a bed that is long enough and wide enough. It should be at least 30 inches wide for each adult sleeper, and long enough so your feet don't hang over. This brings up the matter of double beds versus single. If you decide in favor of a double, there is strong argument for the king-size or various other extra-width beds now on the market, ranging from 60 to 76 inches in width. The standard double bed is 54 inches wide, and when you divide this in two each sleeper gets as much room as he or she would have in a baby's crib. As a compromise, you can always combine the best of both worlds and choose twin beds attached to a single headboard.

Don't Hope Spring's Eternal

As a newlywed you'll want to start married life with a brand-new mattress, but be reasonable about how long it will last. Even the best mattresses get worn out and market experts claim many people are still trying to sleep on them. Some people have an almost marital devotion to their old mattresses and stay by them through thick and thin. If you buy a good mattress, it will be guaranteed to last for many years, costing in the long run no more than a couple of cents a night. Is a good night's sleep worth this price to you? To help you understand why mattresses vary so greatly in price, here are some facts about how they are made.

There are three basic types of mattresses—innerspring, foam and solid upholstered. As to which is best, it's mostly up to you and the one you like. Innerspring and foam, however, are more popular by far than solid upholstered. The latter are stuffed with cotton, horse or cattle hair. These mattresses get their comfort from the resiliency of the stuffing and the foundation under them. Good hair mattresses are exceptionally expensive and not widely available.

Foam mattresses are made from the milk of rubber trees, or a synthetic, which has been treated and whipped up into a foam. They are usually about 4½ to 6 inches thick, considerably thinner than an innerspring mattress, and usually sold in combination with a special box spring that gives the bed the correct height. When you make your purchase be certain it has a one-piece core and not just foam flakes. Generally, good foam mattresses are expensive. Foam mattresses never lump, sag or lose their shape and they will support any weight evenly and strongly. But no matter what type of foam you buy, insist on a particularly good spring foundation for support.

The innerspring mattress consists of strong coil springs of steel with insulating material and padding on both sides of the coil unit. A cover or tick encloses the entire unit. There are two types of coilspring construction. The coils may be sewn into separate cloth pockets which are joined together, or the coils themselves may be linked together with steel spring or wire. Proper design with innersprings gives a mattress just the right amount of resiliency on the surface, plus a firm supporting core.

Values Are Hidden

When you shop for a mattress, you'll see covers beautifully quilted or printed with flowers. But as for the things that really matter, you can't actually see what you are buying. You can't thoroughly test it either, unless they let you spend the night in the store, although it is recommended that you lie down on the mattress to see if the degree of firmness suits you. Primarily, you will have to rely a great deal on the brand name, the bedding label, the type of guarantee and the salesman's answers to your questions.

As important as the mattress itself is the other half of the set—the spring on which the mattress rests. There are three types of spring foundations—flat springs, metal-coil bedsprings and box springs.

Flat bedsprings consist of flat strips or links of steel spring wire than run horizontally and are attached inside a frame at the sides and ends with helical springs. Spring-wire coil bedsprings are similar to box springs but aren't upholstered or covered with ticking. Double-deck coils are extra long and supported through the middle, and are preferable to single-deck coils. Box springs have steel spring-wire coils mounted to a wood frame base, and the outside of the coil unit is padded and covered with ticking to match the mattress. The coils of better box springs are tied to each other and to their base and border with special twine or wire.

Both box springs and open-coil bedsprings provide an excellent foundation for a good mattress. To get the best comfort and service from whatever mattress you buy, you should also buy the bedspring designed especially for it.

How to Buy
Carpets and Fabrics

T HE RIGHT CARPET does wonders for any decorating scheme by adding
warmth and luxuriousness and filling in those bare spots you can't
afford to furnish just yet. But which rug or carpet is the best choice
for you? Actually, your final decision will be based on four separate elements
—color, style, quality and price.

Choose Color First

Color is always important in your home, but never more so than when it's
seen in a big area, such as on the floor. You will want a color that does the
most for the room, decoratively speaking, and one that is practical as well
unless it will be in an area not subject to heavy traffic. No other item of home
furnishings gets walked on every day, and you don't want soil to mar the
beauty of your rug or carpet right from the start. But that doesn't mean you
have to settle for dull, nondescript colors.

All carpet colors available today fall into one of seven basic families—
blue, greens, golds, reds, grays, beiges and browns. Within each family there
are variations from light to dark in solid colors and mixtures of hue. This
wide variety enables you to choose the color you like in a version that is most
practical for your purposes. If you like light colors and want to use them in
a heavy-traffic area, it's best to select a two-tone mixture or tweedy effect.
These don't show soil as readily as solid colors and they can add interest to
a decorating scheme.

Texture and Pattern

The pile surface of a carpet can be plain or show definite texture interest. It
can have a definite pattern, muted pattern or no pattern at all. For formal rooms,
the texture known as plush is particularly suitable—a plain, cut pile with a
luxurious look. Sculptured or carved effects also tend toward elegance, while

65

loops or twists have a more rugged feeling that many people like for informal settings or as a contrast to the sleek look of contemporary design.

Pattern is also important and must be chosen with care. A muted pattern harmonizes with a variety of decorating schemes, but some of the definitive patterns are meant to underscore particular styles—delicate, tiny flowers would suit some small-in-scale traditional furniture, for example, but be wrong with large or heavy pieces. Above all, observe the rule that only one pattern should dominate a room. Since walls and floors are both major surfaces, use pattern on one or the other but not both. Treat sculptured textures and tone-on-tone patterns as if they were solid colors. This effect of "pattern" on the floor is subtle and adds interest without dominating the room or excluding the use of pattern elsewhere. Small patterns are generally best in small rooms and large patterns in large rooms.

If you find a patterned carpet you particularly like, you may want to build a color scheme around it, picking up one or two of the dominant colors in the pattern for solid drapery and upholstery fabrics. Conversely, you may select your carpet color from one of the tones in a patterned fabric. In either case, it is usually best to have the carpet darker in tone than the walls. This gives a room better balance.

Think about Size

Carpeting today is used in three forms—wall-to-wall, room-size rugs and area rugs.

Wall-to-wall covers the floor completely and makes a room seem more spacious because of the unbroken area of color and texture, and it offers the advantage of one surface for easy cleaning. The term broadloom is often erroneously used as a synonym for wall-to-wall, but broadloom is simply a term of measurement and indicates that a rug or carpet was made wider than six feet.

Large rugs are available in pre-finished standard sizes, such as 9 by 12 or 12 by 15 feet, or they can be cut to desired size from rolls of carpet. Room-size rugs generally leave a border of bare floor showing—about 8 to 12 inches. They offer good value because they can be turned to distribute wear evenly and moved to another location.

Area rugs range in size from 3 by 5 feet and upwards and come in varied shapes—round, oval, rectangular or free-form. They define an area of a room, accenting it with color and design. Consider room proportions in selecting size to avoid the "postage stamp" look of a skimpy rug in a large area.

A bright accent rug, in a blend of Avisco rayon and cotton, defines the dining area and repeats the contours of an octagonal table. For economy's sake, the table is a piece of plywood supported by an old pedestal. Paul Krauss, A.I.D., designed the setting.

Select Quality

When you choose a beautiful carpet, you want it to last, so give some consideration to how your carpet will look in use and how long the surface pile and the backing material will stand up.

Actually, you've already considered one aspect of performance in choosing color and texture. Medium colors, color mixtures and patterns are best at disguising signs of use between cleanings, and loops or twists don't show footprints as readily as plain, cut piles. To select the right quality for durability, ask yourself these questions:

1. How long do you expect your rug or carpet to last? Is this an investment for a permanent home or a temporary expedient?

2. How much use will your carpet get? Do you entertain a great deal?

3. Where will your rug or carpet be used? In a daily-traffic area, a guest room, or must it meet the supreme test of a one-room apartment?

Consider your needs, then measure traffic against quality, using the top grades in heavy-traffic areas like the living room, hallways and stairs. Middle grades are suitable for a dining room, study or bedroom. Economy grades will do for guest rooms or for any room in an apartment you expect to vacate soon. If you are buying wall-to-wall carpet, choose from the middle range up, since this is a permanent installation.

How can you tell whether a rug is of good quality or not? "The deeper, the denser, the better" is a good phrase to keep in mind when you shop. The more fiber packed into a carpet, the better its chances for longevity because the yarns support each other and resist bending and abrasion.

Construction

Almost all carpet sold in this country is tufted, woven or knitted. In weaving and knitting, surface yarn and backing are interlocked simultaneously, whereas in tufting, surface yarns are attached to a pre-woven backing. One type is not necessarily better than another—there are different grades of quality in each.

The backing holds the carpet together and prevents stretching, shrinking and buckling. On all tufted and knitted carpets and many woven carpets, the backing is coated with latex for security of surface yarns. Most good-quality tufted carpets have an extra layer of backing for greater strength.

Decide on a Fiber

The surface pile of carpets and rugs today can be made from any number

For an "L" shaped room, try a combination of wall-to-wall carpeting and an accent rug. In the foyer above, a shaggy-textured rug in a blend of russet-gold hues leads into a dining area carpeted in a russet brown hue.

of natural or man-made fibers. The natural fibers are wool and cotton, and those made by man are nylon, acrylic and modacrylic, rayon and polypropylene. Any of these can give good performance, but all do have their own characteristics.

Wool is the classic fiber, with a balance of desirable characteristics. Resiliency, abrasion-resistance, adaptability to styling, warmth and comfort to the touch and soil-resistance are wool's traditional qualities which are at their best in medium-to-higher priced carpets. All carpet wool used by American manufacturers is imported from countries with rugged climates, since domestic wool is too soft and fine for sturdy carpet use.

Other fibers may rate higher on one or more of these desirable characteristics for carpet use. Nylon, for example, is noted for abrasion-resistance and offers outstanding value in medium-price carpets for heavy-traffic use. There are two types of nylon—staple and continuous filament. The latter was designed to eliminate the tendency to fuzzing and pilling. Nylon is a smooth fiber which resists rapid water absorption, which means water-soluble stains are easily removed.

Acrylics and their close cousins, modacrylics, are the synthetics which most closely resemble wool—in abrasion-resistance, resiliency, softness and warmth. Like nylon, they resist rapid water absorption.

Rayons are noted for economy and adaptability to styling. They tend to crush, although less so if the pile is very dense, but they can be used to advantage in low-traffic areas.

Polypropylene is the newest carpet fiber. It is extremely moisture-resistant and high in abrasion-resistance.

Fiber Blends

Two fibers are often combined in a blend in order to give the advantages of both. The higher the percentage of a particular fiber, the more a carpet will be like that fiber. For example, when wool is reinforced by nylon in a blend of 70 per cent wool and 30 per cent nylon, the carpet will look and feel most like wool. At least 20 per cent of a fiber must be used before its characteristics are effective.

Exact fiber content must be stated on a carpet label or on the store's invoice to you, so check and be sure of what you are buying.

The Importance of Padding

Padding adds comfort, quiet and insulation to a carpet. It acts as a shock absorber and therefore extends the life of rugs or wall-to-wall carpet.

Two types of padding are available—the felted type, generally made of hair; and rubber types. Felted hair is somewhat firmer than the bouncy rubber pads, and choosing between the two is a matter of personal preference.

Felted pads are judged by weights based on ounces per square yard. Normally, a 40-ounce pad is good for home use. Rubber cushionings come in various thicknesses ranging from an eighth to a half inch. One-quarter or three-eighths is sufficient for household traffic.

How Much Should You Spend?

Value in a rug or carpet depends on price in relation to performance. A low price for poor quality is no bargain. If you pay a little more, you get a lot more. The cost of a carpet reflects many factors, including construction, fiber content and appearance.

A certain amount of cost must go into the backing and construction of any carpet or rug. For every dollar over this amount, you add ounces of surface pile weight which makes a big difference in wear. That's why two carpets can be made of the same fiber and, at first glance, have a similar appearance, but different price tags. The more expensive one offers a better backing, superior construction and more fiber per square inch.

Unusual styling may add to the cost of a carpet, but today a wide range of style is available in all price ranges. If you want a very unusual color, many carpets can be custom-dyed to your specifications, usually at a moderate extra cost of a dollar or two per square yard.

To determine the real cost, consider the years of expected wear in comparison to price. If one carpet costs $5 per square yard and can be expected to wear about two years, you are actually paying $2.50 per yard per year. Another carpet costing $10 per square yard, but lasting ten years, will cost only $1 per yard per year. The more expensive carpet is actually the better bargain.

The wear life of a carpet will vary according to use and care, but you can estimate the expected life of a carpet by measuring traffic against quality.

Shopping Tips

To sum up, buying a rug or carpet is an important purchase and you would do well to follow this shopping guide:

1. Consider the area in which you plan to use a carpet or rug, make preliminary measurements, then let the salesman help you in making the choice best suited to your needs and preferences.

2. Beware of fantastic "bargains" and don't buy a carpet that isn't properly labeled. Good manufacturers and stores will stand behind products, so look for brand names.

3. Take a look at the many new colors and textures available—don't limit your thinking. Pick a color family you like and look for variations within that range.

4. If possible, take a carpet sample home and see it in relation to your room.

A Guide for Carpet Shoppers

FIBER	SUGGESTED PRICE RANGE	HOW IT WILL LOOK IN USE	HOW IT WILL WEAR*
Wool	$7.95 for light or short-term use only. $9.95 to $12.95 for average traffic. $12.95 and up for heavy use, better style and color selection.	Wool has very good resiliency (the pile springs back after you step on it), soil resistance and cleanability. A good wool carpet has by nature the live, luxurious look and warm, appealing touch that is the goal of all man-made fibers.	Good to excellent depending on price.
Nylon (Du Pont, Chemstrand)	$5.95 for light or short-term use. $8.95 for average traffic. $12.95 and up for heavy use, better style and color selection.	Nylon can be easily cleaned. It resists water-borne stains, so you can wipe up most spilled liquids readily. Carpet nylon is used in two forms—staple nylon, and continuous filament nylon, designed to eliminate a tendency to fuzzing and pilling and seen most often in looped-pile textures.	Nylon is a strong fiber with high abrasion-resistance. It is sometimes used in blends to reinforce the strength of other fibers—e.g., a blend of 70% wool and 30% nylon.
Acrylics (Acrilan, Creslan, Orlon)	$9.95 for average wear. $11.95 and up for heavy use, better style and color selection.	Acrylics have very good resiliency and soil resistance. Like nylon, they absorb very little moisture and are therefore spot resistant. They clean well.	Good to excellent depending on price.

Fiber	Price	Description	Durability
Cotton	$5.95 to $8.95, good color selection at all prices.	Cotton is not resilient and must be vacuumed or carpet swept to restore the pile. It retains its appearance best, therefore, when used in light to medium traffic areas—bedrooms in particular. Cotton cleans well and is washable in small sizes, making it an excellent choice for bath or dressing rooms.	Cotton has good durability.
Rayon (Avisco)	$6.95. Recommended for temporary use or situations where economy is the primary consideration.	Rayon soils and crushes easily, a characteristic which is minimized with dense construction.	Ordinary rayon rates poor to fair in durability. Recommended for temporary use or situations where economy is the primary consideration.
Polypropylene (olefin)	$6.95 to $8.95.	Polypropylene olefin is used most often in looped texture styling, in solid colors or two-tone color effects. It is water resistant and easily cleaned.	A strong fiber with good abrasion-resistance.
All Fibers	Buy the best you can afford. If necessary, cut down on size rather than quality. A good, room-size rug is a better investment than cheap wall-to-wall carpeting.	Medium colors or neutrals hide soil better than pastels or dark shades. Tweeds or multicolors conceal footprints and dirt more effectively than solids. In fairly heavy traffic areas, a loop or twist will retain its appearance better than a cut pile of the same quality.	Durable carpets are well constructed and made with a generous amount of fiber. Examine a swatch closely to be sure tufts are tightly secured to the backing. Rows of tufts should be close together and densely packed with fiber. If you can see the backing, the pile is too sparse. Don't judge by height of pile—some of the best carpets have piles that are very short, but thickly populated with rows of tufts. If the yarn is tightly twisted, the amount of fiber present is even greater.

*In comparing wearing ability of one carpet fiber to another, all factors must be equal, particularly the amount of fiber per square inch. For example, a densely-packed wool will outwear a sparsely-packed nylon.

5. Once you've found the color and texture you like, consider performance in relation to your own needs. Don't hesitate to feel and examine closely the carpets you are considering. Look for density—the closeness of construction, the heftiness of surface pile. It's the best single guide to quality.

6. Don't choose a carpet on the basis of fiber content alone, but do identify the fiber content and consider it in relation to quality of construction and the appearance that pleases you.

7. Don't skimp on quality for carpets and rugs which will see constant duty underfoot. Remember that poor-quality carpeting is not a wise investment, but carpets and rugs of good quality will pay off in years of service and comfort.

CARING FOR YOUR CARPETS

A good carpet will serve you longer and look better if you give it good care. Dirt particles are abrasives, and if you allow them to pile up, footsteps will grind them into your carpet and create damaging friction. Soil also creates a film that dulls and changes the color you chose so carefully.

Daily Care

How much day-to-day cleaning your carpet needs depends on the cleanliness of the air in your neighborhood and how much dirt is tracked into various parts of your house.

Seldom-used rooms require less attention than others. In some homes, light vacuuming or carpet sweeping every day and a thorough cleaning once a week is sufficient.

A vacuum cleaner is essential for proper carpet care. The cleaner that does the best job combines a strong suction with a revolving agitator brush or bar. Upright cleaners are usually of this type. Some canister and tank types have attachments which contain the necessary agitator, but others offer only suction. The straight suction type will remove surface dust, but not imbedded dirt.

For a light cleaning, make three strokes over each area of carpet—forward, back and forward. A thorough cleaning requires up to seven strokes, and if you are using a cleaner that provides suction only, be sure to use it this thoroughly for proper maintenance.

Carpet sweepers take up lint, crumbs and other litter from the surface and remove some dust, but they do not reach imbedded soil and are helpful only for light cleaning. Brooms sweep dust from the carpet, but toss it into the air to fall back or settle on furniture. A light brooming is helpful, however, in brushing up a matted area—but keep it light and never use a metal broom or very stiff brush.

Home-Cleaning Methods

After a time, any carpet becomes dulled by an accumulation of soil not readily removed by regular care, and an occasional brightening of the surface through home-cleaning methods is helpful. Home-cleaning is not a substitute for periodic professional cleaning, but it is a great help in keeping your floor-coverings fresh and bright at all times.

There are two ways to clean your rug—the dry method, using an absorbent powder cleaner; and the wet method, using a water-and-detergent solution. Powders are recommended for large areas, while the wet method is best suited to small areas.

Powder-type cleaners are solvent-saturated sawdust or other inert powdered material. Generally, the method calls for thorough vacuuming, then sprinkling the powder liberally over the area, brushing it into the carpet and vacuuming it out again. Although this procedure will not clean the carpet as thoroughly as the wet method, it has the advantage of less texture distortion, better removal of greasy soil and less drying time.

Wet cleaning is suitable for all types of carpet. Certain precautions must be taken, however, most important of which is to avoid the use of soap, ammonia, washing soda or any strong household cleaning agents intended for hard surfaces. Use instead one of the light neutral detergents which are often sold as special-purpose cleaners for home laundering. A small amount (two heaping tablespoons to a gallon of water) provides a safe solution.

Apply this mixture sparingly with a sponge or cloth and with a gentle motion to avoid distortion of pile. Wet only the face of the carpet, not the backing. Dry as quickly as possible, using a fan if available.

In home cleaning, it is not possible to rinse the carpet as would be done in a plant, and the repeated use of the detergent-water solution may leave a residue which will cause resoiling to occur more rapidly. Frequent home cleanings of this type are not recommended.

Professional Cleaning

About once a year, you should treat your carpets to a professional cleaning that thoroughly removes all the imbedded soil you may have missed. If you have wall-to-wall carpeting, you can have someone come to your home for "on-location" cleaning, which is economical because the floorcovering does not have to be taken up and then relaid.

CURTAIN, DRAPERY AND UPHOLSTERY FABRICS

Shopping was simpler, if less exciting, in the days before test tubes began bubbling in the laboratories of fabric manufacturers. Today, there are dozens

FACTS ABOUT FABRICS	RAYON	ACETATE
SOME COMMON BRAND NAMES	Avisco, Avron, Avi-color, Fortisan, Coloray	Chromspun, Celanese, Celaperm, Avisco, Du Pont
BEST USES	Curtains, draperies, upholstery. Best in blends	Curtains, draperies, upholstery. Best in blends
CARE AND CLEANING	Hand washing or dry cleaning recommended	Dry clean primarily. Washable only if specified
ABRASION RESISTANCE	Fair to good	Fair to good
EFFECT OF SUNLIGHT	Colorfast in solution dyes, average in regular fibers	Colorfast in solution dyes, average in regular fibers
SHAPE-RETENTION	Fair	Good
WRINKLE RESISTANCE	Fair to good	Good
DURABILITY	Fair to good	Fair to good
RESISTANCE TO MOTHS	Not attacked	Not attacked
RESISTANCE TO MILDEW	Attacked	Good

POLYESTER	NYLON	ACRYLIC	GLASS
Dacron, Kodel, Fortrel	Du Pont, Enka, Chemstrand, Caprolan	Acrilan, Zefran, Orlon, Creslan	Fiberglas, Pittsburgh, PPG, Burlington
Curtains and casements	Upholstery primarily	Upholstery and casements	Curtains and draperies
Washable, needs little ironing. Iron at low heat	Dry clean, washable	Dry clean primarily. Hand-washable. Iron at low heat	Washable, drip dries, no ironing needed
Excellent	Excellent	Good	Fair
Excellent behind glass	Average color-fastness	Darkens after long exposure	None
Very good	Good	Very good	Excellent
Excellent	Good	Good	Excellent
Excellent	Excellent	Excellent	Excellent
Not attacked	Not attacked	Not attacked	Not attacked
Not attacked	Not attacked	Not attacked	Not attacked

of different synthetics, some claiming to work miracles right in your living room.

If you don't look for miracles, but merely good performance and a minimum of care, you'll find many synthetic fabrics that will amaze you for their ability to combine high fashion and durability with low price. In addition, the old standbys—cotton and linen—are still popular and better than ever before, thanks to modern finishing techniques and special processes that have endowed nature's own fibers with such man-made characteristics as wrinkle-resistance or spot-resistance.

What To Look For

Curtain and drapery fabrics should be reasonably resistant to sunlight, which can cause fading and deterioration. Upholstery should be firmly woven, strong enough to hold up under tension and to resist abrasion, or the wear and tear of continual contact. All fabrics should hold their shape without excessive shrinkage or stretching, either from use or from laundering or dry cleaning.

Fiber content and the method of weaving determine these important factors of performance. Since no single fiber is perfect, fabrics are often woven in blends—either a combination of synthetics, or natural and synthetic fibers. The Federal government requires that the fiber content of every fabric be indicated on a tag, whether the fabric is sold by the yard or bought in the form of upholstery or ready-made curtains. Percentages must be shown also, and they are your best indication of how a fabric will perform. A fabric will be "wash-and-hang" only if it contains at least 50 per cent of a fiber that needs no ironing. Other fibers will make a significant contribution to the overall quality when they are present in amounts of at least 25 per cent.

Treating your fabrics to a stain-repelling finish is an excellent idea, particularly if your taste runs to white or light colors. "Scotchgard," an invisible coating that resists dirt and keeps stains from penetrating the fabric, is used by many furniture and fabric manufacturers. To be effective, special finishes must be applied at the time of manufacture, so be sure to inquire about having this done when you are buying upholstered furniture.

Elements of Decorating

NOW THAT you've been exposed to the intricacies of selecting furnishings for your home, you are ready for the next phase of your decorating project—coordinating everything into a meaningful whole.

Following certain established rules and devising a preconceived plan are necessary steps if your interiors are to make sense, and no professional decorator would dream of working any other way. But in your zeal for adhering to the right format and basing decisions on practicality, don't overlook the aesthetic nature of what you are doing.

Interior design is the art of taking inanimate objects and making them livable. The objects come from the store, but the life you give them is your own. The adroitness with which you highlight a certain lovely object, the way you arrange furniture, your flair for combining colors—all these intangibles are just as important as furniture, fabrics, floorcoverings and other necessities of daily living.

An interior designer thinks of everything as having both functional value and artistic merit—lighting, for example, can be introduced in a room for purely practical purposes, or it can serve to create a mood as well. Accessories can do nothing more than fill in the bare spots, or they can inject a personal note that tells people something about you.

On the pages that follow, you will find a series of articles written especially for the bride by some of the most outstanding personalities in the home furnishings field. Their messages to you deal with the basic elements of decorating—budget, style, room arrangement, lighting and accessories—and are designed to stimulate your imagination as well as appeal to your practical sense. Color is treated separately in another chapter.

Although you may have a lot to learn and some fairly technical details to cope with, don't lose sight of the fun-and-adventure aspects of decorating. You'll find the sailing much smoother when you're carried along on a wave of enthusiasm.

How to Achieve
a Big Effect on a Small Budget

By Dede Draper, N.S.I.D.

B UDGET-MINDED NEWLYWEDS will find that a little originality and effort can produce a wealth of decorative beauty at minor cost.

A very large part of your home is taken up by walls, floors and windows. If you concentrate on less costly decoration for these areas, you automatically save more of your total budget for other necessary furnishings.

Paint and wallpaper offer many possibilities for creating special effects inexpensively. If you want to make a small room seem larger or dramatize vivid color in other areas, you can paint the walls and ceiling in white or off-white. Or, you may prefer to use wallpaper to introduce color, pattern or texture. Papers are often scrubbable and can be used to cover defective walls in a building that is old or in disrepair. The use of a pattern on walls reduces the necessity for other wall decorations. If you don't want an overall pattern, try a wallpaper border on a freshly painted wall—as a cornice, framing around doors, or on top of the baseboard. For a more traditional feeling, paper trompe l'oeil borders make excellent door moldings or wall panels.

As for floors, it costs next to nothing to paint, stencil or stain them, then add wax and polish. If the budget permits, harmonizing or contrasting area rugs are wonderful accents underfoot. In addition to their decorative value, area rugs are a device for defining conversational areas or setting off a furniture grouping.

Window treatments can be simple, yet attractive with inexpensive casements of cotton, linen, Fiberglas and viscose fibers that are in abundance on the market. The colors and weaves are interesting and marvelous effects can be achieved with them without the necessity for expensive lined draperies. Where the budget cannot allow for curtains, window shades can be made by using one of the fabrics in the room and applying it to a plastic laminated window shade.

To get the most out of your budget, retain any furniture that is useful.

Either refinishing or a fresh application of paint can restore an old piece to usefulness. In the case of sofas and chairs, slipcovers usually cost less than reupholstery and they can be tailored to look like upholstery. If you have a table that is unattractive but serviceable, cover it with a floor-length skirt. Particularly colorful and economical is felt, available in 72-inch widths that can be easily cut and fitted. Near the bottom edge, add a trimming of soutache, braid or fringe.

Shelves holding books and objets d'art are both practical and appealing, particularly in sparsely-furnished rooms. Most book bindings contribute their own color and interest, and colored paper can be used to cover those that are less attractive.

Another secret of creating a big effect for a little money is to avoid selecting all furnishings in the same "budget" price category. Your budget acquisitions will seem less obvious when mingled with more expensive items. Emphasize quality rather than quantity—no one will criticize spaciousness resulting from fewer purchases.

Deciding What You Like

By John Van Koert, A.I.D.
Home Furnishings Designer

MOST YOUNG COUPLES can expect a period of nomad living, but expression of taste preference cannot be postponed indefinitely. Inhabiting a kind of limbo—a home with a permanently adolescent personality, scratched together from little impulse purchases—is the penalty for years of indecision.

Look around you at the middle-aged couples who are still living in a hodge-podge of meaningless tables, foolish lamps that date so clearly from an era of one fad or another, and dubious wall ornaments that become clichés after one season. These are the people who could never quite commit themselves to a plan. Lacking both a knowledge of interior design and the courage to have convictions, they allowed their money to be dribbled away ineffectually through the years on whatever seemed to be in vogue at the moment. Let their plight be a reminder that the harmless vice of impulse buying should be restricted to an occasional can of chocolate covered ants or a momentary fling with a fad in women's dresses. Expediency ought not be a habit in home decoration.

Equally unfortunate is the interior dominated by a single, monumental folly —perhaps a sofa that is imposing, expensive and ultimately unsuitable, bought prematurely to demonstrate the solidity of a marriage or to provide the security of one "important" piece of furniture. It is just as wrong to be stuck with extravagant articles before one's preferences are clear as it is to dodge the issue indefinitely.

Leaving it up to Mother is another kind of evasion. In the long run, you might not be happy perpetuating the image of your family environment. The voice of experience from your background may not fit the present situation and could stunt the growth of a fresh point of view.

How does one acquire the confidence to make clear-cut decisions as to taste? There are no panaceas. Instant decoration does not come in jars, nor does Berlitz guarantee immediate fluency in the language of line, color or form. Somewhere along the way, you must seek to educate yourself in the arts, and the sooner the better.

Two kinds of knowledge are necessary. First, learn what it is possible to accomplish in design and decoration. Then you are ready to acquire a knowledge of yourself and what you should accept or reject.

For the far-sighted and the fortunate, courses in the history of art during student years will now prove their worth. The less provident can acquire background from books, magazines and newspapers, visits to museums and sharp-eyed attention to interiors shown in movies and on television. Store window and floor displays are another source of enlightenment.

Familiarity with concepts, past and present, in architecture, sculpture and painting makes it possible for almost anyone to sift out the permanent values from what is momentarily smart. Once you expand your horizons in the world of home furnishings, you can begin to decipher your own instinctive responses to line, color and form and begin exercising your own powers of discrimination. Many knowledgeable people conclude they don't like Rubens even if he is a certified Old Master. By the same token, a knowledge of home furnishings will enable you to decide, without uneasiness, that Chippendale isn't for you. In the process of learning, make dozens of hypothetical decisions so that when it is time to choose that rug or chair, you can answer with the resounding "yes" or "no" that leads to satisfaction.

Ignorance isn't bliss in this world, and choice should be a pleasant, constant exercise amid the abundance of our society. Count on making some mistakes in furnishing a home, but hope they are little ones, providing the kind of experience that helps build a point of view. Taste develops from being exercised and stagnates from indecision.

How to Arrange Furniture

By Erica Lemle, A.I.D.
Interior Designer

STARTING WITH A FLOOR PLAN is the simplest way to determine how you are going to arrange your furniture for maximum convenience and visual appeal. But much more important, it will enable you to try before you buy and thereby eliminate the possibility of acquiring pieces that are out of scale with your needs.

A floor plan is a very simple drawing representing the interior dimensions of your rooms and showing the location of windows, doors, closets and beams that affect the space. On this plan, which is usually done to a scale of $\frac{1}{4}$ inch or $\frac{1}{2}$ inch representing one foot, you may place little cut-outs drawn to the same scale to indicate the shape and size of furniture you plan to use in each room. By shifting the cut-outs back and forth in various positions and studying the results, you can visualize the way the completed room will look and determine whether or not the furniture you plan to buy will fit the space.

In working out your miniature plan, the establishment of "traffic lanes" is a primary consideration. Traffic lanes are the paths you must leave open for free movement of persons using the room or walking from one room to another. A good rule is to allow a minimum of two feet of unobstructed space wherever passage is necessary. Even more width is desirable in small spaces like foyers and hallways. If you have a three-foot hallway, it is better to leave the area free than to risk cluttering it with a console or table.

If there are numerous windows in a room, you may wish to place seating pieces to take advantage of the view. Where the view is of no particular interest, you might concentrate instead on a conversation grouping, in which seats are arranged so a number of people may chat comfortably with each other. Such a grouping may vary from as little as two chairs to as much as a sofa, several upholstered lounge chairs and side chair. In addition to seating, it is usual to include cocktail tables, end tables or even chests beside chairs when necessary.

A typical conversation grouping might be built around the cocktail table. Place the sofa against the wall, with the table in front. On the opposite side of the table, place two lounge chairs separated by an occasional table or miniature chest.

A fireplace often dictates the arrangement, with a sofa facing the hearth and chairs grouped at the sides. As an alternative, sofas or love seats can extend at right angles from the fireplace wall.

The dimensions of the room have a great deal to do with actual placement. In a small room, furniture placed against the wall saves interior space. Keep in mind, however, that all furniture should not be placed "on" the wall. The result is much more charming if at least one piece, perhaps a desk table, extends out from the wall, even though placing the desk parallel to the wall would be more economical of space.

To achieve a more spacious feeling in any interior, keep enough open spaces. Do not place furniture in areas which stop the continuity of your line of vision. You can accentuate the length of a room by creating arrangements parallel to the walls, and you can diminish the length by a converse arrangement. In narrow rooms, dominant pieces are best placed on end walls.

For a pleasing overall feeling, do not put all your best pieces in one area, but distribute them throughout the room. A good piece will attract the eye and the same time minimize a lesser piece which must be included for its functional value. Distribute "weight" as well so that all furniture that is heavy in feeling is not in one area and all light-looking selections in another.

Also essential for visual appeal is variety of furniture shapes. Avoid putting only rectangular objects in a room. When working out your floor plan, vary size and shape in room areas. If a rectangular desk is used at one end of the sofa, a round table might be used at the other end. If your coffee table is square, have a round table elsewhere.

To make each piece of furniture look as if it belongs where it is, consider the surrounding area. If you place a desk against the wall, the lighting fixture used on the desk and accessories on the wall above it are part of the everall picture. If the desk extends out from the wall, attractive chairs placed on either side will help establish an eye-catching arrangement. When you are placing a large, tall or important piece against the wall—a cabinet or breakfront displaying art objects and books, perhaps—do not confuse the visual appeal of the piece by placing too many other pieces of furniture around or near it. Let this one important selection be a focal point in the overall room arrangement.

Decorating with Light

By David Barrett, A.I.D., N.S.I.D.
Interior Designer

GOOD LIGHTING creates mood and atmosphere in an interior and can add immeasurably to its personality. From a decorative standpoint, the purpose of light is to dramatize furniture, fabrics and accessories and not to call attention to the lighting instrument itself, be it a lamp, fixture or built-in technique.

Although lamps may be found in almost any size, shape or form, simplicity is suggested, and scale is very important. The size of lamps should never dominate a room. Lamps should blend in with the rest of the furnishings. Lamp shades, in particular, are best kept in simplest form and preferably in conventional shapes—round, rectangular, oval or square, with sides straight or tapered out. Variation from the norm causes lamps to stand out when they should be in the background. Floor lamps, recently returned to popularity, should be used in areas where they are out of the way of traffic.

The scale or size of lamps should relate to the furniture with which it is used. It is a good idea to use small lamps in small areas and large lamps in larger areas. If your furniture is low, you might wish to use tall lamps to create a visual impression of height against the background. When placing lamps on either side of a sofa, avoid choosing an identical pair unless you are attempting to create symmetrical balance. Lamps of different types are effective, although they should be of comparable size and height.

Cords should be unobstrusive as possible and preferably concealed altogether by taping them on or under table legs or hiding them behind chests and consoles. As a safety measure, the entire room's lighting should be controllable from a wall outlet near the entrance to prevent stumbling about in a dark room.

Fixtures hung from the ceiling may either be placed in the center of the room or in other more imaginative areas. A lighting fixture with a Tiffany shade, for example, can be suspended in a corner over a round table to highlight a handsome wood finish or dramatize a table draped to the floor with colorful fabric. Fixtures used near doors should clear the door height by several inches.

Since it is possible to create highlights or shadows with light, a little experimentation can produce remarkable effects. A small spotlight placed at the base of a tall plant will cast a shadow of the plant form on the ceiling or a nearby wall—an excellent device for filling in the empty spaces in a room not fully furnished as yet.

Light can be directed, too. By placing a small, round reflector inside the shade above the bulb, you can send light downward. In a room with bad walls, this device can be employed to direct light onto surfaces of furniture and the floor instead of having it spill on the wall and ceiling.

To emphasize certain areas of the room and diminish the importance of others, use bulbs of different wattage. Areas in the outer perimeter of a living room might be lighted with minor visibility, and the major conversational grouping highlighted with increased wattage.

Accessories and the Individual

By Lawrence Peabody, A.I.D.
Home Furnishings Designer

As a bride, you should develop your first home in an individual style— a background that reflects what is important to you and your husband as personalities.

Instead of seeking accessories that will make your home a replica of the room you saw in a magazine photograph, ask yourself what both of you really like and what your interests are. A cozy, warm background should be your goal, and to achieve this you must surround yourself with the things you love or objects that are related to things you love.

America—the whole world, in fact—is full of inexpensive, exciting, individualistic objects that make a house into a home. Here are a few examples:

1. Old books contain wonderful lithographs and drawings that can be photostated at local blueprint houses, mounted on Masonite and hung. Use them in long, horizontal arrangements—three or four in a row—or in a vertical line from floor to ceiling. If you are interested in sailing, photostat some architectural drawings of lovely old ships. These would be stunning in black and white against a yellow ochre wall.

2. Use wicker baskets on the wall, either all in a row or in a free arrangement. Place plastic containers inside the baskets and fill them with Boston ferns, philodendron or some other plant that grows easily indoors.

3. That old Victorian clock from your grandmother's house may not be a priceless Paul Revere. In fact, it may be worthless—but it means something to you. Mount it on a concealed wall bracket and surround it with circular-shaped photostats of clock parts. At practically no cost, you have a very distinctive wall grouping.

4. Candlesticks are romantic and are to be found in thousands of varieties in antique or just plain junk shops. Pick a type—brass, for example—and collect them in odd sizes, then cluster several at one end of your cocktail table.

5. Suspend some of your accessories. Candelabra over tables, hanging baskets of ferns and mobiles animate the space around them.

6. Nineteenth century paintings and prints on any subject imaginable are available today in reproductions at prices that would astound the artists who created them.

7. Weavings—small Oriental prayer rugs, Kashmir shawls and other handiwork—make beautiful wall decorations that lend rich color and texture.

8. Clusters of wooden boxes—some carved and others plain—can be arranged artistically and also put to good use for storing matches, cigarettes, cocktail napkins and the like.

9. Many flowers, plants and weeds are yours for the picking—on roadsides, in the woods and at the seashore—and enable you to introduce a fresh note to your interiors whenever you please. A blueberry branch picked in January will leaf out and last for two or three months. Laurel stays green for months and flowers in the spring. Bayberry, found on the Northeastern coast, will last for years. Wheat is enchanting as decoration—it has an ethereal quality, and the natural wheat color is perfect for mixing with other colors.

Your own hobbies, favorite sports and cultural interests will inspire ideas of your own. Above all, look for real things rather than unimaginative commercial imitations.

Decorating Your
Living and Dining Areas

JUST AS NO TWO MARRIED COUPLES are exactly alike, neither should one living room be much like another, and even in these days when houses and almost everything in them are mass produced, there is no reason why you can't give your home a look no one else has yet achieved.

You are different in the way you live, think, act, dress and respond to beautiful objects. If you design your living room according to your unique way of life, and not according to what you think is chic or proper, the results are bound to be more pleasing and appropriate.

Decide What You Need

As we have already noted, decorating any room should start with a thoughtful summation of what you really need, followed by the drawing of a floor plan. Since living room furniture today comes in so many shapes and sizes, and we have thankfully left behind the old plan of the sofa and two matching chairs as the nucleus of every room, considering all the possibilities is doubly important.

In deciding what to buy now, an appraisal of your future is essential. If you expect to move to a house or a larger apartment within two or three years, think about how current purchases will fit into a home on a grander scale. A small sofa and diminutive upholstered chairs and tables, for example, may be perfectly scaled for the tiny room you have now, but will look lost when transferred to a spacious living room.

There are ways of getting around almost any problem if you anticipate it instead of letting it creep up on you. In the case of settling temporarily in an

An informal furniture arrangement around the fireplace makes this setting by David Eugene Bell a warm and friendly gathering place. The Venetian blind, custom-made in checked fabric and draped with a swag in the same fabric as the sofa, is in perfect harmony with the Chippendale sofa and Queen Anne wing chair.

89

A temporary living room with a future is furnished with inexpensive items that may be used later in bedrooms or dens—foam rubber studio couch, wicker chair and table, modular storage cabinets and cotton accent rug. Fringed cafe curtains and sofa cover are cotton fabrics. The floor is painted to simulate hexagonal tiles.

apartment with a smaller than average living room, you might decide on a simple, inexpensive foam rubber studio couch from the casual furniture department. Later, this can be transferred to the den or guest room and you can buy a new sofa in the size you need. Other alternatives might be to select a love seat or sectionals as a nucleus, then add to them when space permits.

Other purchases to avoid in temporary situations are wall-to-wall carpeting, expensive curtains and draperies, and any piece of furniture that is extremely large in scale. Before you make any purchase, ask yourself "Can I take it with me?" and "Will it adapt to a new situation?" or "Is it inexpensive enough that I can leave it behind without regrets?"

Area rugs, or room-size rugs in average sizes, adapt easily to new settings. Since there are so many different window sizes, it's wise to buy sailcloth, denim, cotton or other economy fabrics until you are more permanently settled. As for furniture, selections that are too large are even more limited than those that are too small—a large breakfront or storage unit requires a lot of wall space and is often difficult to fit into a floor plan other than the one for which it was specifically purchased. Buy the most versatile furniture you can find. Look for modular collections, featuring storage units that stack and bunch so that you can always add on or subtract as needed. When in doubt about future requirements or unable to decide what you really want, don't invest a lot of money.

A single wall can handle a multitude of storage problems and relieve the cluttered feeling that results when there are too many pieces of furniture in a room. The system illustrated, imported from Denmark, can be dismantled and moved to another apartment. In one compact area, there are bookshelves, magazine racks, a television shelf, china cabinet and lots of drawer and cabinet space.

Keeping the future always in mind, make a list of what is necessary for now. Consider these points:

1. The way you will entertain. Having one or two couples over for an evening of cards or conversation and simple refreshments is popular with the young married set, as are informal buffet suppers for larger groups. Depending upon your own plans, you may want a conversational seating group as the focal point of the room, a table and chairs suitable for games, a set of snack tables, or an extension table for buffet service. In cabinets, you may want to provide for hi-fi, record storage and perhaps a drop-lid cabinet for mixing drinks.

2. The way you will spend evenings at home. If either of you has a hobby, attends college or brings work home from the office, special furniture and lighting may be necessary—a cozy corner with a well-lighted desk or table, a large surface for cutting out dress patterns, a place for a music stand or artist's easel. If you are both avid readers, comfortable chairs, properly placed lamps and lots of book shelves are essential. It is particularly important to have a "man-sized" upholstered chair, preferably with an ottoman.

3. The careers you will follow. When both husband and wife are full-time wage earners and time is a precious commodity, it may be necessary to keep furnishings simple so there will be a minimum of housework. Elaborately carved furniture takes longer to dust, delicate fabrics must be pampered, light-colored rugs require more frequent vacuumings and home cleanings. If you have time for frills, they're wonderful. If you don't, make compromises and look for easy-care fabrics and finishes.

4. The need for dual-purpose living areas. Space is so expensive that it pays to make the most of it, and often one room must serve two or more purposes. If your living room is too small to accommodate a dining area without looking cluttered, or you're not ready to buy a dining table and chairs, a cocktail table that rises to dining height may be perfect. You may need a sofa that converts to a single or double bed, end tables with space for linen storage, dining chairs comfortable and attractive enough to seat guests in the living room, or chairs and tables on casters so they may be shifted about to give greater usefulness. If you are not familiar with all the ingenious dual-purpose designs now on the market, take a long and leisurely shopping trip and see the latest innovations. You may come home with a whole new slant on what can be accomplished.

WORK SHEET FOR FURNITURE ARRANGEMENT

Measure your own living and dining room and outline on this graph sheet. One square, or ¼″, is equal to one square foot. Be sure to indicate windows and door frames. Then cut out templets of furniture pieces and find the arrangement best suited to your needs.

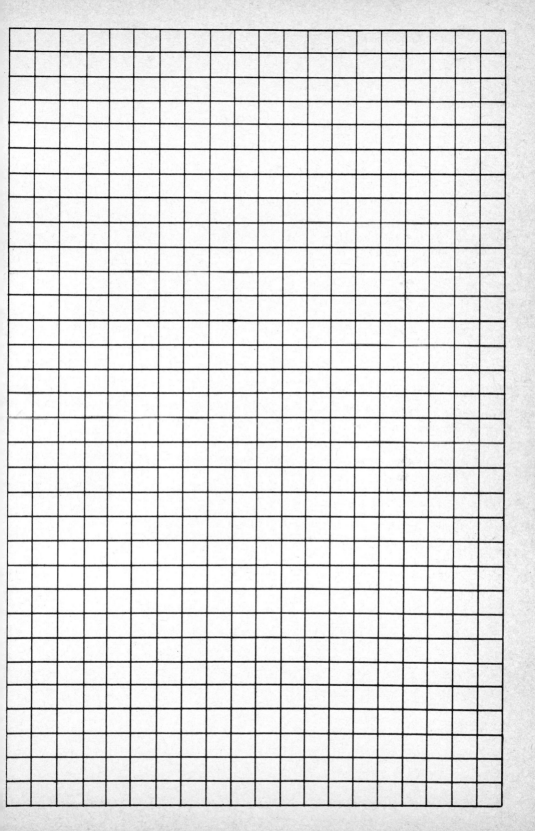

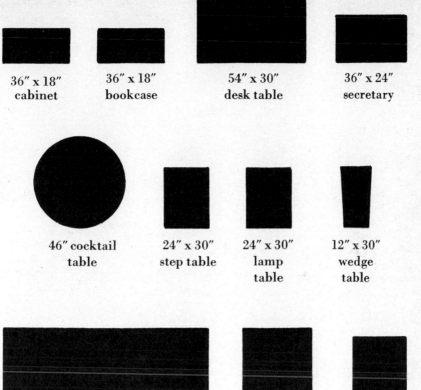

36″ x 18″
cabinet

36″ x 18″
bookcase

54″ x 30″
desk table

36″ x 24″
secretary

46″ cocktail
table

24″ x 30″
step table

24″ x 30″
lamp
table

12″ x 30″
wedge
table

102″ x 34″ sofa

36″ x 36″
lounge chair

30″ x 30″
ottoman

36″ x 36″
lounge chair

46″ x 30″
drop leaf table

66″ x 42″
extension table

Cut-Outs For Creating Your Own Furniture Arrangements

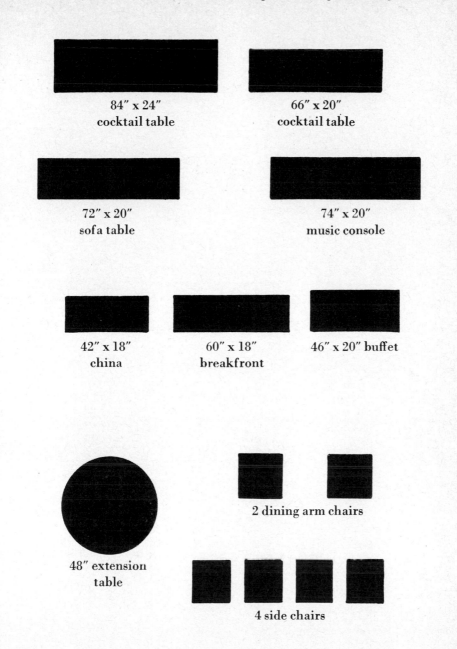

84" x 24"
cocktail table

66" x 20"
cocktail table

72" x 20"
sofa table

74" x 20"
music console

42" x 18"
china

60" x 18"
breakfront

46" x 20" buffet

2 dining arm chairs

48" extension
table

4 side chairs

Cut-Outs For Creating Your Own Furniture Arrangements On Graph Paper

Wall Furniture

If you find you need too many separate pieces of furniture to accommodate seating, serving and storage needs, think about using wall furniture. Along with dual-purpose designs, the advent of wall furniture has been one of the major victories in the conquest of inner space. There are various types of installations that give the effect of being built-in, but which are actually portable and can be easily disassembled for a move to a new location.

On a single wall, it is possible to house almost every furniture need for the entire living room—television, phonograph and record storage, bar cabinet and serving area, book and curio shelves, magazine rack, and even a drop-lid desk or dining table.

Consider the Dining Area

Separate dining rooms are not a thing of the past. But for many newlyweds, they are often a thing of the future. Fortunately, there is much that can be done in the meantime to make a dinette, dining "L" or even a corner of the

Placing a dining table before a window is pleasant as well as space-saving. Grasscloth shades and an abstract reed-patterned drapery fabric are fitting companions for the contemporary styling of the furniture.

living room into an attractive background for showing off your trousseau linens, china, silver and glass. No matter how limited the facilities, you can still dine graciously and attractively, and even give small dinner parties to repay the many social obligations you will have as a bride.

The variety of drop-leaf, extension and console tables available is endless and includes such unbelievable design feats as tables that take up less than a foot of floor space and open to seat eight or ten—or more realistically, to make room for a lavish buffet supper.

You will probably need a hutch or cabinet of some kind for your lovely new tablewares. This is an important purchase, for unless your china and other accessories are in a convenient place, you aren't going to use them as often as you should. Keep them handy so that on evenings when you have a promotion, a birthday or some other occasion for just the two of you to celebrate, it won't be too much trouble to set a pretty table.

Make Up a Floor Plan

Since there are so many different areas of activity in the living room, particularly when it incorporates a dining area, it is essential to draw up a floor plan and see if it works before you buy anything. Use the graph paper and furniture cut-outs in this chapter for trying out your ideas.

When you have worked out a trial arrangement, study it to see if it meets these requirements:

1. Are the chairs and sofa arranged so that people can face each other at a range that is comfortable for conversation?

2. Are there tables where necessary for lamps, smoking necessities and other conveniences?

3. If there are chairs around a dining table or desk, is there sufficient room for pulling them out?

4. Is the television set visible from the main seating area?

5. Do you have a free-flowing traffic pattern without stumbling blocks?

6. From the standpoint of appearance, does it look like a well-balanced room, or do you have too much weight in one area and not enough in another?

It helps to imagine typical situations and see if you have provided for them. Picture yourself greeting guests, seating them at the card table, then serving them refreshments. This will enable you to spot flaws and deficiencies. Even more important, you'll be thinking of your main living area as a place for living and not a showcase for furnishings.

Let the art of conversation thrive amid the cozy surroundings of your living room by arranging the most comfortable seating pieces near each other. Occasional tables should be handy for snacks and smoking accessories. If you have a fireplace, make it a focal point—and provide a man-size chair nearby.

How to Choose a Color Scheme

By Emily Malino, A.I.D.

OLOR IS ONE commodity that doesn't depend on a price tag—it costs no more to enjoy the right colors than it does to be surrounded by the wrong ones. Using color in a big way, in fact, may be just what the small-budget interior needs to make it seem important.

Although the study of color is actually a science, it's wrong to take a strictly scientific approach to working out a color scheme for the home. Color appeals to the senses, fires the imagination and determines moods. People react to color with their emotions—somber colors make them feel sad, gay colors make them happy and color clashes disturb them. So while it is important to know some of the basic scientific facts about different colors and the established rules for using them, don't get so wound up in studying color charts and learning terms like "monochromatic," "analagous" and "adjacent complementary" that you fail to let your own feelings be your guide.

How To Start

In almost any task you undertake, getting off to a good start is half the battle, and this is certainly true of color. Think about these three basic points:

1. Your color preferences. Most of us have emphatic likes and dislikes in colors and their combinations. An evening spent by you and your fiancé in simply looking at a color wheel or set of paint chips and discussing your feelings about each hue will be helpful. Think about colors you like. You may be partial to the brilliant hues of anemones and he may be impressed by the subtle, rich red of a painted barn. Don't discuss colors without samples in front of you— a man's idea of peacock blue may be entirely different from yours. Either or both of you may have stereotyped notions and prejudices about color, too, but

Yellow, the sunshine color, brings added light and spaciousness to a small bedroom when used in generous quantities. The secondary color, green, is used in proportionately smaller areas to offer a pleasing contrast.

103

when you actually see various schemes in front of you, it's very possible you'll have a change of heart.

2. Functions of the room. Will this be a room in constant use? If so, there are practical consideration—colors should be easy to live with for long periods of time, and not apt to show soil too quickly. If you have a yen to try a very vivid, exotic color scheme, it's best to reserve this for a room used less often or to use brilliant colors in accents only. Human nature is fickle and we tend to tire of too much intense color, even though it excites us in the beginning. Will there be a need to define separate areas? If so, you may want to plan on having an area rug or one wall in a different color to set off a study corner or dining area.

3. Architectural features. Background makes up a major part of the overall color picture. The shape of the room itself, its advantages and disadvantages must be considered before you are ready to make selections. For example, in a room where there is one wall unbroken by doors, windows or archways, you may decide to make this wall a dominant color area and play down the other three walls. In a bedroom, this can be accomplished by having the bed and wall behind it in the same color. On the other hand, if all the walls are broken up with architectural detail, you will want to make them unobtrusive by painting them all in the same subdued color—a light background for a room with a dark color scheme, or a dark background for a room with a light color scheme.

4. Be flexible. It's possible to defeat your own purpose by being overly conscientious about color coordination. In building a color scheme around the colors in a print fabric, don't insist on exact matches. If the various tones are related rather than exactly the same, such as a deep aqua slipcover to correlate with the medium aqua of the drapery print, the results will be more interesting and easier to accomplish.

How Not To Start

Next to knowing what you should do, knowing what not to do ranks high in importance. Here are some common mistakes to avoid:

1. Never copy a color scheme exactly. Magazine pictures and model room settings are meant to help and stimulate you, but not to do your work for you. The chances are the photograph you've fallen in love with may not be suited to your particular problems. The colors may have been chosen to enhance architectural features your living room lacks or to contrast with a furniture finish different from yours. Or, the scheme may just not be practical enough for the kind of punishment your room will have to take. Adapt, don't adopt, and you'll get the maximum benefit out of examples set by others.

2. Don't buy anything until your scheme is complete. No matter how much you love that bedspread, wait until you have worked out all the details of the bedroom color scheme before you buy it. A decision to paint the wall another color may change all your plans.

3. Don't start by trying to "work around" furnishings in colors you don't like. Many newlyweds inherit draperies, sofas or chairs in colors they would not have chosen themselves, but don't want to discard or have recovered. Trying to build a color scheme around such handicaps is asking for trouble, and in the long run, it's cheaper to replace or redo them than to compound the felony by making new purchases to harmonize with the old.

Once you have some idea of the colors you want, start collecting fabric swatches, paint chips and rug samples and try them out in various combinations until a plan begins to take shape.

Types of Color Schemes

You can get very technical about defining the various types of color schemes, but a common sense approach and an understanding of what effect each color has on a room and the people in it will serve much better. There are three simple color plans you may find it helpful to follow—balanced, predominant and accented.

A balanced scheme involves starting with a figured pattern—an upholstery or drapery fabric, perhaps—and repeating the colors in this pattern in solid color fabrics, paint, floor coverings and accessories. This scheme works particularly well in a living room. Its effectiveness depends on placing colors in proper relation to each other so that the major color is balanced. For example, you've selected a drapery pattern of green, blue and gold flowers on an off-white background. Paint the walls off-white. Upholster the sofa in a green solid, the club chairs in a blue and green tweed, occasional chairs in gold, and balance the whole on a neutral carpet of beige, or a deep blue area rug.

In the predominant or one-color scheme, a single color is chosen and used throughout the room in as many different shades and tints as desired. One-color schemes are excellent for bedrooms and well suited to anyone with an outstanding color preference. Suppose you and your husband both are fond of blue and decide to use it in the bedroom. Paint the walls pale blue, or white with a blue tint. The bedspread could be a floral combining muted shades of blue, lavender and aqua. Have curtains of white with a fine dark blue stripe or simply a dark blue border on all sides, or a blue fringe. Cover an occasional chair in a solid shade of pale aqua. Your rug could be a deeper shade of the wall color.

Also simple for beginners is the accented scheme, in which the entire background of the room is done in white or a light color, accented by bright touches of color in dramatic contrast. For an exciting scheme, cover your sofa and lounge chairs in off-white or beige, and keep the walls and floor light. Try various pillows on the sofa in shades of red, orange and pink. Then bring out these colors in a small chair, a bowl of flowers, a good print and some ash trays.

Whatever plan you follow, limit yourself to no more than three colors per room. While rooms or areas that open into each other should be coordinated, there is no need for color coordination on a house-wide basis. By all means, choose entirely different schemes for bedrooms as opposed to main living areas if you like.

Working with Swatches

When you have found the right combination of colors, the next step is to study the relationships of one color area to another until you know what amounts of each color to use. As a general rule, the predominant color should occupy about two-thirds of the area. In any case, never use equal amounts of two colors—this is displeasing to the eye.

To see if your proportions are right, gather all your swatches and cut them to the correct sizes in relation to each other—an upholstered chair swatch would be about one-third the size of the sofa swatch, with pillows and other accessories represented by smaller samples. It is helpful to work with a floor plan, setting your swatches down exactly where they will be in the room. But don't forget about vertical surfaces—be sure to lay paint chips and drapery swatches next to the floor plan and try to visualize the whole effect. Is there so much green that it overpowers the blue carpet? Are your bright red and shocking pink accents too small in scale to be significant? Would the print you have chosen look better if you used it just on the windows and chose a coordinating solid for the sofa? When looking at swatches, bear in mind that a busy print will be busier and an intense color more intense in large doses. Now is the time to make decisions and substitutions. If you are in doubt about any of your fabric choices, buy a half yard of each and study them together, preferably in the room where they will be used. It's well worth the money spent to be sure.

What Color Can Do

While having what you like is the primary consideration, there are tricks of the trade to be aware of that may affect some of your decisions. Different colors cause certain reactions and it is wise to think about whether or not the effect will be suitable for your setting.

First of all, there are warm colors, or those in which yellow and red predominate; and cool colors, which contain a lot of blue. If your room is dark or cold, you will want to admit light and warmth with a "sunshine" color scheme—lots of bright yellow, warm orange or orange-red. If you want to tone down a sunlit room or create a cool, relaxing atmosphere, blues and greens should be stressed.

If your color scheme is warm, meaning about two-thirds of the room features warm colors, you might wish to introduce a contrasting cool note in accent colors. Conversely, a touch of warm color can accent a cool setting.

The secondary colors may be warm, cool or in between, depending on which primary color is present in the larger amount—greens with yellow added are warmer than bluish greens, and reds with a blue tinge are cooler than orange reds.

Equally important is the principle that light colors retreat and dark colors come forward. Thus you can use light tints to make a small room look larger— an off-white rug and walls, for example, with a darker or brighter color on furniture. To create the maximum illusion of spaciousness, cover almost the entire room with a single color like beige, light blue or green, then add accent colors in small amounts. Large proportions of accent color can seem crowded in a small area.

If a room is too long and narrow, paint the narrow ends in a strong color to bring them closer and the long walls in a pale color to push them backward. For a room that is square in shape, paint two opposite walls in one color and the others in a different color. To lower a high ceiling, use a darker shade than you choose for the walls; to raise a low ceiling, use a lighter shade.

To unify a room with unattractive architectural detail, such as too many windows, coordinate the colors of the walls and windows. If the windows are not all the same size, unify them by using the same fabric, but not necessarily in the same way. Print draperies may be chosen for the picture window, and a matching fabric shade for a smaller window.

Which Colors Go Together?

There are no magic rules for determining which colors go together, since so much depends on the shade of each. Blue and green, for example, are popular as a decorating team—but in the wrong shades, they clash. By studying good examples and making an effort to be aware of color, you can learn to recognize pleasing combinations.

To sharpen your color sense, be guided by the natural beauty around you. Learn about color by looking at it, then relate what you see to your own home. Observe the autumn foliage, and you'll see that on one tree, there are dozens of different shades of yellow. Then ask yourself why those toss pillows must be the exact shade of yellow picked up from the drapery print. Aren't variations on a color theme more imaginative?

For a lesson in proportion, visit flower shows and landscape gardens and observe the way in which one area of color highlights another. To understand color harmony, visit museums and see the works of artists renowned for their use of color. Buy several inexpensive prints of famous paintings and examine their colors to stimulate your own imagination.

Color exists in abundance all around us. It is you, though, who must see it.

Decorating Your Bedroom

A S REFRESHING as a good night's sleep is the sight of a cheerful, colorful bedroom that offers convenience without clutter. To achieve this result, consider first the practical and then the decorative aspects of what you are trying to accomplish.

The Practical Aspects

First and foremost, this is a room for sleeping, so be sure to buy a good mattress set in the size necessary to allow ample room. Then you are ready to think about storage.

Bedroom storage furniture comes in all shapes and sizes and answers every need for keeping one's clothes in order. Be sure the choices you make fit not only the amount and type of possessions to be stored, but the size of the room. High, narrow chests may be best in a small room with wall space interrupted by multiple doors and windows. In other situations, one or two long pieces or a series of stacking units might be best for utilizing space efficiently.

Don't forget to consider the closet as part of the room when deciding how many drawers and cabinets will be adequate. If the closet is large enough, you can have it fitted with racks and shelves for hats, handbags, shirts, sweaters, gloves and other accessories that might normally go into a wardrobe or chest. If bedroom closet space is limited, or there is no linen closet in the apartment, an extra piece of furniture may be necessary. Be on the lookout for "bonus" storage — night tables with roomy cabinets, seating benches that are also blanket chests, and bookcase headboards with sliding door compartments.

Hinged panels from an old barn or carriage house door are the novel focal point of this bedroom. If no door is available, buy the lumber and hinges and make this unusual headboard yourself. Other decorative features are the checked rug on a vinyl tile floor and the use of one table lamp and one floor lamp instead of twin boudoir lamps on nightstands.

Mixing instead of matching makes a bedroom more interesting—rattan head-board and blanket chest, painted secretary and both light and dark wood fin-ishes. A note of the unexpected is supplied by the use of a long cocktail table as a combination night table and television stand.

Decorative Aspects

While the cliché of the bed, dresser, chest and twin night tables may have sufficed some years ago, today's generation is intent on avoiding such a stereo-typed background. Naturally, you still need a bed, some lamps and lots of drawer space—but no longer need all of these be from the same matched bed-room suite. Look for furniture collections that include surprising innovations, or make up your own. You can vary textures, for example, by including one or two pieces in materials other than wood—a cane headboard, rattan blanket chest or wrought iron desk chair. A change of pace in wood finishes also makes for interest—one painted and decorated accent piece, perhaps.

Bedroom lighting should be free from glare, colors interesting but restful, and accessories used in moderation to avoid the "busy" feeling that may jangle the nerves. For inspiration, think of what represents a peaceful setting in your own mind, and try to capture this feeling through the medium of interior decorating. Is it a favorite lakeside retreat in spring or summer? Then a blue or green color scheme may be your choice. Do the tensions of daily living fade away for you amid Early American surroundings? Perhaps you should turn your bedroom into a bit of Americana. Do you relax best when you feel pampered and luxurious? French Provincial furniture and lush fabrics are one solution.

A triumph in efficient use of space is this wall of modular storage units. The angular corner piece, teaming a one-drawer desk with lighted television hutch, is flanked by 60-inch and 72-inch dressers.

Dual-Purpose Aspects

If you take the trouble to set the mood for relaxation, why waste it by not using this room when you're awake? Properly equipped with a few extras, a bedroom is ideal as a second living room.

By working out a floor plan that makes economical use of square footage, you can find the right spot for one or two comfortable reading chairs, or perhaps a small table for playing cards or serving midnight snacks. A desk can be incorporated easily, either as a separate piece of furniture or part of a wall of stacking units, thereby providing a quiet corner for studying or paper work.

Even in small rooms where extra furniture is out of the question, the bedroom can be made more versatile simply by installing adequate lights over the headboard for reading in bed, and choosing night tables with slideout shelves for snacks. Add a small portable television set and you have an added attraction.

Advice to Wives

In your approach to decorating, certain compromises may be necessary so the result will be his private world as well as yours. There are men who are indulgent about the feminine yen for frills in the bedroom and others who rebel. If your husband is in the latter category, don't be insulted when he refuses to use the desk you put there just for him. If it faces those frilly pink ruffled curtains, who can blame him?

Somewhere between the pastel ruffles that make men feel silly and the austere "bachelor browns" that women find depressing lies the perfect decorating scheme. With his male conservatism and your frivolous femininity to balance each other, you can achieve better, more professional results than either of you might have done on your own, so be sure to make this a joint project.

WORK SHEET FOR FURNITURE ARRANGEMENT

Measure your own bedroom and outline it on this graph sheet. One square, or ¼″, is equal to one square foot. Be sure to indicate windows and door frames. Then cut out templets of furniture pieces and find the arrangement best suited to your needs.

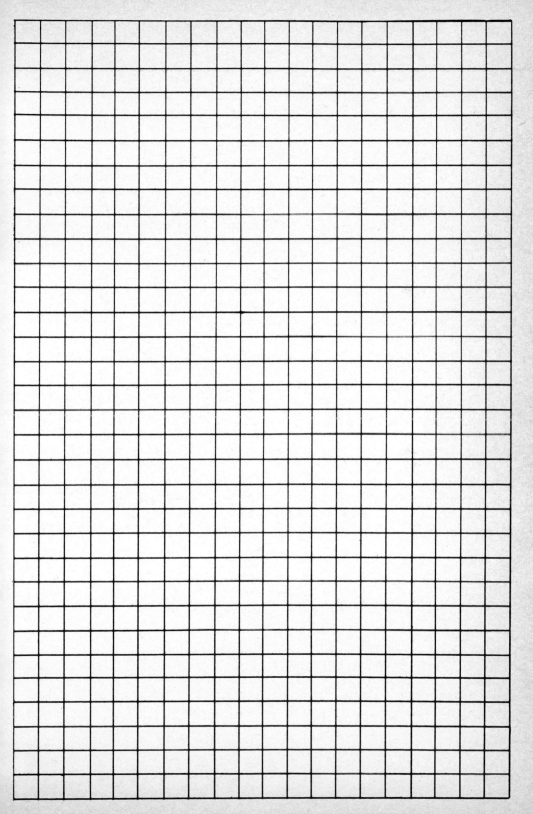

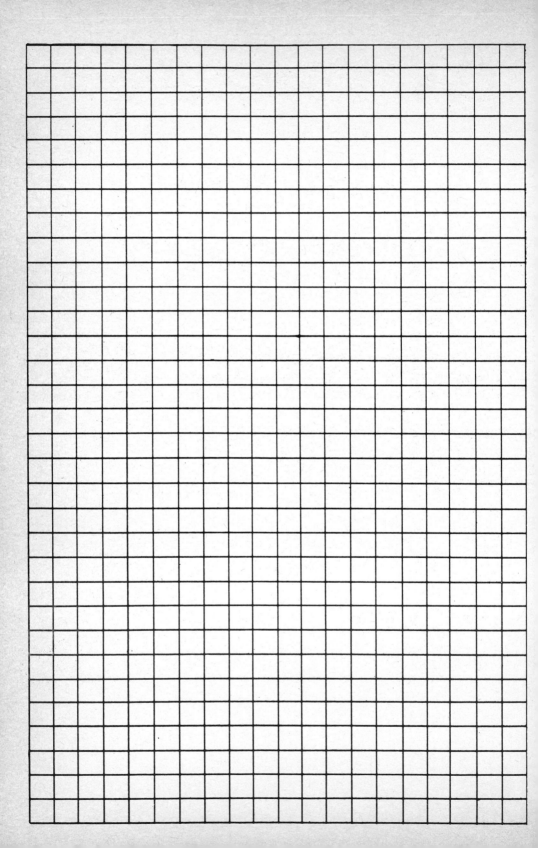

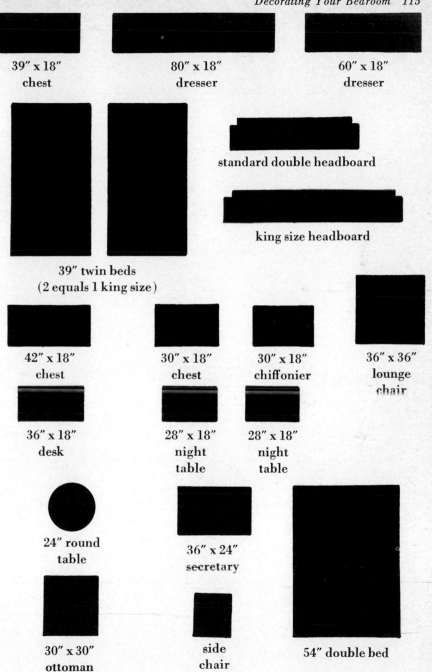

39″ x 18″
chest

80″ x 18″
dresser

60″ x 18″
dresser

standard double headboard

king size headboard

39″ twin beds
(2 equals 1 king size)

42″ x 18″
chest

30″ x 18″
chest

30″ x 18″
chiffonier

36″ x 36″
lounge
chair

36″ x 18″
desk

28″ x 18″
night
table

28″ x 18″
night
table

24″ round
table

36″ x 24″
secretary

30″ x 30″
ottoman

side
chair

54″ double bed

Cut-Outs For Creating Your Own Furniture Arrangements

The World of Windows

EVERY DECORATING SCHEME needs the bright outlook that only well-dressed windows can contribute.

Windows are something of a compromise and should be treated as such. On the one hand, we want our homes to be secluded corners where we can shut out the rest of the world. But on the other hand, we don't wish to exclude sunlight, air and natural beauty. Any trimmings added to windows, therefore, should be designed to accomplish the dual function of affording privacy, yet bringing in the benefits of the great outdoors.

Depending on where you live and what type windows you have, you may be able to satisfy all your needs for decoration with a single covering for each window, but in many cases two are required.

In most city apartments or suburban developments, the need for privacy is greater than in rural or secluded locations. By the same token, windows that are very large—picture windows, in particular—or those strategically placed at eye level, require extra thought as to coverup. Bear in mind that at night, every home is a potential spotlight in a field of darkness.

Blinds, Shutters and Shades

For affording privacy, controlling light and ventilation, venetian blinds, vertical blinds and shutters are advantageous. They may be purchased ready-made or custom-made, depending on whether or not your windows are standard sizes.

Wood shutters are particularly charming in Early American and other informal interiors when stained to blend with the furniture. They also look fresh and attractive in almost any interior if painted white or a color, either to match or contrast with the surrounding wall area.

Blinds, too, are versatile from a decorative standpoint. Although most often seen in white or light tones, they can be made up in prints and textures or trimmed with decorative tapes.

117

*An awkwardly placed window above an exposed radiator is turned to decora-
tive advantage by Paul Krauss, A.I.D., through the use of a fabric-covered
lambriquin built of pre-cut lumber. He staples the fabric over the wood, then
uses the same plaid rayon to cover an old foot locker.*

Window shades are a story in themselves. They run the gamut from translucent cloths that admit a great deal of light to the opaque fabrics that completely
darken a room. Room-darkeners are fine for bedrooms, while translucent shades
filter glare and lend privacy in rooms used primarily by day. For decorative
effect, you may choose anything from the conventional plain white shade to
textured, striped, printed, puckered, nubbed and embroidered types. You may
even have a fabric of your own choosing vinyl-coated and made into a washable
window shade. Or, create your own custom touches with appliques and other
trimmings.

Similar to window shades are matchstick or bamboo blinds that roll up and
down, and admit some light through their narrow slits.

Curtains and Draperies

From the simplest pair of curtains to the most elegant lined draperies, fabric can be used to achieve any effect you want in an interior.

For combinations of daytime light and evening privacy, opaque draperies on a traverse rod are both decorative and functional—leave them open during the day and enjoy the view, and draw them when the sun goes down. Where the view is not desirable or more seclusion is necessary, two fabrics may be preferable—a semi-sheer curtain combined with draw draperies. Two or more tiers of cafe curtains may be used to achieve double function—the top tier remains open to admit light, while the bottom tiers keep passersby from looking in.

Window coverings may be lined or unlined. A lining lengthens wear and

White shantung shades decorated with black tape are an effective door-and-window treatment designed by Emily Malino, A.I.D. Slim shutter-screens act as borders. Glass shelves on either side show off a collection of objets d'art that may be concealed behind white cabinet doors when desired.

makes the fabric drape more gracefully. If you are buying an expensive fabric, it's well worth spending a little more and adding the lining.

Combining blinds or shades with curtains is another way of obtaining maximum control over the functional possibilities of windows and creating the decorative look you want.

Decorating Tips

Conformity is a word architects strike from their vocabularies when they decide on the size, shape and placement of windows. Add to this the fact that the decoration of the surrounding walls and the view outside must be considered, and you have some idea of how wrong it is to make blanket statements about how windows should be embellished.

There are, however, a few tips applicable to almost any situation. In deciding how to decorate any window, you must first determine whether you want it to be a feature of the room, or would prefer that it all but disappear into the wall. Unattractive windows can be made unobtrusive by covering them to match

A two-shaded window treatment provides sunlight and privacy by day and total blackout at night. The room-darkener is a paisley print. Behind it is a white translucent shade with wide paisley border. John Van Koert, A.I.D., designed the room.

The simplest treatment is often the best, as illustrated by Howard Williams, A.I.D., who uses blinds to deal with an entire window wall.

the walls. If you have a patterned wallpaper, for instance, a very simple curtain or window shade in a matching fabric will give the effect you want.

Your windows will stand out, conversely, if you choose the prettiest pattern or color you can find to contrast with the walls, and perhaps repeat a fabric used on upholstery or a bedspread. As an added attention-getter, "frame" the window as you would a picture by using a cornice or shadow box.

If you are unhappy with the shape of a window, by all means change it. Instead of placing curtains on the window, place them on the wall to make a small window look wider. If the window is too short, raise the curtains to the desired height, using a shade to conceal the tell-tale wall area. Valances are also helpful in adding inches and hiding unattractive moldings.

Finishing Touches

As ANY WELL-DRESSED WOMAN KNOWS, there is no such thing as an unimportant detail in the creation of the total costume. The bright little scarf, the flash of gold jewelry and the gloves should be chosen with as much care as a suit or dress.

The same meticulous attention to finishing touches is mandatory in decorating a home. Once the furniture is in place, the rugs are down and the curtains are hung, you have an incomplete picture that awaits a final burst of creativity in order to be worthy of admiration.

Decorating the Walls

By virtue of the amount of space they occupy, walls are particularly important as areas that demand attention in the final stages of a decorating project. In addition to pictures, three-dimensional objects make impressive wall decorations, so consider using both to make arrangements more interesting.

If you own only a few frame pictures and objets d'art at present, group them together instead of trying to scatter them to the four walls. Nothing looks lonelier than an isolated piece of art, unless it's large enough to command attention by itself. To supplement your store of accessories inexpensively, buy travel posters, inexpensive prints and old maps.

In addition to the sketches that follow, these hints will help you to frame and hang your pictures attractively:

1. Choose the right frame for the type picture—a simple, provincial style for fruit and floral prints or primitives; a more elaborate traditional frame in metal, gold leaf or rich wood for formal subject matter; and a modern frame for bold, dynamic 20th-century art.

Accessories can help bring the flavor of a country kitchen to a city apartment. For contrast, polished copper utensils are mingled with brilliant fruit and flower paintings. The floor is vinyl tile in an 18th century Delft pattern.

123

2. The frame should focus attention on the picture and draw the eye to the center of interest in the picture.

3. Select a frame that harmonizes in color and weight with the subject matter of the picture.

4. Be sure the frame does not dominate the picture, particularly when the art is in a light or delicate mood.

5. Measure carefully before you start hammering. A single picture should be at eye level for a person of average height standing in the center of a room.

The Importance of Plants

Accessories that live and grow inside your home make a contribution no inanimate object can rival. Even if you are a complete amateur at gardening, it is possible to maintain vigorous and healthy plants indoors by following the advice of the person who sells them to you on watering, exposure to light and other simple tips on care.

The decorative effects that can be achieved with potted plants are endless. Large plants may be placed on the floor for accent. Use them in hallways, alongside doors, fireplaces, stairs or picture windows. Medium-sized plants are at home on wall shelves, benches, window sills and dining tables; or in room dividers, hanging baskets or window boxes. Small plants are appropriate in planters and dish gardens or on narrow shelves.

While plants enhance any setting, certain species lend themselves to contemporary rather than traditional design. For large-scale contemporary furniture, an increasing number of designers are showing the large foliage plants, often placed directly on the floor. Among these are philodendron of many varieties, Norfolk Island pine, podocarpus, dracaena, scheffler and dieffenbachia.

A revival of Victorian furniture has brought back into popularity many plants that were once considered a trifle old-fashioned. These include potted palms, rubber plants and ferns, especially the Boston fern.

Those whose preference is for French Provincial, or such periods as Louis XV, Louis XVI, Georgian, English or French Regency, should select smaller plants to blend with the more delicate scale of their furniture. Flowering plants —including white and pink azaleas, geraniums, kalanchoes and the small chrysanthemums—are excellent choices. Also appropriate are the smaller foliage plants, particularly flowing types like ivy and sprengeri. Floor plants—in the more delicate of the large-foliage plants, like dracaena and cypress—are suitable, especially in front of windows and near doorways. Stylized plants— including bonsai, succulents and snake plants—are also very attractive in settings of this type.

Plant containers, too, must be geared to the theme of the room. Clay pots, which have the advantage of providing healthy growing conditions, look well in most settings, but some period furniture is best complemented by decorative

Lots of foliage plants, all in clay pots, provide a center of interest on the shelves of a modern room divider. For a change of pace, the plants may be replaced occasionally, perhaps you might introduce flowering varieties that complement a color scheme.

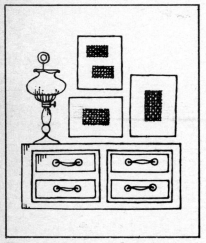

Experiment with informal placement. Instead of lining up three pictures in a row, try an asymmetrical arrangement.

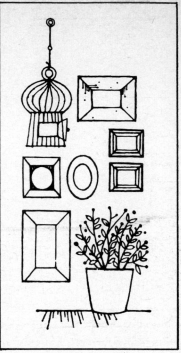

With pictures, plants and potpourri, a bare corner or a foyer can be "furnished" attractively and inexpensively.

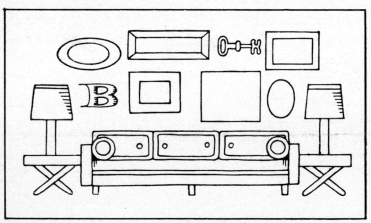

Work around lamps and other tall accessories so they won't obscure the pictures. Notice the perfect balance achieved between this grouping and the long, low sofa.

Use cardboard or fabric mats, in color or plain
white, to make small pictures appear larger. Mats
are especially right for delicate art.

Relate all objects to the scale
of the furniture. Large pictures would overpower this
small, light desk and chair.

Sketch your arrangement first by
drawing outlines on a huge piece
of paper. Above is an example of
formal balance.

Single pictures appear more
decorative when coupled
with other accessories—preferably of contrasting shape
and size.

jardinieres. In the latter case, you can always double-pot your plants by slipping the clay pot into a decorative outer container and packing the space with vermiculite or sphagnum moss.

Lighting Your Way

Aside from the obvious purpose of keeping you out of the dark, lighting has an important contribution to make in interior design. It can make rooms seem larger, colors richer, and you more attractive against the background of your new home. Don't skimp on lighting. After you have drawn up the floor plans for each of your rooms, analyze your lighting requirements, using this list to remind you of what may be needed:

1. Living rooms. About five portable lamps are necessary in the average living room. A three-light lamp, placed close within each furniture grouping, provides light for typical home activities. You may want to have some concealed lighting behind a cornice or valance for a soft, flattering effect that is also easy on the eyes. Valance lighting is ideal for televiewing—it won't reflect on the screen. If you have a card or game table, try a suspended ceiling fixture over it for proper down-light.

2. Dining rooms. A ceiling fixture, centered over the table and adjustable in height and position, offers the most desirable conditions for dining. Combine this with wall lighting to brighten the entire area.

3. Bedrooms. A close-to-the-ceiling fixture gives convenient all-over lighting throughout the room and helps you see into closets and bureau drawers. For reading in bed, night table lamps are fine, but a wall bracket over the headboard provides even light across the bed and allows more freedom in reading positions. Try two portable lamps on the dresser for good grooming as well as decoration. If you have a desk, of course, you will need a lamp there.

4. Kitchens. Good lighting helps avoid fatigue on days when you must spend hours in the kitchen. You should have either a large central fixture, fluorescent wall brackets or indirect ceiling units. In addition, specific work areas—sinks, ranges and counters—should be lighted to avoid shadows.

5. Bathrooms. Three fixtures are necessary in most bathrooms to take care of shaving and applying cosmetics. Shielded fluorescent tubes on each side of the mirror will light both sides of the face. To complete the picture, install a ceiling fixture above the wash basin to light the top of the head and reflect under the chin.

When selecting table lamps for any area, be sure they are the correct height. The bottom edge of the shade should be at eye level with the reader. Sit in a chair or sofa and measure the distance from eye level to table top, then take a tape measure when you shop.

How to Keep House

NOW THAT YOU'RE about to play the role of Mrs. Homemaker, why not become a "method" actress? It's the lady with the method who gets things done the fastest, thereby saving precious time and energy for more creative endeavor.

In order to keep house efficiently, you need a schedule, just as if you were running a business or managing a factory. Although many women keep their schedules in their heads, it's a much better idea to write yours down in the form of a work chart.

How to Draw Up a Work Chart

Once you are settled in your new home, study your housework patterns over a period of a week or two. Analyze the number and types of jobs that must be done and the time you usually allot to them. Then see how a little thoughtful planning can help you do a speedier job with less effort. Follow these guide lines:

1. List in separate columns the jobs you do daily, weekly and occasionally. Note the order in which you usually do them and the time required. Add the grace notes, too—the little finishing touches you would like to do if you could find time for them.

2. Study this list and see how you can rearrange jobs to save steps. Try grouping together those that require the same equipment or are located in the same area.

3. Schedule weekly cleaning tasks on the most logical days for each operation. For instance, defrost the refrigerator the day before your major weekly marketing. Apportion these jobs over a five-day period so that no one of them disrupts the usual daily cleaning.

The following suggestions on daily, weekly and occasional cleaning tasks provide a basis for setting up your own schedule. You will probably want to make additions or substitutions to conform with your own thinking.

Daily Routine

Swab the kitchen floor with a mop wrung out of hot soap or detergent suds. Wipe the range burners and refrigerators with a sudsy sponge. Empty trash baskets and replace paper liners.

Dust and tidy rooms. Vacuum or carpet sweep. Use a dry mop on uncovered floors.

Wash the bathtub, basin and toilet with hot suds. Wipe the bathroom floor with a mop wrung out of suds.

These tasks, of course, are in addition to the essentials—dishwashing, bed-making, marketing and cooking.

Once-A-Week Tasks

Scrub the kitchen floor with warm suds, rinse, and mop up excess moisture. Clean the range thoroughly, inside and out. Defrost the refrigerator, remove contents, and wash with suds inside and out. Wash trash and garbage containers with hot suds and scalding rinses.

Vacuum upholstery, draperies, blinds, window and door frames, rugs, floors and baseboards. Vacuum or brush fabric lamp shades. Swab plastic shades with a sudsy sponge.

Clean the bathroom, scrubbing or mopping the floor thoroughly and swabbing down tile walls.

Do the laundry and ironing. If this requires multiple loads, space them over two or three days.

Polish silver and decorative metals. Swab railings and doorknobs with a sudsy sponge. Wash mirrors and glass table tops. Rub up wood furniture.

Occasional Chores

Remove contents of closets. Wash floor, walls and fittings with a sudsy sponge. Empty drawers, wipe clean and reorganize contents.

Shampoo upholstery and rugs. Launder washable curtains, draperies and slipcovers.

Vacuum the walls. Wash the kitchen walls with soap or detergent suds.

Wash wood floors, woodwork, blinds and furniture. Wax or polish those surfaces which require it.

Empty, wash and rearrange cabinets, medicine chests, cupboards and shelves.

Wash light bulbs, window shades and fabric lamp shades with warm suds.

Suds-sponge flower pots and the leaves of houseplants.

Wash the windows.

Now you are ready to draw up a chart on a large sheet of paper, indicating days of the week and hours in the day. When you have decided on your schedule, list each task and the estimated time allotted in its proper place.

Just how you arrange this chart is your own personal decision. When you are tempted to stray too often from your arbitrary format, remind yourself that housework will never become a problem if you don't let things go.

HOW TO CLEAN EVERYTHING

Today's bride sets up housekeeping in a washable world. A home and its contents, with few exceptions, can be kept clean with water and soap or detergent suds. Time-tested cleanliness methods are listed alphabetically:

BATHROOM: Wash tile or painted walls, or plastic-coated wallcovering, with cloth or mop wrung out of hot suds; rinse with damp cloth. Mop or scrub floor, cleaning between tiles by dispensing a solution of suds and bleach from a squeeze bottle along the grout. Go over fixtures with sudsy sponge, removing stains with scouring powder. Pour hot suds and bleach in toilet bowl before scrubbing with long-handled brush. Bathtub rings can be prevented by adding a spoonful of detergent to the daily bath water.

CURTAINS: To test for soil, hold several folds of the fabric together. If this reveals dinginess not visible on a single layer, the curtains need washing. A second clean sudsing is advisable, since curtains literally "sieve" soil out of the air. Most fabrics used for window dressing today are no-iron as well as washable and can be hung back up while still damp.

Dacron, nylon and *Orlon* may be washed by hand or by machine after putting them into a mesh laundry bag to prevent snags and "roping." Use warm suds and rinses, and hang without wringing to drip dry, or use a dryer. To wash these synthetics by hand, use warm suds in bathtub or deep sink. Lightly fold the curtains into quarters, immerse, press suds through with palms of the hands, then rinse the same way. This avoids rubbing or wringing that could cause deep creases.

Fiber glass may be machine-washed only if so stated on the manufacturer's directions. After washing and rinsing, blot in a towel, then rehang, smoothing hems with fingertips. *Rayon* may be handled like nylon, using a cool iron and pressing lengthwise when fabric is nearly dry. *Cottons* are machine-washable in warm suds (for colors) or hot suds (for whites) and may need no ironing if dried in a dryer. Four to six average size pairs make a load.

FABRICS: To insure laundering success, buy washables. Save and refer to manufacturers' instructions on hang-tags or labels which come with purchases. Here are general rules to guide you in deciding what and how to launder:

Blends of fibers should be washed by the method prescribed for the dominant fiber.

Cottons, linens and rayons are machine-washable in hot suds and rinses if white or colorfast; warm suds if colors are doubtful. All but the most delicate cottons can be machine-washed, but consult labels as some need special care, such as cottons treated with resin finishes for soil- and crease-resistance.

Silks may be washed by hand or machine in warm suds and rinses. Press with a warm iron while still damp. Avoid sprinkling which can cause water spots. If fabric becomes dry, wrap in damp towel to distribute moisture evenly before pressing.

Stretch fabrics may be hand- or machine-washed in warm suds and rinses. Drip or dry automatically at low heat. Replace stretch covers on furniture while they are still damp.

Synthetic fiber fabrics, such as Dacron, Dynel, nylon and Orlon, are machine-washable. Check labels to determine proper time settings for sturdy or delicate materials. Cool-to-warm water helps prevent creases, but does not remove deep-set soil or wrinkles ingrained by wear. Therefore it is advisable to use hotter water for every fifth or sixth washing, followed by a cool rinse before the first spin to minimize wrinkling.

Water repellent finishes are machine-washable unless otherwise stated on hang-tags or labels. Use warm suds and extra thorough rinsing. Pressing with a cool iron tends to renew the effectiveness of the finish.

Wools are best washed by hand unless pre-treated for shrink-resistance. Use lukewarm suds and rinses, keeping in mind that this fiber is very absorbent and requires more suds than other materials. Lay flat to dry, or place in automatic dryer at Off setting.

FLOORS AND FLOOR COVERINGS: A good general rule is to wash the floor with a brush or mop wrung out of soap or detergent suds to avoid excess moisture, then wipe speedily with an almost-dry cloth or mop. Never apply wax until floor is completely dry.

Asphalt tile: Mop with warm suds and rinse.

Concrete: Scour with a stiff brush and hot suds. Flush-rinse with hose if the floor has a drain.

Cork tile: Wash with warm or cool suds and rinse. Wax as desired.

Hardwood (shellacked or varnished) : Wash at intervals with warm suds. Rinse and mop dry quickly, never letting water stand.

Linoleum: Wash at least once a week with warm suds and rinse. Wax if desired.

Painted: Wash with warm suds, rinse and dry quickly.

Vinyl tile: Wash with cool-to-warm suds, rinse and dry promptly. Some plastic tiles are best left unwaxed, so follow manufactuer's instructions for daily and occasional care.

FURNITURE, Wood: Use "dry" suds (made by beating a handful of soap or detergent with a little water until the mixture peaks like meringue), applied with a soft cloth, to remove soil and old wax or polish from wood surfaces. This thorough cleaning is needed occasionally even by the finest antiques. Wash with the grain of the wood—haphazard motions leave streaks. Rinse with an almost-dry cloth, then rub with completely dry cloth, always using the same methodical strokes to enhance the pattern. If possible, use a wood block, of pine or other soft wood, to stroke wood surfaces after rinsing. This smooths down any fine "hairs" which have been raised by moisture. A piece of an old orange crate will serve as a block. Only when furniture is thoroughly dry should the appropriate oil or wax finish be applied.

GLASSWARE: Protect from extreme and sudden changes of temperature. Let icy glasses warm to room temperature before washing. Use suds as hot as the hands can comfortably stand, and rinse with almost scalding water. Glassware may be left to "air" dry in drainer, or polished with a soft cloth. Precious cut-glass pieces should be washed individually, using a sudsy brush. After drying, rub with a soft tissue to add luster. As a general precaution, rubber mats in sink or dishpan and on drainboard guard against chipping. With an automatic dishwasher, follow directions as to temperature.

LAMPS AND SHADES:

Bases of ceramic, glass, glazed pottery, plastic, metal and wood can be wiped clean with a sudsy cloth, rinsed with a damp cloth, then wiped dry.

Bulbs should be removed from sockets to wash the glass with a sudsy cloth, but never wet the metal neck. Dry before replacing.

Cords should be disconnected and drawn taut through a sudsy cloth or sponge, then wiped and allowed to dry completely before being connected.

Shades may be sponged clean with "dry" suds or immersed in sudsy water, depending on material and construction. Coated fabric, plastic, paper parchment or parchment shades should be given the "dry" suds treatment, rinsed with damp sponge or cloth and wiped dry. This method is also recommended for fabric shades which are glued. Stitched fabric shades may be plunged into deep warm suds, using sponge or soft brush on stubborn spots. Rinse in clear water, or use a spray. Shake off excess water and dry in a current of air or near an electric fan.

Reflectors may be put into hot suds, rinsed and wiped dry.

Indirect lighting fixtures may include luminous ceilings, wall brackets, cornices and valances—with plastic panels, corrugated sheeting, frosted glass, louvers or other translucent shielding. All need regular washing in warm suds. Plastic panels are lightweight and easy to remove from suspension bars. Corrugated plastic in sheets may be unfastened, rolled and carried to a large washtub or bathtub. Do not use abrasives on plastic—a soft cloth or sponge wrung out of suds is safest. Let plastic "air-dry" before replacing, because rubbing creates static electricity which acts as a magnet for dust. Wearing soft white gloves while handling plastic panels will prevent leaving fingerprints.

MATTRESSES, COVERS AND PADS: Mattresses should be aired daily, turned and vacuumed or brushed once a week. Use "dry" suds to wash soil spots from the surface. Once or twice a year, remove for thorough scrubbing, taking outdoors on a sunny day if possible. Go over entire surface on both sides with brush and stiff suds, rinsing with damp cloth or sponge as each area is cleaned. Allow to dry thoroughly, exposing each side to air and sun.

Covers may be machine-washed in hot suds and put in the dryer. If line-dried, pull edges straight when hanging. Plastic covers may be kept clean by sponging regularly with warm suds, rinsing with damp cloth and wiping dry.

Pads are machine-washable in hot suds. They benefit by dryer-drying which fluffs them. If line-dried, hang lengthwise over parallel lines and shake vigorously to fluff the stuffing.

METALS, *Decorative:*

Aluminum may be washed with warm-to-hot suds, scoured with fine steel wool if needed. Rinse with hot water, dry, and polish with a soft cloth.

Brass, if lacquered, should be washed in lukewarm suds, rinsed, and rubbed dry. Badly tarnished unlacquered brass needs hot suds followed by polish when dry. A piece of lemon dipped in salt, or hot vinegar and salt, will remove corrosion. After polishing, wash again thoroughly.

Chromium needs only warm suds and rinses, followed by polishing with a soft cloth.

Copper should be washed in warm suds. Add a little ammonia to remove spots caused by corrosion. Rinse, dry and apply polish.

Pewter normally comes clean with warm suds. If heavily tarnished, cover with silver polish; then while still wet, apply suds generously. Rinse in hot water and dry thoroughly.

Silver, when used regularly, stays bright simply through hot sudsing and rinsing. Polish is needed only occasionally. If ornamental, polish at regular intervals after washing. Use clean soft cloth to buff.

Stainless steel responds promptly to washing in hot suds, as deposits of all kinds come off easily. Use a well-lathered sponge, fiber brush or cloth; then rinse and wipe dry. No polishing is necessary.

How to dine without a dining room is the lesson to be learned from this thoughtfully-planned living room. The large, round cocktail table is set buffet-style for six guests who can luxuriate on the sofa, pull up a chair or relax oriental style on a floor pillow.

PILLOWS: If there is an inner lining, remove and wash ticking separately. Or rip a few inches of ticking seam and baste or safety-pin the opening as a vent to allow suds to float out soil but not the stuffing.

Feather, down, Acrilan, Dacron and Orlon filled pillows are machine-washable and dryable. Wash two pillows at a time or add towels to balance the load for one. Use warm suds generously. Turn pillows during washing if possible. Rinse well, re-stitch opening in ticking, then put into dryer or hang out on a breezy day. Shake and punch pillows during drying to plump them up and distribute filling evenly.

Latex foam rubber: Put pillows into cases with the open ends loosely basted, then machine-wash in warm suds for five minutes. Press between bath towels to remove excess moisture, then hang with clip-type clothespins. Do *not* use a dryer. Foam rubber is slow-drying, so allow ample time.

Polyurethane foam: Wash by hand, pressing warm suds and rinse water through the pillow with palms of the hands, or a plunger. Dry by machine or air.

PLANTS: Swab dust and soot from foliage with sponge or cloth wrung out of cool soapsuds. Rinse in same manner, protecting earth in pot with a sheet of plastic or waxed paper slit at one side and fitted around plant stem. Or turn the pot upside down and dip foliage into suds, then into rinse water, holding plant firmly in place. An atomizer may be used to apply sudsy solution and rinse water to very delicate foliage. Swab plant containers with sudsy sponge, rinse, and wipe off excess moisture. Allow plants to dry away from sunshine. With a small brush, apply mineral oil to make leaves shiny.

PLASTICS: Many plastic items, such as tablecloths, shower curtains and raincoats, can be washed by machine with towels added to the load as buffers. Use warm suds and rinses, short cycles, and remove as soon as the washer shuts off. Hang to drip, wipe dry, or use a dryer at Off or lowest heat setting. Plastic draperies, slipcovers and bedspreads can be washed "on location"— sponge the surface with suds, rinse with a clean damp cloth and wipe dry. Because plastics are non-porous and non-absorbent, soil is easily removed. So between machine-washings, a quick going-over with suds is effective, using a well-lathered brush to clean soil from textured surfaces.

Freeze, cook and serve in the same dishes—then set them back on the shelf to be admired as decorative accessories. What more can you ask of any cookware? Made of Pyroceram, they may be used for top-of-the-stove cooking as well as in the oven or broiler.

POTS AND PANS: When pre-soaking, use cold water for utensils containing residues of milk, eggs, starchy foods; hot water for sugary or greasy residues. Washing directions are as follows:

Agate and enamel: Handle gently, treating as glass. Wash only with hot suds as abrasives encourage chipping. If food is burned on, soak in suds until crust can be scraped off with a rubber or wooden spatula.

Aluminum: Wash in hot suds, using steel wool if necessary to remove discolored spots. Scald and wipe dry.

Chrome: Wash with hot suds, rinse and wipe dry, polishing with soft cloth.

Copper: Wash in hot suds, rinse, dry carefully with soft cloth. If badly soiled, apply a paste of hot vinegar, salt and flour in equal parts, allow to dry, then wipe off. Follow by sudsing, rinsing and drying thoroughly to restore the original lustre.

Glass: Wash with hot suds and rinses. Never use coarse abrasives. Air dry or wipe with soft cloth.

Iron: Use hot suds, and a stiff brush or steel wool if necessary. After rinsing, wipe completely dry.

Nickel: Wash in hot suds and rinses, wipe with dry cloth.

Stainless steel: Wash in hot suds, rinse and rub dry with soft cloth. Prompt and thorough drying will prevent water spots.

Electric cookware: Many newer items may be submerged in hot suds for thorough washing. Follow manufacturer's directions carefully, however. If the electrical unit is not detachable, the appliance should not be completely immersed in water.

RANGES: Wipe up spills as they occur. Use a sudsy sponge or cloth to wash enamel surfaces daily, when cool; rinse and wipe dry. Wash removable parts— drip pans, broiler racks, oven shelves, burner grates or reflectors—in deep hot suds at the sink. Rinse and dry thoroughly before replacing. Electric units will burn themselves clean; gas burners should be removed for sudsing with a stiff brush. Wash deepwell cooker with hot suds after each use. Swab inside of oven with sudsy sponge; if grease has collected, leave a bowl of suds and ammonia in the cooled oven overnight to loosen the deposit. After this is wiped away, wash again.

REFRIGERATORS: At least once a week, defrost, remove food and shelves, and swab the interior with a sudsy sponge or cloth. Wipe with damp rinse cloth. Put removable parts such as shelves and containers in deep hot suds and wash ice trays in warm suds. Rinse thoroughly and dry all parts before replacing. Wash the rubber door seal and go over inside surfaces with a sudsy sponge. Even if your refrigerator defrosts automatically, it still needs this weekly cleaning to get rid of stale food odors.

RUGS (scatter types, carpeting panels): Many small rugs and mats can be machine-washed and dried. If line-dried, shake briskly during drying to fluff up pile. Washable carpeting laid in sections or panels small enough to go into the washer can be machine-washed and dried piece by piece. Or hang over two parallel lines, set two or three feet apart, to prevent line marks. (For care of large rugs and carpets, see page 74).

SALAD BOWLS: Contrary to some theories, wooden salad bowls can be washed, but should not be soaked. Use warm suds and rinses, then wipe dry. When bowl is thoroughly dry, rub in coating of oil and let it remain overnight. Then wipe with paper toweling until all oily residue is removed.

SHOWER CURTAINS: Launder often, by hand or machine. An easy way is to swish through warm suds and rinses in the bathtub. If badly soiled around hem and edges, use a soft laundry brush. Re-hang on shower rod to dry, weighting hem with skirt hangers for smooth drying.

SLIPCOVERS AND DRAPERIES: In general, cottons and linens, whites and pastel colors can take hotter water than synthetic fabrics, deep tones and prints. Synthetics, and natural fibers treated with stain-resistant and wrinkle-resistant finishes, require warm suds.

Slipcovers: Shake, brush or vacuum to remove dust and lint. Close zippers or grippers. Rub thick suds into soiled spots, and let set for 10 minutes. Wash one large or two small pieces per machine load. Or soak briefly in a tub, then use a plunger for sudsing and rinsing. Dry by machine or hang over parallel lines. In either case, remove covers while still slightly damp and replace on furniture. Stretch seams and welts, pull pleats into place and smooth flat areas. Set an electric fan nearby to complete drying.

Draperies: Follow manufacturer's instructions on whether to wash by hand or machine. When hand-washing, do one panel or one pair at a time, in deep laundry tub or bathtub with plenty of room to swish them through suds and rinses. After drip-drying over parallel lines, or machine-drying, remove slightly damp and press at once. If pressing is optional, re-hang at windows and stretch edges and seams. In machine-washing synthetic fiber fabrics, keep both wash and spin cycles short.

STARCHING, BLEACHING, BLUING:

Bleaching: Chemical bleaches are no substitute for efficient washing, because only a solution of soap or detergent can emulsify and remove soil. But occasionally adding bleach to the wash cycle helps remove some stains and retards a tendency of some fabrics to yellow with use and age. Never use chlorine on silk, wool, acetate, spandex or on cottons treated with certain resins.

Since you can't predict the effect of chlorine on fabric, follow directions on the label. If in doubt, use a perborate, oxygen-type, or other non-chlorine bleach. Always rinse thoroughly after bleaching.

To whiten cottons and linens safely, coat pieces with thick suds and, without rinsing, hang to dry in the sun. After this natural bleaching, launder fabrics in clean hot suds and rinses. If necessary, repeat the process.

Bluing does not make fabrics come clean, but does brighten colors and make white fabrics appear whiter. Varieties include dry, liquid, stick and tablet forms. Follow printed directions for each.

Starching: Depending on crispness desired, use heavy starch for shirt collars and cuffs and children's dresses; medium for dresses and aprons; light for sheer rayons and cottons, synthetic fabrics, curtains and lace. Follow directions to prepare hot or cold starch. Liquid starch is convenient for small items. Plastic starch, which lasts through many washings, should be used sparingly. Some starches and plastic finishes come in spray cans to apply as you iron.

TABLE LINENS: It is wise to launder new table linens before using to remove the factory finish, soil and finger marks due to handling, pasted labels, machine oil or embroidery stamping ink. Don't try to use them just once more before laundering. Any food or beverage stains should be pre-treated at once. Then cloth and napkins can be laundered later when convenient.

Many plastic and plastic-coated cloths can be machine-washed, so follow manufacturer's directions. Always press "real" linen quite damp with a hot iron—first on the wrong side, then on the right for luster. To reduce wear, change the fold lines from time to time when storing linens. Or roll them on cardboard cylinders to eliminate creases.

UPHOLSTERY: If the fabric can safely take water, it can be shampooed with "dry" suds applied to upholstery with rotary motions. Wash small sections at a time, overlapping strokes and scraping off soiled suds with dull edge of a knife as you work. Then rinse with clean cloth wrung out of clear water. Wrap cloth around a ruler to work suds into crevices between seat and back and along arms. Rinse with same method.

VENETIAN BLINDS: Dust or vacuum, then tilt slats down and wipe with cloth or sponge wrung out in warm suds. Rinse with clean damp cloth and repeat with slats turned up. Occasionally, remove blinds and immerse in deep warm suds. Scrub tapes on both sides with a well-lathered brush. Rinse, wipe, and let blinds hang full length while tapes are drying to prevent shrinkage.

WALLS AND WOODWORK: Most wall finishes can be safely washed with soap or detergent suds. If in doubt, test with sudsy sponge on hidden area.

Painted walls: After dusting with wall mop, apply thick suds with sponge or cloth—one section at a time, with overlapping strokes. Rinse with sponge wrung out of clear water, and wipe dry. Change to clean suds and rinse water as needed. Always work from the baseboard up to prevent water from dribbling down over soiled walls, leaving hard-to-remove streaks.

Wall coverings: For asphalt, cork, vinyl and other wall tiles, use same sudsing method as above. Also for coated or plasticized fabric and linoleum.

Woodwork: Go over moldings, door and window frames, sills and cupboards with sponge or cloth wrung out of warm suds. Wash thoroughly to remove gummy old wax; then rinse and allow to dry before applying fresh wax.

WINDOWS: Wash with warm soap or detergent suds, adding a few drops of vinegar or kerosene and a little bluing for extra sparkle. A bottle brush dipped in suds will pick up dust from corners of window pane molding. Rinse with warm water and polish dry with clean, lintless cloth.

WINDOW SHADES: Spread washable shade flat. Scrub with stiff suds and sponge or brush, using overlapping strokes on one section at a time. Rinse-wipe with clean damp cloth, avoiding excess moisture. After completing one side, turn shade and wash reverse side. Re-hang at window, leaving unrolled to dry thoroughly.

STAIN REMOVAL GUIDE

Soap or detergent suds alone will remove many common stains from washable materials if tackled while fresh. But a two part treatment is necessary for stubborn stains—first loosening, then laundering. Directions follow:

Adhesive tape: Apply kerosene, then wash in hot suds.

Alcoholic beverages: Soak or sponge promptly with cool water, then wash in warm suds. For old stains on white cotton or linen which have turned brown, use a weak solution of household bleach and re-launder.

Blood: Soak or rub in cold water, then wash in warm suds. If stain persists, soak briefly in a weak solution of bleach; then re-launder.

Candle wax: Scrape off excess and press stained spot between white blotters, using a hot iron. Then rub any remaining spot with cold lard or turpentine and wash in warm suds.

Chocolate or cocoa: Wash in warm suds. Treat any remaining stain with a weak solution of household bleach or hydrogen peroxide and re-launder in hot suds.

Cod-liver oil: Sponge with glycerine or carbon tetrachloride, rub lightly to loosen the stain, then rinse. Follow by laundering in warm suds. Old stains are almost impossible to remove.

Coffee and tea: Pour boiling water from a height of 3 or 4 feet through the stained fabric stretched taut over a bowl. Then wash thoroughly in hot suds.

Egg: Scrape off excess; soak in cool water. Then wash in warm suds.

Fruits and berries: Sponge peach, pear, cherry and plum stains at once with cool water and rub with glycerine. After two hours, apply a few drops of vinegar for a minute or two, then rinse and launder in warm suds. For other fruits, stretch the stained portion of fabric over a bowl and fasten with an elastic band or string. Pour boiling water through it from a height, then launder in suds.

Glue: Soak in warm suds until dissolved, then launder in clean warm suds.

Grass and foliage: Scrub with hot water and suds. If necessary, use a mild bleach. Then wash promptly in warm suds.

Gravy and white sauce: Soak in cool water, then wash in hot suds.

Grease, oil and tar: Pure fats and oils usually come out by rubbing with thick lather. Rub tar-like or heavy grease spots with lard, then wash in very hot suds.

Iodine: Warm suds remove fresh stains. If set, moisten and place in the sunshine; or cover with a paste of starch and ammonia, let this dry, and brush off. Then launder.

Lipstick and rouge: Soften with glycerine and launder in hot suds.

Mayonnaise: Sponge with cold water to remove the egg, next with warm suds to remove oil, then wash in hot suds.

Meat juices: Soak in cool water, then wash in hot suds.

Mildew: Wash in sudsy water and hang outdoors with mildewed spots exposed to sunlight. If spots persist, rub with lemon juice and salt, bleach in the sun, then launder in hot suds.

Milk or cream: Sponge or soak with cool water, then wash in hot suds.

Paint: If fresh, use lots of hot suds; if set, apply turpentine, kerosene or lard and wash in hot suds. Still-wet *water emulsion paint* usually comes out in hot suds. There is no practical solvent for dried latex-base or casein-base cold water paints. *Plastic paints* require professional treatment with strong solvents. Use a solvent such as carbon tetrachloride on *spray paints,* then launder with suds.

Scorch: If light, launder in hot suds. If deep, rub with suds and bleach in the sun or dampen with hydrogen peroxide. Then launder in hot suds.

Soft drinks: Sponge at once with cool water or equal parts of alcohol and water, as these stains may turn brown with "age." Rub stain with glycerine, let stand for half an hour, rinse, then launder in hot suds.

Tomato and tomato catsup: Dampen stains with cool water and rub with glycerine. Let it stand for half an hour, then wash with hot suds.

Note: Use carbon tetrachloride and other solvents sparingly in a well-ventilated room away from fire.

For Bridegrooms Only

GETTING SETTLED in a new apartment is a task that's big enough for two. It will take a lot of hammering, painting and puttering before your home acquires the lived-in look your bride longs to see.

Today, with so much attention being focused on the walls as a source of extra storage space as well as decorative beauty, a man who knows how to wield a few simple tools is really something to boast about. On the next page, you'll find a chart to help you cope with the intricacies of hanging all sorts of objects, from towel bars to heavy furniture.

Meanwhile, the job of furnishing a home awaits both of you. If you are one of those men who has never bought anything but sports jackets and fishing rods, here are some suggestions:

1. Take an active part in preliminary budget sessions on home equipment buying. As the head of the household, it isn't fair to leave all these decisions to your wife.

2. Speak your mind about what you want or expect in your new environment. If you must have a desk for doing sales reports or a place to display your gun collection, now is the time to plan for it.

3. If you have an aversion to a particular color or style, don't suffer in silence because you feel this isn't a male prerogative. A married couple's home should reflect the tastes and personalities of two people.

4. You may be color blind, but it's nice to have you along when buying furniture. While women are influenced by style and color, men usually consider comfort and practicality first.

5. Be observant when you shop. Read labels, ask questions and study the differences in workmanship and quality of merchandise in different price categories. Two heads are better than one, and with both of you able to make intelligent appraisals, you will get more for your money.

6. Grumble all you want. It *is* a man's prerogative to show disdain for shopping, even though he may secretly enjoy it.

ITEM	PLASTER
Pictures, mirrors, clocks and other wall accessories up to 100 pounds	Use conventional picture hooks in correct size for weight you are hanging. To avoid chipping plaster, put a piece of masking or cellophane tape over area where nail will be inserted and hammer gently. For heavy mirrors and other items 50 pounds or more, locate the studs * and nail to them a piece of plywood ($\frac{1}{4}''$ by 3'' by width of item), Then nail picture hooks to plywood.
Book shelves supported by bracket arms.	Best procedure: locate studs,* then secure the metal strips to the studs with wood screws. If studs cannot be located, substitute toggle bolts for wood screws.
Towel bars, tie racks, knick-knack shelves and other items supporting light weights.	Use long self-threading screws. (At least $1\frac{1}{2}''$).
Wall-hung furniture.	Locate the studs.* Affix cabinet to studs with lag screws (2'' to 3'' long). If studs cannot be located, use toggle bolts.
Curtain and drapery rods hung from wall or ceiling.	Use self-threading screws.
Curtain and drapery rods hung from window jambs.	For wood jambs, use wood screws. For steel jambs, affix rods to surrounding plaster or sheet rock whenever possible. If not possible, drill into jamb with electric drill and use sheet metal screws.

SHEET ROCK	WOOD PANELING	BRICK OR TILE
Same as plaster, but protective tape not necessary.	Use conventional picture hooks or wood screws	For brick, obtain steel-cut nails and nail them into the mortar. For tile, or brick that has been plastered over, use a masonry or star drill to make openings for lead expansion shields.
Same as plaster. If studs cannot be located, substitute Molly bolts for wood screws.	Use self-threading screws ($\frac{3}{4}''$ to $1''$ long).	Same as above.
Same as plaster.	Same as plaster.	Same as above.
Same as plaster. If studs cannot be located, use Molly bolts.	Locate studs.* Affix cabinet with wood screws. ($1\frac{1}{2}''$ to $2''$ long). If studs cannot be located, use self-threading screws at least $1\frac{1}{2}''$ long.	Same as above.
Use Molly bolts.	Use self-threading screws.	Same as above.

* To find studs, rap on wall, moving along until you detect a change in sound from hollow to solid. The stud is behind the solid area and others are usually spaced 16'' apart. Or, buy a stud-finder at the hardware counter—a magnetic device that points out studs by attracting nails.

The Bride in the Kitchen

GOOD FOOD BEGINS with a sound knowledge of the fundamentals of cooking. Once a homemaker learns the basic principles she can add a spice here, a condiment there, and can adapt a basic recipe to suit the special flavor preferences of her husband and friends.

This is when cooking becomes an adventure, when it is no longer a chore to prepare the necessary meals and what would normally be considered work becomes a creative outlet.

It takes just as long and costs just as much to put indifferent meat, overcooked vegetables, and a soggy dessert on the table as it does to prepare good food, food with integrity that satisfies not only the inner man but sooths the discords of modern living. Dusting a table or scrubbing a floor offer little joy to those who must perform these tasks, but cooking can be creative. It can add a new and fascinating dimension to life, and any woman, who has delighted her husband with a triumphant dinner, need not be told how sweet culinary compliments are to the feminine soul!

What is good food? Is it a spectacular dish, using expensive ingredients, extravagantly prepared over many hours of labor in the kitchen? Indeed, it is not, and don't let anybody tell you it is.

The best food in the world is a dish carefully prepared from good wholesome ingredients, attractively presented on a pretty table. It may have taken only a few minutes to make from start to finish. It may be a simple casserole of macaroni and cheese, prepared in the morning and heated before serving. But the macaroni was cooked just eight minutes. It was not undercooked or cooked to a mush, the cheese sauce was creamy and golden, made with good aged American cheddar, and it was served hot on hot plates. That's good food! That's good eating!

The kitchen with a French farmhouse look can still offer all the modern conveniences. Above, textured woodgrain Formica appears on cabinets, ceiling beams, curved stove hood. Moveabout Formica-covered cubes, set for breakfast for two, can be used for buffet serving in living rooms or on terraces.

147

The following chapters in this book will, it is hoped, start you off on the right culinary foot. They do not pretend to take the place of a good general cookbook, such as *The Joy of Cooking* or *The New York Times Cookbook,* which you may have been lucky enough to receive as wedding presents, nor can they be considered a specialty cookbook, many of which you will want to collect and accumulate as you become more and more proficient in the kitchen. If these chapters can succeed in interesting you to provide a good table for your husband and can awaken in you the creative urge that is so satisfied by the art of cooking, it will have done its job, and you will be well on your way to being a really fine cook. Good food can go far to make your marriage a success, for a well-fed husband is a happy one and, being a good hostess to his business friends and acquaintances can help tremendously in furthering his career and your lifelong happiness together.

EQUIPPING THE KITCHEN

The housewares department of your favorite department store is burgeoning with gadgets which can contribute much toward making your life in the kitchen easier and more pleasant.

We don't suggest that you try to rush out and buy them all at once. At first you will need only a few of the most important. You can add additional equipment as your interest in cooking increases. Most gadgets are relatively inexpensive and you can add them at a rate equal to your enthusiasm.

In addition to a well-regulated stove with a dependable thermostat and a refrigerator with an adequate freezing compartment, an electric blender is a basic small appliance for all cooks. Then you need an adequate supply of the right size of pots and pans and skillets to feed you and your husband, and guests. High on the priority list in this category is a double boiler to allow you to make sauces without constantly stirring. You need several wooden spoons with which to stir, without scratching your pans or imparting a metallic flavor to your foods.

A swivel-bladed paring knife is essential for peeling fruit and vegetables quickly and economically. A pastry brush is vital for spreading melted butter or beaten egg on pastries and you should have a pair of tongs for turning chops, chicken, and other foods. Forks should not be used for they puncture the meat and allow valuable juices to escape. A wire whisk for making sauces can turn an amateur into a professional overnight.

Several rubber spatulas, the slim bottle scraper kind, are handy for folding in egg whites and scraping mixing bowls clean. And no cook should lack a pepper mill. Freshly ground pepper from whole peppercorns is much more pungent than the ground varieties. For other freshly ground seeds and spices you need a small mortar and pestle. This can be a decorative addition to your kitchen as well as useful.

Any cook who enjoys wine needs a sturdy metal corkscrew and everybody needs a food mill for pureeing soft fruits and cooked vegetables if they don't have an electric blender.

Nice to have, but not vital, are a wire salad basket for shaking excess moisture out of salad greens, an egg slicer to slice eggs uniformly, a cheese grater, such as the Mouli cheese mill, imported from France, cheesecloth for straining aspics, and a melon ball cutter to add festive touches to fresh fruit mixtures. Finally a pastry bag with several sizes and shapes of tubes belongs in the kitchen of any bride who likes to add decorative touches to salads and cakes or for making fluted borders and rosettes from mashed potato. For further details, photographs and lists, see the chapter, *Equipping the Kitchen.*

STOCKING THE SHELVES

Part of the first day in your new home will be devoted to a trip to your local supermarket. You may have to make more than one trip, or enlist the co-operation of your husband, if you are going to have to carry home enough supplies to begin housekeeping. Many markets have a delivery service which you may wish to take advantage of during the first few days of stocking your kitchen. Plan to spend some time in the market to familiarize yourself with how the products are grouped and where each category is located. You will also want to inspect the meat, vegetable and dairy counters to be sure that produce is fresh and stored under ideal conditions. You will only want to buy the bare essentials on your first day's shopping. You have many other things to attend to and, besides, it is going to take more than the average amount of your food budget to get started. Additional ingredients can be accumulated over a period of weeks or even months.

Before shopping, plan your first luncheon and dinner menu, keeping them simple, and make a list of every ingredient you are going to need for these meals. Then check your list to make sure you have included the following foods, which should be kept in constant supply in your refrigerator or on your shelves:

Butter or margarine	Bread
Cream	Sugar
Milk	Salt
Cheese	Pepper
Eggs	Tea or coffee
Parsley	Fruit juice
Lemons	Jam, jelly or marmalade

STAPLES FOR THE WELL-STOCKED KITCHEN

The following staples can be accumulated as you need them in recipes over a period of weeks. Put them in orderly categories in your kitchen cabinets and renew the supply as needed:

Baking Staples

Flour, all-purpose

Flour, cake

Baking powder

Baking soda

Cream of tartar

Chocolate, bitter and semi-sweet bits

Cocoa

Cornmeal

Flavoring extracts

Food coloring

Molasses

Brown sugar

Confectioner's sugar

Walnuts, pecans, or almonds

Salad Ingredients

Vinegar, Cider and wine

Salad Oil

Mustard, dry and prepared

Garlic, powder or fresh (optional)

Onions

Canned Foods

Canned shortening

Canned soups, including chicken and beef stock

Canned beef gravy

Canned vegetables (favorites including tomatoes)

Evaporated milk

Tomato paste

Canned fruits

Canned fish

Bottled and Preserved

Catsup

Chili sauce

Olives, pickles, gherkins

Capers

Tabasco

Worcestershire

Sparkling water

Soft beverages

Gingerale and Tonic

Peanut butter

Mayonnaise

Maraschino cherries

Dried Foods

Dried beans

Peanuts

Gelatin

Yeast

Noodles, macaroni, spaghetti

Instant dry milk powder

Pudding and cake mixes

Cornmeal or cornmeal mix

Rice

Loaf sugar

Crackers

Cereals

THE EMERGENCY SHELF

In case guests drop in unexpectedly for lunch or cocktails, you will want to save a portion of one of the upper shelves for ingredients reserved for such emergencies. Such ingredients alone or in combination with your supply of milk, cream, eggs, cheese, etcetera, can be made quickly into savory appetizers or an appetizing luncheon dish. We are suggesting a few ideas, recipes for which will be found in the following chapters, but must leave the detailing of all but the basic ingredients up to you.

For Cocktail Dips
 Potato chips
 Devonshire rounds
 Crackers, a variety of
 Canned minced clams (for the dip)

Cocktail Nibble-Food
 Salted nuts
 Olives, black, green, and stuffed
 Cocktail onions, gherkins, dill pickles

For Tea
 Dainty cookies
 Canned salmon, crabmeat, sardines for dainty sandwiches

Always Good as an Appetizer
 Canned anchovies and canned pimiento
 Cold Deviled eggs (eggs in your refrigerator)

For Soups
 Can of cream of chicken soup (Blender Senegalese)
 Canned potatoes (Blender Vichyssoise)
 Canned beets (Blender Borscht)

Luncheon or Supper Dishes
 Canned Crab Meat (Crab Meat Louis)
 Dried Beef (Chipped Beef Royale)
 Canned Salmon (Salmon Souffle or Scalloped Salmon)
 Canned Minced clams (Linguini with Clam Sauce)

There are many possibilities from just cheese, eggs, and milk or cream, such as creamed hard-cooked eggs on toast, or Welsh rarebit.

And, if you are lucky to have enough space in your freezer to be able to allot a corner to emergency foods, you can increase your repertoire greatly with such dishes as Chicken Livers Chasseur, Vegetables Mornay, Eggs Florentine. Keep a package of frozen patty shells on hand to use in place of toast. These may be baked anytime you have a free moment, and kept in a tightly closed container where they stay fresh for weeks. Simply reheat.

THE HERB AND SPICE SHELF

Oregano, Rosemary, Basil, Tarragon, and Bay Leaf were well known to our forefathers, yet by the twenties these herbs were scarcely used by any but professional chefs. Fortunately for all of us, the public appetite has once more been sharpened for herbs, and today an impressive list of herbs, spices, and seeds are available at local grocery stores and supermarkets, and a well-stocked herb and spice shelf is taking its place in thousands of American kitchens beside the salt shaker and the pepper mill.

Successful seasoning is an art and herbs and spices must be added with a knowing hand to enhance a dish and not overpower it. Certain seasonings have an affinity to certain foods, yet fail to improve others. Basil, for example, is particularly well suited to almost any cooked tomato dish, salad, aspic, or soup. An herb bouquet, that tiny bundle consisting of a spray of parsley, a pinch of thyme, and a piece of bay leaf, known in early Roman times as a faggot, improves almost any stew, and rosemary is a perfect compliment to lamb or poultry. Both tarragon and dill are exquisite with eggs, fish, and poultry, and make delicious additions to soups and sauces. Nutmeg is particularly good with creamed chicken or spinach, while ginger compliments beef and duck and mace is perfect with fish.

Dill, fresh, is often available in the fall months, during the pickling season. If not, the dried dill, known as dill weed, makes an admirable substitute, providing it is bright green in the jar when you buy it, otherwise its strength and flavor are gone. Dill is one of the most popular herbs in Scandinavian countries where it is used to flavor and decorate poached fish and is added to meat balls and loaves. Try adding chopped fresh dill (use sprays not stems) to a green salad or to sour cream for a dip for vegetables.

Season to taste makes a lot of sense when it comes to using herbs, for some are fresh and some are dried, some are old and some are new, and some, both fresh and dried, have more strength than others. The flavor of herbs and spices diminishes with age, so buy them in small quantities and store them in tightly closed containers away from the heat. To increase your knowledge of herbs and your repertoire of dishes using them, you may wish to buy, *The Herb and Spice Cookbook,* by Craig Claiborne.

A List of A few Herbs and Spices

Some you will need for basic cooking and baking. Others can be added gradually. A fun idea is to buy and try a new herb or spice each month.

Allspice	Mustard
Basil	Nutmeg
Bay leaves	Oregano
Cardamom, ground	Paprika
Cayenne pepper	Parsley
Celery salt	Peppercorns
Chili powder	Poultry Seasoning
Cinnamon, powdered and stick	Red Pepper flakes
Cloves, powdered and whole	Rosemary
Coriander, powdered and whole	Saffron
Curry powder	Sage
Dill weed	Tarragon
Garlic powder	Turmeric
Ginger	Thyme
Marjoram	Vanilla beans
Mint	

Seeds

Caraway seeds	Poppy seeds
Cardamom seeds	Sesame seeds
Celery seeds	

WINES AND SPIRITS

In addition, if possible, it is nice to have a bottle of brandy handy and one or two liqueurs to add their fragrance to cooking. Dark rum is also delightful to flavor desserts.

As for wines, Margaret Williams, has this to say in a charming book entitled, *The Well-Fed Bridegroom.*

A WORD ON WINE

A little wine added to many dishes will endow them with an incalculable amount of grace, glamour and, literally, good taste.

Please, I beg of you, don't waste your money on buying so-called cooking wines (and this includes sherry); a respectable wine will well repay you for the little extra that you may spend for it.

The only time that a really downright cheap red or white wine can be recommended is for the marinating of a particularly tough piece of meat.

In this case, cover the meat with wine, add herbs or spices, and allow to marinate for many hours. Turn the meat from time to time. One cannot lay down hard-and-fast rules as far as the uses of wines go—you will certainly find exceptions, but in general, use dry white wines for white meats and fish and dry red wines for red meats. "Dry" means the wine is not a sweet one.

Sherry and Madeira are excellent for soups, sea foods, and meats; sweet wines, liqueurs, and brandies are useful in desserts.

If you are having wine with your dinner, you can always extract a small amount from the bottle to use in whatever dish you are preparing that calls for it. Otherwise the thriftiest bottle is the half size, but unfortunately this is not easy to find, particularly in the imported wines; however, there are several excellent California wines that are available in small bottles and these should do very nicely.

Here are some wines and their types:

ALSATIAN AND MOSELLE WINES These are dry, light wines.

AMERICAN Aside from the California wines, we have wines from many other states: North Carolina, New York, New Jersey, and Ohio, to name a few. There are American types of Champagne, Bordeaux, Chablis, Graves, sauternes and Moselle.

BORDEAUX Both red and white; Graves, a white Bordeaux, is somewhat less dry than Chablis. Red Bordeaux is usually called "claret." Sauternes and Barsac are sweeter white Bordeaux.

BURGUNDY Also white or red; rich, warm, full wines. Chablis is a dry, white Burgundy.

CHAMPAGNE May range from extra-dry to sweet. (Shun the latter.)

TERMS USED IN COOKERY

A LA KING	Food, usually chicken or sweetbreads, served in a rich cream sauce, often flavored with sherry.
A LA MODE	The addition of ice cream as a garnish for pies and cakes. Also applied to some braised foods.
ALMONDINE	Foods, chicken or fish usually sauteed, garnished with shredded blanched almonds toasted in butter.
ASPIC	A well seasoned clear jelly made from stock, broth or tomato juice.

AU GRATIN	Food creamed and baked or broiled until top is brown. Surface frequently sprinkled with buttered bread crumbs or cheese.
AU JUS	Meat served in its natural juice, thickened with butter.
BAKE	To cook in the dry heat of an oven. Applies to all oven-cooked foods except meats, which are oven-roasted.
BARBECUE	To roast meat over coals or on a spit. Also applies to broiled meats served with a barbecue sauce.
BASTE	To pour liquids over food while it is cooking or roasting. Such as syrup over baking apple, or pan juices over roasting meat.
BAVARIAN	A rich pudding containing cream and gelatin.
BEAT	To blend by lifting mixture rapidly up and over with fork, spoon, wire whisk, rotary or electric beater.
BISQUE	A rich cream soup usually of fish or seafood.
BLANCH	To parboil or dip in boiling water, generally to loosen skin from almonds, tomatoes, peaches.
BLANQUETTE	A savory stew with a white sauce.
BLEND	To combine two or more ingredients thoroughly.
BOIL	To cook in a liquid, usually water, which bubbles actively during the cooking period.
BOMBE	A rich frozen cream or custard.
BOUILLON	Clarified soup stock.
BOUQUET GARNI	A small bundle of vegetables and herbs tied together for easy removal. Used to flavor soups, stews, and sauces.
BRAISE	To brown food in shortening and then cook, tightly covered, with a small amount of liquid.
BREAD	To dip food into an egg-milk mixture and then into crumbs.
BROIL	To cook under or over direct heat.
BROTH	Liquid in which food has been simmered.

BROWN	To cook a food by frying, toasting, broiling or baking, until brown.
BRUSH	To spread thinly with a pastry brush, usually melted butter or beaten egg.
CANDY	To cook in sugar or syrup until transparent and glazed.
CANAPE	An appetizing mixture spread on a small base of bread, toast, or cracker.
CARMELIZE	To heat sugar until light brown in color and caramel in flavor.
CHARLOTTE	A creamy gelatin dessert molded with cake or lady-fingers.
CHOP	To cut in small pieces with a sharp knife.
COMBINE	To mix ingredients together thoroughly.
COMPOTE	Fruit stewed in sugar syrup.
CONDIMENT	Any food seasoning such as spice, vinegar, relish, or spicy sauce.
CONFECTIONERS' SUGAR	Sugar ground to consistency of flour.
COURT BOUILLON	A highly seasoned broth for poaching fish.
CREAM	To mix soft shortening and sugar with spoon or electric beater.
CREOLE	A highly-seasoned tomato sauce containing green pepper, garlic, and chopped onion.
CROQUETTES	A mixture of chopped or ground cooked food bound with thick cream sauce, dipped into egg and crumbs and fried.
CROUTON	Cubes of bread toasted or fried crisp, used to garnish soups and other dishes.
CRUMB	To cover with fine crumbs.
CUT	To divide with knife or scissors.
CUT IN SHORTENING	To work cold shortening into flour with pastry blender or two knives.

DEMITASSE	A small cup of strong, after-dinner coffee, "half-a-cup."
DEVILED	Highly seasoned food.
DICE	To cut into square pieces.
DISSOLVE	To mix a dry substance with liquid until it is in solution.
DOT	To scatter bits of butter or shortening over surface of dish to be cooked.
DRAWN BUTTER	Melted butter used as a sauce.
DREDGE	To coat with flour or sugar.
DRIP	Method of making coffee in a "drip" pot.
DRIPPINGS	Residue left in pan in which food has been cooked.
DUST	To sprinkle lightly with flour or sugar.
EGG AND CRUMBS	To roll food in crumbs or flour, then into beaten egg and finally in crumbs. Used to prevent fat soaking into foods, or to form a crisp surface.
EGGS, TO SEPARATE	Break egg shell carefully in half, let white run into one cup or bowl, put yolk in another.
EN BROCHETTE	Food cooked or served on a skewer.
ENTREE	The main dish of an informal meal or a dish served between main courses of a formal dinner.
ESPAGNOLE	A basic brown sauce.
FILLET	A boneless piece of fish or lean meat.
FINES HERBS	A combination of finely chopped herbs such as parsley, chives, tarragon.
FLAMBE	To pour warm brandy or liquor over food, ignite and let flame burn out.
FLAKE	Separate into small pieces.
FOLD	To combine ingredients with an up and over folding motion.
FONDUE	Melted to sauce consistency, such as cheese.
FRAPPE	Sweetened fruit juice frozen to a mush.

FRENCH	To trim meat away from the end of a bone, such as lamb chop, or to cut into thin slivers, such as green beans.
FRICASSEE	To stew fowl or meat and serve in thickened broth, often with dumplings.
FRY	To cook in hot fat. When small amount is used, process is known as pan frying; when food is partially covered with fat, process is known as shallow frying; when surrounded with hot fat, process is known as deep frying.
FRIZZLE	To cook very quickly in a small amount of hot fat.
GARNISH	To add something extra to a dish to make it more attractive.
GLAZE	To cover food with a glossy coating such as jelly, mayonnaise, or fruit or meat juices.
GOULASH	A thick stew of meat or poultry.
GRATE	To rub through a grater.
GRILL	To broil.
GRIND	To put through food chopper using fine, medium or coarse blade.
HOLLANDAISE	A delicious sauce of butter, egg yolks, and lemon juice.
JULIENNE	To cut into narrow lengthwise strips.
KIPPERED	A method of preserving fish, usually herring.
KNEAD	To fold and press dough with palms of hands.
LARD	To cover meat with strips of fat, or to thread strips of fat salt pork through lean meat with skewer or larding needle.
LEAVENING	Ingredients needed to make mixture rise, such as baking powder, soda, yeast.
MACEDOINE	A mixture of fruits or vegetables.
MARINATE	To let stand in a sauce to improve flavor. The sauce itself is known as the marinade.
MASH	To beat or press to a soft pulp.

MASK	To cover with a mayonnaise or cream sauce containing gelatin or with a clear jelly.
MELT	To heat a solid to liquid form.
MINCE	To cut or chop very finely.
MINESTRONE	A thick vegetable soup.
MIX	To combine ingredients, usually by stirring.
MOCHA	A flavor combination of coffee and chocolate.
MOUSSE	A mixture containing beaten egg whites, baked, chilled, or frozen.
NESSELRODE	A sweet dessert or sauce containing chopped fruit and chestnuts.
PAN-BROIL	To cook in frying pan over high heat.
PAN-FRY	To fry quickly in small amount of fat.
PARBOIL	To partially cook in boiling water.
PARE	To remove skin or rind with sharp knife.
PARFAIT	A dessert of ice cream, fruit, and whipped cream served in a parfait glass.
PEEL	To remove skin.
PERCOLATE	Method of making coffee.
PETITS FOURS	Small iced cakes.
PICKLED	Foods preserved in brine of salt and vinegar. Sugar and spices often added.
PILAF	Rice cooked with butter, onion, and spices.
PLANKED	Food, usually fish or steak, served on a wooden board or plank made especially for the purpose.
POACH	To cook in liquid below boiling point.
POT ROAST	Method of cooking less tender meats in heavy pot with tight fitting cover.
PREHEAT	To heat oven to desired temperature in advance of baking or roasting food.
PUREE	Press food through a sieve to obtain a thick pulp free of skins and seeds.
RAGOUT	A savory stew.

RAMEKINS	Individual baking dishes.
RENDER	To remove fat from meats by heating slowly at low temperature.
REDUCE	To reduce amount of liquid by boiling off part of the liquid in steam.
ROUX	A smooth blend of fat and flour used to thicken a liquid.
SAUTE	To cook slowly in small amount of fat.
SCALD	To heat liquid to a temperature just below boiling point or pour boiling water over food.
SCALLOP	To bake food in an oven-proof dish.
SCORE	To make shallow slits across surface with a sharp knife.
SCRAMBLE	A method of cooking eggs, or mixture containing eggs, by stirring over low heat while thickened.
SEAR	To brown food quickly on all sides on top of stove or in oven.
SHRED	To cut or tear in thin strips or pieces, or press through a shredder.
SHERBET	A frozen mixture of fruit juice often containing beaten egg whites.
SHORTENING	Any kind of cooking fat or oil.
SIFT	To put dry ingredients through a sieve.
SIMMER	To cook in liquid just at or below the boiling point.
SKEWER	To fasten meat with a thin wooden or metal pick.
SLIVER	To cut into very fine strips.
STEAM	To cook over or surrounded by steam.
STEEP	To let stand in hot liquid.
STEW	To cook in liquid below the boiling point.
STIR	To mix with a circular motion.
STOCK	Liquid in which meat, fish and/or vegetables have been cooked. Used to make soups, sauces and gravies.

STUFFING   A mixture of bread or crackers, usually flavored with onion and spices.

TOAST   To brown by direct heat or in a hot oven.

TOSS   To mix lightly by lifting with fork or fork and spoon.

WHIP   To beat rapidly in order to incorporate air.

TABLE OF MEASUREMENTS

Oven Temperatures

Slow oven	275° – 325° F.
Moderate oven	325° – 375° F.
Moderately hot oven	375° – 425° F.
Hot oven	425° – 475° F.
Very hot oven	475° – 500° F.

Size of Cans

No. ½	7¾ to 8½ oz.	Approximately 1 cup
No. 300	13½ fl. oz.	Approximately 1¾ cups
No. 1	1 lb.	Approximately 2 cups
No. 303	1 lb. or 15 fl. oz.	Approximately 2 cups
No. 2	1 lb. 4 oz.	Approximately 2½ cups
No. 2½	1 lb. 13 oz.	Approximately 3½ cups

Weights and Measures

Pinch or dash	less than ⅛ teaspoon
1 teaspoon	⅓ tablespoon
3 teaspoons	1 tablespoon
2 tablespoons	⅛ cup
4 tablespoons	¼ cup
5 tablespoons plus 1 teaspoon	⅓ cup
10 tablespoons plus 2 teaspoons	⅔ cup
12 tablespoons	¾ cup
16 tablespoons	1 cup
2 cups	1 pint
2 pints	1 quart
4 quarts	1 gallon
16 ounces	1 pound
1 fluid ounce	2 tablespoons
16 fluid ounces	1 pint (2 cups)

EQUIVALENTS

Ingredient	Quantity	Equivalent
Butter	1 pound	2 cups
	1 stick	½ cup
	½ stick	4 tablespoons
Chocolate	1 square	1 ounce
Cheese	1 pound	4 cups, grated
	4 ounces	1 cup, shredded
Cream	1 cup	2 cups whipped
Date	1 cup, chopped, pitted	about 6 ounces
Eggs, whole	5	1 cup
	1 large	¼ cup or 2 ounces
Egg yolks	16	approx. 1 cup
Egg whites	8 to 9	approx. 1 cup
Flour, bread, sifted	4 cups	1 pound
Flour, cake, sifted	4½ cups	1 pound
Green peas	1 pound	1 cup hulled
Lemon	1, squeezed	2 to 3 tablespoons
Lemon rind	Rind of 1 medium	2 tablespoons grated
Macaroni	8 ounces raw	5 cups cooked
Meat	1 cup ground	approx. 8 ounces
Noodles	8 ounces raw	5 cups cooked
Nut Meats	1 cup chopped	4 ounces
Pecans	2½ pounds in shell	3 cups chopped nut meats
Potatoes	3 medium	1 pound
Rice	2⅓ cups, raw	1 pound
Rice, whole grain	8 ounces (about 1 cup)	4 cups cooked
Onions	3 medium	1 pound
Shortening	1 pound	2⅓ cups
Sugar, brown	2¼ cups, firmly packed	1 pound
Sugar, granulated	2 cups	1 pound
Sugar, confectioners'	4½ cups, sifted	1 pound
Tomatoes	3 medium	1 pound

SUBSTITUTIONS

Ingredient	Substitute
1 square (ounce) chocolate	3 tablespoons cocoa plus 1 tablespoon shortening

1 tablespoon cornstarch	2 tablespoons enriched flour
1 cup fresh milk	½ cup evaporated milk and ½ cup water or 3 tablespoons non-fat dry milk solids and 1 cup water
1 cup sour milk	1 cup fresh milk and 1 tablespoon lemon juice or vinegar

ABBREVIATIONS OFTEN FOUND IN COOKBOOKS

Gal.	Gallon	Tsp.	Teaspoon
Oz.	Ounce	Tbsp.	Tablespoon
Pkg.	Package	In.	Inches
Pt.	Pint	Min.	Minutes
Lb.	Pound	Sq.	Square
Qt.	Quart		

HOW TO MEASURE

Use standard measuring cups and spoons and measure accurately.

Measuring liquids

Glass measuring cups with graduated markings and lip for easy pouring should be used for liquids. Hold glass level with eye to make sure liquid comes to desired amount.

Dry measure

Use the nested unit measuring cups and standard measuring spoons. Fill to the top and level off with straight edged knife or spatula.

Flour

If recipe calls for sifted flour, this means to sift before measuring. The new presifted flours have eliminated this step in baking.

Brown sugar

Pack firmly into dry measure cup and level off.

Shortening

This can be measured by displacing water. If ½ cup is specified, fill liquid measure ½ full of water, then add shortening until water reaches the 1 cup mark. Pour off water and remove fat, which will not stick to sides of cup.

HOW TO BE A GOOD COOK

1. Be accurate.
2. Read recipes carefully and assemble ingredients and utensils before starting to cook.
3. Make necessary advance preparations before beginning to cook such as mincing an onion, dicing celery. In France this advance preparation is called *mis en place*—everything in its place—and many chefs have assistants who do nothing but prepare the *mis en place* for the master chef, who then takes over. The bride must be both master chef and assistant but, anyone who begins to cook without first having "everything in place" is not a well organized person and is apt to have more failures than success.
4. Preheat oven to degree specified.

The Bride Cooks Breakfast

ONCE THE HONEYMOON IS OVER, the daily breakfast will settle down pretty much to routine, based on the type of work your husband is engaged in, his working hours, and his eating habits.

If he likes cereal or cream of wheat every morning, that is, undoubtedly, what you will give him. If he's a ham 'n' eggs man, that is what you will cook for him.

Nevertheless, breakfast need not be monotonous. Regardless of the personal preferences of your spouse, providing him with an appetizing breakfast is your first step in seeing that his day begins in a cheerful fashion. You can always add variety to your breakfast menu by the fruit you serve before the cereal or eggs, and by a selection of homemade hot breakfast breads, muffins, or coffeecakes.

Then, on Sunday, go all out for a revolutionary breakfast. Refuse to give your husband the same breakfast menu on the seventh day. Make Sunday breakfast a special once-a-week treat . . . an intimate hour to be anticipated and treasured.

A little planning the night before can make every breakfast a pleasant way to start the day and not a harried affair. Most fruit or juice can be prepared the night before, covered, and stored in the refrigerator. You can fill the tea kettle with fresh water for the tea or coffee and set the breakfast table or trays. All necessary utensils for preparing the meal can be assembled close to your kitchen work area, so that morning duties are pared to a minimum.

The morning meal should provide from one-fourth to one-third of the daily caloric intake. This means it should be almost as large a meal as the other two. And it should contain some protein as well as carbohydrates.

A serving of juice, fresh or stewed fruits, or berries in season should begin the breakfast menu. Certainly, canned or frozen fruit juices are convenient, but nothing can take the place of the fresh-squeezed juice of oranges, grapefruit, or tangerines (extra special!). Canned or bottled apricot nectar, prune or grape juice all make a good beginning. Always serve juices well chilled.

This breakfast chapter begins with a variety of fruit suggestions to help you keep your breakfast menus varied.

BREAKFAST FRUITS

SLICED ORANGES WITH MINT

Peel oranges with a paring knife, cutting away not only the orange rind but all the white pith that lies beneath. Slice thinly and sprinkle with a little chopped fresh mint.

GRAPEFRUIT

One grapefruit is all you need for two people. Cut in half and, with kitchen scissors, clip out the center white core. For segments, peel the grapefruit deeply with a paring knife, removing the yellow rind and all the bitter white portion next to the rind. Then remove the pulp, a section at a time, by cutting it free from the membrane on both sides. Garnish with a cherry, a strawberry, a few raspberries, or a sprig of mint.

ORANGE JULEP FOR TWO

Put 2 tablespoons fresh mint leaves, 1 teaspoon sugar, and 2 tablespoons water or orange juice into container of an electric blender. Cover and blend on high speed for a few seconds. Divide into two tall glasses, fill with cracked ice, and pour juice over all. Garnish with sprig of mint.

SLICED PEACHES

Peel peaches by putting each peach on a slotted spoon and lowering into a saucepan of boiling water for 1 minute. The skin will strip off easily. Slice and serve with sugar and cream. They are also delicious sprinkled with a little sugar and soaked in orange juice.

SLICED BANANAS

Always a delicious beginning to a meal. Serve with cream or with a fruit juice such as apricot nectar, prune, pineapple, or orange juice.

BERRIES

All berries in season are a fine way to begin the day. Serve strawberries, blueberries, raspberries with sugar and cream or with a fruit juice.

MELONS

Summer is a good time for melons, when citrus fruits are not at their peak. Select a cantaloupe, honeydew, Casaba, Persian, papaya, or other melon that is fully ripe. A ripe melon gives off a fragrant odor when pressed close to the nose and the portion of melon around the "eye" yields to the pressure of the finger. Cut into wedges or cut into small balls with a French ball scoop and always chill well before serving. There is nothing more refreshing on a hot summer morning than a large slice of chilled watermelon!

PERSIMMONS
This exotic fruit is in season in November, December, and January. Peel, slice, and serve with cream or lemon wedge, or cut into petals, beginning at pointed end, open up like a flower, and serve whole with a fruit knife and fork.

BAKED APPLES
Core 2 baking apples and peel them about ⅓ of the way down. Set them upright in a small baking dish. Mix ¼ cup sugar, 2 tablespoons chopped almonds, and a good pinch of cinnamon or nutmeg. Divide mixture and fill cavities in the apples. Put a slice of butter on top of each. Add ¼ inch boiling water to the pan and bake in a preheated 400° F. oven for 30 minutes, or until apples are tender when tested with a fork, basting several times during the baking with the liquid in the pan. Serve warm or chilled with cream.

RHUBARB
An excellent breakfast fruit in early May, when cherry rhubarb is tender and at its best, although hot house rhubarb is available in February and home grown lasts through June.

To Stew Rhubarb in its own Juice
   In top of double saucepan combine 2 cups sliced rhubarb and ½ cup sugar. Let stand for 1 hour to bring out natural juices. Cover saucepan, set over simmering water, and simmer for 30 minutes, or until rhubarb is tender.
To Bake Rhubarb
   Combine 2 cups sliced rhubarb, ½ cup sugar, and juice and grated rind of 1 orange. Put into an oven casserole, cover, and bake in a preheated 350° F. oven for 45 minutes.

PRUNES OR APRICOTS
. . . . or a combination of these fruits make a wonderful beginning to mid-winter breakfasts, when fresh fruits and berries are scarce. Simply follow directions on the package of the dried fruit. Serve plain with the juice, or with the juice plus cream.

CANNED MANDARIN ORANGE SECTIONS
Put 1 8-ounce can of the segments in the refrigerator to chill. Open can and drain, reserving the liquid. Divide segments into two serving dishes and sprinkle each with about 2 tablespoons of the juice from the can and a dash of lemon juice or, if this is too sweet, use orange or pineapple juice.

MIXED FRESH FRUIT
This is called a *macédoine*. Sounds difficult, but is nothing more than an assortment of fresh fruit, either mixed together or arranged on a serving plate. Use any fresh fruit in season: melon balls, pitted sweet cherries, sliced bananas, strawberries, blueberries, or raspberries, citrus fruit segments, pineapple cubes, or sliced pears. Sprinkle with a little sugar and a little fruit juice.

FRUIT WITH RASPBERRY SAUCE
This is a really elegant way to start the day. To make the puree for sauce, simply blend a 10-ounce package of partially defrosted raspberries in an electric blender for 20 seconds, and pour through a sieve to remove the seeds. Without a blender, you can force the berries through a sieve or use a food mill. Pour the puree over sliced, chilled pears, peaches, or strawberries.

PINEAPPLE
To prepare fresh pineapple: Cut off and discard the fronds. Slice pineapple crosswise about ½ inch thick. Then, with a sharp knife, cut away the thick surrounding skin from each slice. This will leave small eyes in the flesh which must be trimmed off. Cut each slice into segments, radiating from the center core and discard the core. Sprinkle with sugar and a little pineapple juice and chill. Pineapple combines beautifully with other fruits or berries in season.

BAKED EGGS AND BACON FOR BREAKFAST

Individual ramekins containing eggs nestled in a ring of bacon, baked with a topping of grated Parmesan cheese and Tabasco-seasoned butter, are a sunny-side-up way to begin a busy day. Selecting good bacon is sometimes difficult: Ideally, the lean meat, bright pinkish red in color, should be streaked through with clear white fat. If the bacon is too fat it will shrink a great deal in cooking, and if too lean it is apt to be tough. Experience is your best teacher. When you find a brand that you like, stick to it.

BAKED EGGS AND BACON   *Serves 2.*
4 strips bacon   2 tablespoons grated Parmesan cheese
4 eggs   1 tablspoon melted butter
4 dashes Tabasco

1. Cook bacon until partially done, but not crisp; drain on absorbent paper.
2. Place 2 strips in each ramekin or individual baking dish.
3. Carefully break 2 eggs into each dish and sprinkle with cheese.
4. Combine butter and Tabasco and pour half over eggs in each dish.
5. Bake in a preheated 350° F. oven for about 15 minutes, or until eggs are set.

The recipes for these Buttermilk Tea Biscuits and Lemon Curd may be found on page 268.

A CONNUBIAL BREAKFAST

Helen Evans and Philip Brown, west coast food experts, give the menu for a Connubial Breakfast, in their charming book, *Breakfasts and Brunches for Every Occasion*. They selected ham and eggs because, "ham and eggs are said to be a 'marriage made in heaven' and the bride, unsure of her mate's morning preferences, might well serve them, for they bring that proverbial bliss."

Menu
Scalped Oranges
Ham and Eggs
Applesauce   Whole-Wheat Toast
Coffee

SCALPED ORANGES
Cut a slice from the top of a whole orange and serve with a tiny spoon. It should be eaten from the shell. Serve well chilled.

HAM AND EGGS
"The ham should be of the finest, preferably an old-fashioned one, naturally smoked. Slice it thin as you wish—say from $1/8$ to $1/4$ inch—allowing a slice a serving, and cook it quickly in a lightly buttered skillet. The ham should be pinkly moist, just tinged with amber. Keep warm while you do the eggs. Add more butter to the pan so that the bottom will be completely covered. Carefully break in the eggs—1 or 2 to a person—making sure that they are extra fresh. Cover and turn heat very low. Cook until the whites are set but tender, and only very lightly browned at the edges. Slip onto the platter with the ham, and garnish with crisp cress."

A LOW CALORIE BREAKFAST

The Browns are firm believers in a high protein breakfast and Mr. Brown lost twenty pounds in five months on the following Low Calorie Breakfast. He never regained the weight he lost since he gave up his usual morning meal of black coffee! They say, "skipping breakfast is the worst possible way to try to lose weight." This is the menu they prescribe for keeping a trim figure.

Menu
Melon Wedge with Lime
Lean Broiled Hamburgers   Sliced fresh Tomatoes
Melba Toast   Black Coffee

This Apple-Beef Ring is filled with Green Bean Succotash. The recipe is on page 250. The Cranberry Tart recipe is on page 259.

LEAN BROILED HAMBURGERS

"No trick, except that the hamburgers should be freshly ground from rump or chuck with all fat trimmed off and discarded. For rare hamburgers, broil the patties 3 minutes on each side, without butter or oil. Add salt and pepper after cooking."

A PANCAKE BREAKFAST

Grapefruit is a favorite at the breakfast table. You can give it a different twist, if you like by broiling it briefly before serving. Or you may wish to substitute baked apples. But regardless of the fruit course, there is no more heart-warming breakfast than a stack of hot homebaked pancakes served with crisp bacon and molasses.

BROILED GRAPEFRUIT

Cut grapefruit into halves. Clip out center core with kitchen scissors and loosen fruit segments from membrane without cutting around outer edge. Top each grapefruit half with 1 tablespoon unsulphured molasses. Place on broiler rack 3 inches from heat. Broil slowly for 10 to 15 minutes, or until grapefruit is slightly browned.

MOLASSES PANCAKES

Makes 6 large cakes.

1 cup all-purpose flour
2½ teaspoons baking powder
½ teaspoon salt

¼ cup unsulphured molasses
¾ cup milk
1 egg, lightly beaten

2 tablespoons of melted shortening

1. Sift flour, baking powder, and salt into mixing bowl.
2. Combine molasses and milk and add to beaten egg.
3. Slowly add milk-egg mixture to dry ingredients and stir only until blended. Stir in melted shortening.
4. Bake on hot greased griddle, using ¼ cup batter for each pancake.
5. Serve hot with butter and molasses, or desired topping.

A PLAYDAY BREAKFAST

This is designed for one of those pleasant times when late sleeping is in order, and active sports are in the offing. It is another suggestion made by Helen Evans and Philip Brown in the book *Breakfasts and Brunches for Every Occasion.*

Menu
Fresh or Canned Figs with Cream
Corned Beef Hash   Broiled Tomatoes
Cinnamon Coffeecake   Coffee or Tea

FRESH OR CANNED FIGS WITH CREAM

If fresh, peel, quarter or slice; if canned, they can usually be left whole. Serve with cream, or not, as you prefer.

CORNED BEEF HASH

"This all-American favorite is very good when made from canned corned beef, though of course you can cook your own or use leftover beef, if you prefer. Cook ¼ cup chopped onion in 1 tablespoon of butter until wilted. Chop 1 pound of corned beef, add the onion and 2 cups of chopped boiled —or, better, baked—potatoes. Moisten with 6 tablespoons of cream and season to taste with salt and freshly ground pepper. Melt 3 tablespoons of butter in a skillet, add the hash, and press down with a spatula. Cook very slowly until bottom is crisply brown. Fold like an omelette and turn out onto a hot platter. This mixture may be formed into patties, sauteed on both sides, and topped with a poached egg. It may also be baked in a shallow buttered dish for 30 minutes at 350° F., or until crisply brown."

CINNAMON COFFEECAKE

"Combine 1½ cups of sifted flour, 1½ teaspoons of baking powder, and ½ teaspoon of salt. Cream together ½ cup of butter and ½ cup of sugar: beat in 1 egg and add dry ingredients, alternating with ½ cup of milk. Spread in a buttered 9 x 9 inch pan and sprinkle top with a mixture of ¾ cup of sugar and 2 tablespoons of cinnamon. Dot butter lavishly over the top, and bake in a 350° oven for 45 minutes, or until brown and puffily crusty. The butter sinks into the batter and makes little rich sugary hollows. Serve at once, cut in squares."

A FRENCH TOAST BREAKFAST

Menu
Chilled Fruit Juice
French Toast   Sausages
Milk, Coffee, or Tea

FRENCH TOAST   *Serves 2.*

1 egg   ¼ teaspoon salt
½ cup milk   4 slices day-old bread

2 to 3 tablespoons butter

1. Beat egg slightly, add milk and salt, and stir. Pour into shallow dish.
2. Dip bread slices into mixture, turning so they are coated on both sides.
3. Heat a little butter in a skillet. Lift bread slices with a pancake turner and place in skillet. Cook until a delicate brown on both sides, adding extra butter as needed.
4. Serve hot with Honey Butter and sausages.

SAUSAGES

Buy small breakfast-type sausages and keep chilled until ready to cook. Separate and put into a skillet. Cook over low heat, turning occasionally, until well browned on all sides.

HONEY BUTTER

Blend equal parts of soft butter and honey together. Store in refrigerator. Also delicious with breakfast toast, biscuits, or muffins.

A SPECIAL HOLIDAY BRUNCH

Holiday breakfasts have a warm, companionable aura all their own. Generally speaking, they are late, relaxed, unhurried and cheerful. They are also generous and ample. On holidays and week-ends, there's time to prepare and enjoy special treats. Time, too, to indulge in that second or even third cup of coffee.

Among the foods that belong to leisurely mornings are waffles, baked right at the table. They can be whisked to the plate hot and tender, with pats of butter melting down through them. For a glorious touch, try Piquante Fruited Topping, thick, rich, and syrupy.

PIQUANTE FRUITED TOPPING FOR WAFFLES   *Makes about 3 cups.*

2 cups plumped pitted prunes
  (see below)
½ cup dark brown sugar
1 teaspoon cinnamon

1 teaspoon nutmeg
2 tablespoons lemon juice
1 No. 2 can pineapple chunks
Slivered toasted almonds

1. Combine prunes, sugar, cinnamon, nutmeg and lemon juice. Heat.
2. Remove from heat and add pineapple and syrup. Heat.
3. Just before serving, top with slivered toasted almonds.
4. Serve over waffles.
5. Store leftover topping in refrigerator and serve over ice cream.

*TO PLUMP PRUNES

Just Cook Method: When a rich heavy juice is desired. Cover prunes with cold water. Bring to a boil and simmer for 10 to 20 minutes. Let stand overnight in the liquor.

A LAZY BRUNCH FOR FOUR

Menu
Chilled Fruit Compote
Crepes Filled with Cheese Scrambled Eggs
Sauteed Ham Slices
Milk, Tea, or Coffee

BREAKFAST CREPES

Makes 8 thin crepes.

1½ cups flour

½ teaspoon salt

3 eggs

1½ cups milk

1. Sift flour and salt into bowl.
2. Blend eggs and milk and add to dry ingredients. Mix until smooth.
3. Bake in lightly buttered 6 or 7-inch skillet, one at a time.
4. Fill crepes with Cheese Scrambled Eggs, arrange on a hot serving platter and surround by sauteed ham slices.

CHEESE SCRAMBLED EGGS

8 eggs

½ cup milk or half and half

¾ cup shredded American cheese

1 tablespoon chopped parsley

Salt and pepper to taste

2 tablespoons butter

1. Combine all ingredients in a bowl and beat lightly until blended.
2. Melt butter in a skillet, without letting it brown.
3. Pour in egg mixture and reduce heat to very low.
4. When mixture begins to set, stir gently with a wooden spoon until eggs are cooked, but are still moist and glossy.

Another wonderfully delicious idea for a lazy-day breakfast is ·...

PRUNE COFFEE CAKE

Serves 9.

½ pound prunes, *plumped, pitted, halved

3 marachino cherries, halved

1 tablespoon grated orange rind

⅓ cup firmly packed brown sugar

3 tablespoons melted butter or margarine

1½ cups sifted all-purpose flour

1¾ teaspoons baking powder

¾ teaspoon salt

¾ cup sugar

2 eggs, well beaten

½ cup milk

1 teaspoon vanilla

⅓ cup melted shortening

Confectioners' sugar

1. In bottom of greased 9 x 9 x 2 inch pan arrange prune halves, cut side up, and cherries to form a design.
2. Sprinkle with orange rind, brown sugar, and melted butter or margarine.
3. Combine flour, baking powder, salt and sugar.
4. Combine eggs, milk, and vanilla and gradually add dry ingredients, stirring until mixed. Stir in melted shortening.
5. Beat vigorously 1 minute or until creamy and pour batter over prunes.
6. Bake in a preheated 375° F. oven about 45 minutes.
7. Remove from oven. Let set on cake rack about 2 minutes. Loosen edges and invert on serving plate.
8. Sprinkle with confectioners' sugar and serve warm, cut into squares.

HOT BISCUITS FOR BREAKFAST

Rich crusty baking powder biscuits are so very easy to make that they take little longer than using a packaged mix. They cost less than the packaged mix and, besides, you made them yourself! Serve them with marmalade, jam, or honey.

RICH CRUSTY BISCUITS
Makes 16 2-inch biscuits.

2 cups all-purpose flour
3 teaspoons double-acting
  baking powder
1 teaspoon salt
½ cup shortening
⅔ cup milk

1. Set oven at 425° F.
2. Assemble ingredients.
3. Assemble utensils: You should have a pastry board, pastry board cover, rolling pin and rolling pin stocking. A mixing bowl, pastry blender and a 2-tined fork. A biscuit cutter and a baking sheet.
4. In mixing bowl combine flour, baking powder, and salt.
5. With pastry blender cut in shortening until it is cut into fine particles. (You can make this much of the biscuits on the evening before, if you wish.)
6. Add milk all at once and stir gently with a fork until dough holds together.
7. Gather dough into a ball, place on lightly floured board, and knead gently with floured fingers, about 12 kneading strokes.
8. Roll out dough gently to about ½ inch thickness and, with floured biscuit cutter, cut into 2-inch rounds.
9. Place biscuits on baking sheet about 1-inch apart.
10. Bake for 12 to 15 minutes, or until golden.

CHEESE KNOTS—wonderful with salad
Makes 40 knots.

Add ½ cup shredded American cheese to flour mixture before adding liquid. On floured board, roll dough into a rectangle ¼ inch thick and 6 inches wide. Cut crosswise in ½ inch strips. Carefully tie each strip into a loose knot and place knots 1-inch apart on baking sheet. Sprinkle lightly with cayenne pepper and bake for 10 to 15 minutes.

THIMBLE BISCUITS—delightful with soup
Makes 36 tiny biscuits.

Add ½ cup finely chopped parsley to flour mixture before adding liquid. On floured board roll dough ¼ inch thick and cut into 1-inch rounds with floured biscuit cutter. Bake for 10 minutes.

COCKTAIL BISCUITS

Split and butter Thimble Biscuits. Place a thin slice of Virginia ham between each biscuit and reheat in a slow oven.

POPOVERS—ALWAYS ON SUNDAY

PERFECT POPOVERS   *Makes 8*

1 cup milk   1 cup all-purpose flour
2 eggs   ¼ teaspoon salt

1. Preheat oven to 425° F.
2. Grease 8 muffin pans or custard cups.
3. Combine milk and eggs.
4. Add flour and salt and beat with rotary beater until smooth. Or blend in electric blender for 15 to 20 seconds.
5. Pour into prepared containers and bake for 40 minutes.

HOT MUFFINS FOR BREAKFAST

It's just as easy to make a dozen muffins as it is to make half the quantity. So whip up a batch of muffins either in the morning or before bedtime. Serve piping hot from oven or wrap in aluminum foil and reheat in a slow oven.

BASIC MUFFINS   *Makes 12 2½ inch muffins*

2 cups all-purpose flour   ¼ cup sugar
3 teaspoons double-acting baking   1 cup milk
   powder   1 egg
1 teaspoon salt   ¼ cup melted butter

1. Set oven at 400° F.
2. Rub 12 muffin cups with shortening
3. Assemble ingredients
4. In mixing bowl combine flour, baking powder, salt, and sugar.
5. Mix milk and egg with a fork, add to flour mixture, and stir just until dry ingredients are moistened to make a lumpy batter.
6. Stir in butter.
7. Fill muffin cups ⅔ full.
8. Bake for 20 to 25 minutes.

NUT MUFFINS

Add ½ cup chopped pecans or walnuts to flour mixture before stirring in liquid.

BLUEBERRY MUFFINS

Add 1 cup washed, drained blueberries to batter before spooning into muffin pans.

CORN MEAL MUFFINS

Follow directions for Basic Muffins, using only 1 cup flour. Add ¾ cup yellow cornmeal to flour mixture before adding liquid. Bake 25 to 30 minutes.

RAISIN BRAN MUFFINS

Follow directions for Basic Muffins, using only 1 cup flour. Use brown sugar in place of white. Add 1 cup bran flakes to flour mixture and fold into batter before putting into muffin cups 1 cup seedless raisins and ½ cup chopped nuts.

QUICK BREADS

A slice of homemade Banana Bread or Date Nut Loaf is a great way to start the day. They are as easy to make as biscuits or muffins and stay wonderfully fresh for days. Thinly sliced and buttered, they make perfect tea sandwiches. Wrap the baked loaf in aluminum foil and keep in refrigerator. Try these breads sliced, toasted, and buttered while hot.

BANANA BREAD   *1 loaf 8 x 4 x 3 inches.*

⅓ cup melted shortening
¾ cup sugar
2 bananas, sliced
1 egg
2 cups all-purpose flour

1 teaspoon double-acting baking powder
½ teaspoon baking soda
1 teaspoon salt
¾ cup buttermilk

1 teaspoon vanilla

1. Set oven at 350° F.
2. Grease loaf pan and assemble ingredients.
3. In mixing bowl beat shortening, sugar, and bananas. Add egg and beat until well blended.
4. Combine dry ingredients and gently stir into banana mixture alternately with buttermilk and vanilla.
5. Turn batter into loaf pan and bake for 1 hour.

DATE NUT LOAF   *1 loaf 8 x 4 x 3 inches.*

2 cups pitted, chopped dates
1 cup chopped walnuts
⅓ cup shortening
1 cup boiling water
5 tablespoons cold water
1 teaspoon soda

¾ cup brown sugar
1 teaspoon vanilla
1 egg
2 cups all-purpose flour
1 teaspoon double-acting baking powder
1 teaspoon salt

1. Set oven at 350° F.
2. Grease loaf pan and assemble ingredients.
3. In mixing bowl combine dates, walnuts, shortening, and boiling water and beat until shortening is broken into small lumps.
4. Add cold water and stir in soda, brown sugar, vanilla, egg, and flour mixed with baking powder and salt.
5. Beat until well blended.
6. Pour batter into loaf pan and bake for about 1 hour.

HOW TO MAKE GOOD TEA

There are three different types of tea. These are black, green, and oolong. All three types of tea come from the same tea bushes cultivated in the same careful way in the same rich tropical lands. What happens after the leaves are picked is what makes them different.

BLACK TEA

This tea undergoes a special processing treatment that turns the leaves black. This gives the tea a rich, hearty flavor—the kind most Americans like best.

GREEN TEA

One of the steps—oxidation—is omitted here. As a result, this tea is green in appearance and has a light color when brewed.

OOLONG TEA

This is a compromise between black and green tea. It's semi-processed so its leaves are partly brown and partly green. Oolong tea also has a light color.

From the Tea Council of the U.S.A. came these rules for making a delicious and refreshing cup of tea.

THE FOUR GOLDEN RULES FOR BREWING TEA

1. *To make the best tea, use your teapot.*
   A teapot is best because it helps keep the water hot during the brewing period.
2. *Bring fresh cold tap water to a full rolling boil.*
   Water that has been reheated in a kettle gives tea a flat taste. Only boiling water poured over the tea produces the full flavor.
3. *Use one teaspoon of tea or one teabag per cup.*
   Don't guess. A teabag is equivalent to a teaspoon of tea . . . just enough to give you a full-bodied cup of tea.
4. *Brew by the clock—3 to 5 minutes*, depending on the strength you like. It takes time for the leaves to unfold and release their flavor. So don't guess—time it by the clock.

HOW TO MAKE REALLY GOOD ICED TEA

Nowadays, when you're hot and thirsty, you automatically think of a glass of iced tea. It's as easy to prepare as hot tea. Follow the four golden rules but use 50% more tea to allow for the melting ice. For example, you'd use 4 teabags to make 4 cups of hot tea. But to make 4 glasses of iced tea, you would use 6 teabags.

HOW TO MAKE GOOD COFFEE

There could be no better source of information on how to make really good coffee—every time, than the Coffee Brewing Institute. Here are its rules.

A FEW BASIC RULES

There are a few basic rules that apply to all types of coffee makers. If you follow them, you can be certain that your coffee will be dependably good, every time.

1. Make certain that your coffee pot is sparkling clean. This means it should be thoroughly scrubbed after each use. Mere rinsing is not enough to remove the oils which coat the inside of your coffee maker.
2. Be sure that the coffee itself is fresh and that it is the proper grind for your coffee maker.
3. If your coffee is sometimes good, but more often too strong or too weak, it's likely that you do not measure the coffee and water accurately. Here are the proper measurements: Allow *one Approved Coffee Measure* (or its equivalent, two level measuring tablespoons) of *fresh* coffee to each *three-quarters of a measuring cup of fresh, cold water*. This makes enough for one serving, and will give you a flavorful, dependable brew, strong enough to please the average palate.
4. You will get best results when you brew coffee to the full capacity of your coffee maker. After it is brewed, serve it as quickly as possible and serve it piping hot.

DIFFERENT METHODS OF COFFEE MAKING

DRIP COFFEE

Bring water to a full rolling boil. Measure coffee carefully into coffee basket. Then measure the exact amount of boiling water to allow three-quarters of a cup to each Approved Coffee Measure of coffee. When water has dripped through, remove coffee basket and water container. Then—and this is an important point—stir the hot coffee thoroughly to insure a brew of even strength. Never attempt to make a small amount of coffee in a large drip pot. You will find that the brew will be weak if you make less than two-thirds of the pot's capacity.

VACUUM COFFEE

For this type of brew, measure freshly-drawn water into lower bowl. Place over heat and, while it is reaching the boiling point, insert filter in upper bowl. Then measure out correct quantity of finely-ground coffee. When water boils, lower heat and insert upper bowl. After most of the water has risen into the upper bowl, stir water and coffee briskly. After two to three minutes, remove coffee maker from heat. When all the coffee has returned to the lower bowl, remove upper section and serve. Cloth filters should never be allowed to dry, once they have been used. Keep them in water in the refrigerator between uses. Rinse them in clear water—no soap, please!

PERCOLATOR COFFEE

Measure cold water accurately into pot and place on heat. When water boils, re-. move it from heat and then measure the proper amount of coffee into the basket. Cover, return to heat and allow it to percolate gently for six to eight minutes. If it is necessary to keep coffee hot for a time, the coffee maker should be placed on an asbestos mat over low heat.

Cooking for Two

THE HONEYMOON IS OVER; the die is cast. You and you only stand between your husband's and your own starvation. Either you surrender to the can-opener method of cooking, to allow you more time at the beauty parlor, or you make up your mind to follow a more rewarding path. You decide to learn to cook well, to experiment and master culinary techniques, and to set interesting and nourishing meals on an attractive table.

Feeding a husband successfully starts with feeding him the things he likes to eat, for a clever bride cooks to please her man. She goes out of her way to keep mealtimes pleasant and comfortable. She knows that experts say "happy mealtimes are as important to health as proper food." And whether the meal is served informally in the kitchen, at the dining table by candlelight, or on trays in the living room with soft background music, the surroundings should be neat, the atmosphere one of relaxation, and there should be some special touch—a single flower floating in a glass saucer, a colorful napkin tied in a knot, a pretty china figurine—just to remind your husband how lucky he is to have "caught" you.

The menu itself should be thought out in advance to provide essential nutrients, contrasting colors and textures, and the same element should not be repeated in two or more courses of the same meal. If the meat has a sauce with cream in it, the soup will not contain cream, neither will the dessert. If the soup contains tomatoes, you will not serve broiled tomatoes with the meat or sliced tomatoes for salad.

The wise young homemaker will use a touch of color on the serving plate—a sprig of parsley or water cress, a dash of paprika, a lemon slice, or a radish rose—to make the dish attractive. Varying shades of green add interest to a salad.

Beyond these common-sense rules, the sky's the limit.

A WORD ON NUTRITION

No more concise advice on nutrition can be found than that written in a small booklet, *"and she does it so easily and so well,"* by Margaret Jane Suydam, Home Economist for the National Dairy Council, in Chicago. Miss Suydam says:

"The feeling of zestful living that lasts round the clock and calendar has its foundation in food—the right foods for health and vitality.

We invest time and money in three meals a day. It's smart to be sure that they help keep us on top of the world. A lack of certain nutrients in the diet can account for grouchiness, nervousness, depression, fatigue, and lessened ability to concentrate. Food can help prevent and cure all these? Sounds more like a barker for a patent medicine? No, you can save the dollar that the unwary spend for nostrums and build your husband's health and yours soundly and scientifically by serving and eating the foods that meet body needs.

WHAT ARE THESE?
Everyone needs foods to do three things:
1. Build and repair tissues—bones, muscles, nerves, blood, all vital organs, fingernails, skin, hair.
2. Regulate body processes—to keep the body working at its best.
3. Supply energy—for every conscious and unconscious action.

Proteins, minerals, vitamins, fats, carbohydrates, and water are the substances found in foods that perform these three tasks. Combinations of all these food elements are necessary in order to make the most profitable use of the food you eat. Most foods combine several food nutrients. Milk combines more than any other food and some of all known to be essential. But no one food combines all the nutrients in the amounts needed.

PROTEINS rank first as body builders. We can't live without them. If what we eat is short of proteins, we may suffer lowered resistance to infection, muscular weakness, mental and physical fatigue.

The best proteins come from animal sources—milk and its products—cheese, ice cream—meat, poultry, fish and eggs. Second best proteins—less expensive and valuable when used with proteins from animal sources—come from dried beans, peas, peanut butter, cereals and breads.

MINERALS both build and regulate. Calcium and iron are the ones about which to be alert. If you choose foods rich in these, the dozen or so other minerals you need will trail along in the same foods.

Calcium is vital to bones and teeth but it is also necessary for healthy nerves and muscles, for normal blood clotting and to regulate your heart beat.

To get enough calcium every day you should drink at least two large glasses of milk and eat cheese and ice cream often, unless you prefer to eat large quantities of turnip greens. Turnip tops, kale, and mustard greens are the next best sources of calcium. But a serving of these greens contains much less calcium than a glass of milk—and few people want to eat such greens every day.

Iron is necessary to build red blood cells. It enables the blood to carry oxygen from the lungs to every cell in the body. Lack of iron causes nutritional anemia, pallor, and fatigue. It's necessary to both your good looks and your good health.

Many foods supply iron but liver gives you the most from any food. Lean meats, egg yolks, green leafy vegetables, enriched and whole-grain cereals, dried fruits, and molasses are other foods from which you can get iron.

VITAMINS are well known to most of us. Some 20 odd have been found to be important to people. If you watch your A B C's in the vitamin group you'll do all right. (Vitamin D is especially important to growing children, pregnant and nursing mothers.)

Vitamin A maintains the health of your skin and the linings of all the organs you learned about in physiology class. It is also important in building the enamel of your teeth and in helping your sight, especially at night.

Milk, cream, butter, ice cream, cheeses made from whole milk, liver, egg yolks, and the green and yellow vegetables supply this vitamin. Your body most readily uses the vitamin A from animal sources.

Vitamin B turned out to be more than one when the scientists explored the matter more thoroughly. Of these, often called the B-complex vitamins, thiamine, riboflavin, niacin, and vitamins B6 and B12 are the most important ones. Without enough of these in your diet, fatigue, irritability, poor digestion, listlessness, lowered vitality, and depression can plague you.

Milk, meats—especially liver and heart, eggs, legumes, peanut butter, and the whole grain and enriched breads and cereals, put these vitamins on your table.

Vitamin C is necessary, yet found in a limited number of foods so that special care must be taken to get it. Its every day job is to help in the formation and maintenance of teeth, gums, bones, blood vessels, and muscles. The need for it is increased in illness or injury. It hastens the healing of wounds.

Citrus fruits—oranges, lemons, grapefruit—and tomatoes are the best sources of Vitamin C. Strawberries, cantaloupe, cabbage, and peppers are good sources: potatoes, too, if eaten regularly.

Vitamin D, the "sunshine" vitamin, is necessary with the minerals calcium and phosphorus, to build bones and teeth.

Vitamin D milk, as well as fish liver oils, can supply the additional amount of vitamin D needed by children, pregnant and nursing mothers, or people who are indoors most of the time.

CARBOHYDRATES AND FATS are dietary essentials and are the chief sources of energy in your diet. Without enough of them anyone will be hungry, tired and lack zest for either job or hobby. If eaten beyond the amount required for work and play they will cause excess weight.

All foods supply some energy but foods that contain much sugar, starch or fats give you the most calories. (A calorie is the unit which measures the amount of energy the body gets from a given amount of food.) A good guide to good meal planning is to choose the foods first that supply proteins, minerals, and vitamins and then add carbohydrates and fats for fillers or flavor.

To capsule all the above information into easy meal planning, you can think of the foods that help make man, woman, or child feel "healthy, wealthy and wise" as falling into two groups: Animal Foods and Plant Foods. Everyone needs some variety of animal and plant foods at each meal. They complement each other to provide all essential nutrients. It is as simple as that."

SOUPS

Few foods are more satisfying or easier to make than a bowl of really good soup—a hearty chowder in cold weather, a well-chilled cream soup in summertime. Followed by a sandwich or a salad, soup makes a delicious, nourishing, and economical lunch.

FRENCH ONION SOUP   *Serves 2.*

2 tablespoons butter

2 large onions, thinly sliced

1 13½ ounce can beef consomme or 1 10½ ounce can plus water to measure 1¾ cups

¼ teaspoon pepper

Salt to taste

1 teaspoon lemon juice

2 thick slices French bread, buttered

2 tablespoons grated Parmesan cheese

1. In saucepan heat butter and in it cook onions over low heat until tender, but not browned, stirring often to separate onion slices into rings.
2. Add stock and pepper and bring to a boil. Simmer for 10 minutes.
3. Add salt and lemon juice and keep hot.
4. When ready to serve, ladle soup into individual oven-proof casseroles, place a slice of French bread in each and sprinkle each with 1 tablespoon cheese. Place under broiler for about 3 minutes, or until cheese is brown and bubbly.

For a special touch, stir in 2 tablespoons Port wine before serving.

INSTANT BLENDER VICHYSSOISE *Serves 4.*

1 thin slice small onion
¾ cup chicken broth
¼ teaspoon salt
Dash pepper

¾ cup cooked or canned potatoes, sliced
1 cup crushed ice
½ cup milk or cream

Chopped chives or green onion tops

1. Into container of the electric blender put onion and ½ cup chicken broth. Cover and blend on high speed for 6 seconds.
2. Add salt, pepper, potatoes, and remaining broth, cover, and blend for 8 seconds.
3. Add ice and milk or cream, cover, and blend for 10 seconds longer. Serve immediately or keep cold. Garnish each serving with chopped chives or onion tops.

SENEGALESE *Serves 4.*

1 can (10 oz.) cream of chicken soup
1 teaspoon curry powder

½ cup milk
1 cup crushed ice

¼ cup cream

1. Into blender container put soup, curry powder, and milk. Cover and blend on high speed for 15 seconds.
2. Add ice and cream, cover, and blend for 10 seconds longer.
3. Serve garnished with a sprinkling of paprika, chopped chives, or chopped cucumber.

BRUSSELS SPROUT CHOWDER *Serves 2.*

2 slices bacon
½ clove garlic
1 package (10 oz.) frozen California Brussels sprouts, quartered
½ cup water
3 tablespoons raw rice
¾ cup chicken stock

1 cup milk
½ teaspoon salt
Dash pepper
¼ teaspoon oregano
¼ cup cooked peas
¼ cup cooked diced carrots
2 tablespoons grated Parmesan cheese

1. Rub bacon slices with garlic and cook in heavy saucepan until translucent.
2. Add Brussels sprouts and water. Cover and simmer for 30 minutes.
3. Stir in rice, stock, milk, and seasonings and simmer for 20 minutes longer.
4. Discard bacon and stir in vegetables and cheese.
5. Serve hot with additional grated cheese, if desired.

SOUPS FROM A CAN

When serving a canned soup, add a special touch to enhance their flavor and appearance. Sprinkle individual servings with chopped parsley, chives, or dill, or a dash of paprika. Add crisp croutons, frankfurter slices, sliced hard-cooked eggs, chopped mushrooms, celery, cucumber, diced ham, or crumbled crisp bacon. Stir in a pinch of curry or nutmeg, a touch of lemon juice, or a dash of sherry, Port, or Madeira. Blending canned soups for a few seconds in an electric blender aerates them and removes any can flavor.

PUREE MONGOLE
Mix or blend 1 can cream of pea soup and 1 can measure of tomato juice. Heat and serve.

CREAM OF CLAM
In electric blender blend 1 can (7½ oz.) minced clams with 1 cup chicken stock and ½ cup cream. Serve hot or cold.

CREAM VERT
In electric blender blend 1 can condensed cream of chicken soup, 1 can measure chicken stock, ½ cup cooked broccoli, spinach, or asparagus, and ¼ cup cream. Serve hot or cold.

CREAM OF PIMIENTO
In electric blender blend 1 can condensed cream of asparagus soup, 1 can (4 oz.) pimientos, drained, ¾ cup water, ¼ teaspoon salt, ¼ teaspoon pepper, 2 tablespoons dry sherry, and ¼ cup cream. Heat over simmering water.

CUCUMBER SOUR CREAM SOUP
In electric blender blend 1 medium cucumber, peeled and cut into chunks, 1 can condensed cream of chicken soup, ¾ cup milk, and 1 cup sour cream. Season to taste with celery salt and cayenne pepper. A dash of curry powder is excellent. Serve chilled and garnish with chopped chives.

CURRIED SHRIMP BISQUE
In electric blender blend 1 can frozen shrimp soup, 1 can measure milk, ¼ cup parsley clusters, and ½ teaspoon curry. Serve hot or cold.

POTAGE NIVERNAISE
In electric blender blend a 1-pound can sliced carrots, drained, 1½ cups chicken broth, ½ small onion, 2 teaspoons chicken-stock base (or 2 chicken bouillon cubes, ¼ teaspoon dry marjoram, ⅛ teaspoon pepper, and ½ cup cream or milk. Heat over simmering water.

CREAM OF BEAN SOUP
In electric blender blend 1 cup of baked beans, 1 thin slice of medium onion, 1½ cups of chicken broth and ½ cup cream. Heat over simmering water.

BASIC SAUCE AND VARIATIONS

It is strange that the most feared recipe by a young homemaker is, perhaps, the easiest and most simple recipe to make—the basic sauce, the basis of all creamed dishes, scalloped potatoes, chicken gravy and a thousand other dishes. From it springs a myriad of other sauces, all the essence of simplicity, once the technique of making the basic sauce is mastered.

BASIC SAUCE   *Makes 1 cup thick sauce.*
2 tablespoons butter   ½ teaspoon salt
3 tablespoons flour   ⅛ teaspoon pepper
                1 cup hot milk, beef, or chicken stock

1. In top of double saucepan melt butter over low heat.
2. Remove pan from heat and stir in flour, salt, and pepper. Use a wooden spoon or wire whisk.
3. Add hot liquid all at once, stirring vigorously.
4. Return saucepan to direct heat and cook, stirring or whisking rapidly, until sauce is smooth and thick. It will thicken almost immediately when made by this method. Be sure to mix well from bottom and sides of pan so there will be no lumps.
5. Cover saucepan, set over simmering water, and let cook for 10 minutes.

THIN SAUCE
Use only 1 tablespoon flour in above recipe.

MEDIUM SAUCE
Use only 2 tablespoons flour in above recipe.

CREAM SAUCE
Make Basic Sauce with hot milk. When cooked, stir in ½ cup heavy cream.

MORNAY SAUCE
Add to Cream Sauce 2 tablespoons each grated Swiss and Parmesan cheese. Cook, stirring, until cheese is melted.

ROYAL SAUCE
Stir into Cream Sauce 1 egg yolk beaten with 3 tablespoons of the hot sauce.

SHERRY CREAM SAUCE
Make Basic Sauce with chicken stock. When cooked, stir in ½ cup heavy cream and 1 to 2 tablespoons sherry to taste.

NEWBURG SAUCE
Make Basic Sauce with milk. When cooked, stir in ½ teaspoon paprika, a dash cayenne, 2 egg yolks lightly beaten with ¼ cup cream, and 2 tablespoons sherry.

CREAMED ON TOAST

The following recipes are a few of the many dishes which have one of the sauces on the preceding page as their base. Serve on toast, in patty shells, with rice or a baked potato.

CHIPPED BEEF ROYALE   *Serves 2.*
Shred 4 ounces chipped beef into a saucepan and cover with boiling water. Drain and mix with 1 cup Cream Sauce, Sherry Sauce, or Sauce Royal. Heat over simmering water and serve hot.

CHICKEN A LA KING   *Serves 2.*
Make Sherry Cream Sauce but saute 1 tablespoon minced onion in butter before adding the flour. When sauce is cooked, stir in 1 cup diced cooked chicken and ½ cup sliced mushrooms cooked in 1 tablespoon butter. Serve hot.

LOBSTER NEWBURG   *Serves 2.*
Make Newburg Sauce. Stir in 1 teaspoon brandy and 1½ cups cooked lobster meat. Cook over simmering water until lobster is heated through.

CREAMED EGGS   *Serves 2.*
Make any one of the sauces on the preceding page. When cooked, add 4 hard-cooked eggs, sliced. Stir gently to avoid breaking egg slices and serve as soon as eggs are heated through. If desired add chopped parsley, chives or green onion tops, or chopped pimiento.

Creamed dishes such as Creamed Deviled Ham, make a hearty supper dish when served on a baked potato as in photograph on the opposite page. It is equally good served on cooked noodles. Flaked, cooked white fish may be substituted for the ham.

DEVILED CREAMED HAM   *Serves 2.*
1 tablespoon minced onion	Dash cayenne
1½ tablespoons butter	1 cup hot milk
1½ tablespoons flour	½ teaspoon Worcestershire sauce
1 teaspoon prepared mustard	1 cup diced cooked ham
1 tablespoon minced parsley	

1. Cook onion in butter until tender but not browned.
2. Stir in flour, mustard, and cayenne pepper.
3. Add hot milk, stirring vigorously, and cook, stirring rapidly, until sauce is smooth and thickened.
4. Stir in Worcestershire sauce and ham, cover, and cook over simmering water for 10 minutes. Stir in parsley.

An attractive luncheon menu is suggested in this photograph. The Creamed Deviled Crab is baked in fluted scallop shells (real or ceramic ones can be used), and served with half a Bartlett Pear on a bed of cole slaw with mayonnaise dressing. A wedge of lemon, a stalk of celery and some ripe olives add color to the plate.

CREAMED DEVILED CRAB
Serves 2 to 3.

1½ tablespoons butter
1 tablespoon minced onion
2 tablespoons diced celery
1 tablespoon flour
¼ teaspoon dry mustard
¼ teaspoon salt
½ cup hot milk

½ teaspoon Worcestershire sauce
1 teaspoon lemon juice
Dash Tabasco
2 canned pimientos, chopped
1 hard-cooked egg, chopped
 (optional)
1 6½ oz. can Alaska King Crab

2 tablespoons buttered bread crumbs

1. In saucepan melt butter and in it cook onion and celery until onion is tender, but not brown.
2. Stir in flour, mustard, and salt.
3. Add hot milk, stirring vigorously, and cook, stirring, until sauce is smooth and thickened.
4. Add remaining ingredients, except crumbs.
5. Put mixture into buttered shells or ramekins.
6. Sprinkle with crumbs and bake in a preheated 400° F. oven for about 20 minutes, or until browned.

VEGETABLES MORNAY

Cook 1 10-ounce package frozen vegetables, such as cauliflower, string beans, carrots, peas, or artichoke hearts, according to package directions. Drain and stir in 1 tablespoon minced parsley, ¼ teaspoon dry tarragon, and 1 cup Mornay Cream Sauce. Keep hot over simmering water until ready to serve. *To Serve Au Gratin:* Fill small oven-proof casseroles with the vegetable-sauce mixture. Sprinkle with a mixture of 2 tablespoons each bread crumbs and shredded cheese, and bake in a preheated 350° F. oven for 15 minutes.

CRAB MEAT LOUIS

Make Basic Cream Sauce but saute 2 green onions, chopped, and 2 tablespoons minced green pepper in the butter before stirring in the flour. When sauce is cooked, stir in ½ teaspoon dry mustard, 2 dashes Tabasco, ¼ cup shredded American cheese, 1 tablespoon minced parsley, and the contents of a 6½ oz. can Alaska King crab meat, flaked. Keep hot over simmering water until ready to serve.

ELECTRIC BLENDER CREAM SAUCE

The Basic Sauce or Cream Sauce used for creamed dishes and as a base for many meat, fish, or vegetable casseroles can be made in seconds in an electric blender. It cooks to smooth perfection in only 3 minutes with just occasional stirring, or may be poured immediately over other ingredients in a casserole to be baked without cooking it at all.

MEDIUM CREAM SAUCE   *Makes 2 cups.*

4 tablespoons flour   ½ teaspoon salt
4 tablespoons soft butter   ⅛ teaspoon pepper
            2 cups hot milk or part milk and cream

1. Put flour, butter, salt, pepper, and ½ cup hot milk into container of an electric blender. Cover and turn motor on high speed.
2. As soon as blades are fully in motion, remove cover, and gradually pour in remaining hot milk.
3. Pour into saucepan and cook over low heat for 3 minutes, stirring occasionally; or pour over other ingredients in a casserole and bake.

CREAMED IN CASSEROLE

EGGS FLORENTINE   *Serves 2.*

½ cup cooked, chopped spinach   Dash pepper
1 tablespoon butter   1 cup Mornay Sauce
1 teaspoon lemon juice   2 poached eggs *
¼ teaspoon salt   1 tablespoon grated Parmesan cheese

1. Heat spinach and butter and stir in lemon juice, salt, and pepper.
2. Make a layer of spinach in bottom of 2 casseroles or ramekins.
3. Spoon 2 tablespoons sauce over spinach and place a poached egg on top.
4. Cover egg generously with sauce and sprinkle with cheese.
5. Bake in a preheated 350° F. oven for 15 minutes.

* *Poach Eggs* in a small frying pan in enough salted water to cover. When eggs are set, cut carefully around each egg yolk with a 2¼ to 2½ inch cooky cutter. Lift eggs out of water with a slotted pancake turner.

HAM AND BROCCOLI CASSEROLE   *Serves 2.*

1 package frozen broccoli   2 tablespoons shredded cheese
2 slices cooked ham   1 teaspoon prepared mustard
1 cup Cream Sauce   ¼ teaspoon salt
                       1 teaspoon minced onion

1. Cook broccoli according to package directions. Drain.
2. Arrange broccoli in bottom of a small casserole.
3. Arrange ham slices on top.
4. To Cream Sauce, add cheese, mustard, salt, and onion and cook, stirring, over low heat until cheese is melted.
5. Pour sauce over meat and broccoli.
6. Bake in a preheated 400° F. oven for 30 minutes.

Note: Sliced leftover chicken or turkey meat may be used in place of the ham.

A truly delicate and delicious dish has its cream sauce flavored with white wine. Although a little more time-consuming to make than previous creamed dishes in this chapter, it is well worth the trouble. Make it for some special celebration—your first month's anniversary, for instance! What a lucky bridegroom!

SCALLOPS POULETTE AU GRATIN   *Serves 2.*

2 tablespoons butter   ¼ teaspoon salt
1 teaspoon minced onion   Dash pepper
½ pound scallops, quartered   ¼ cup cream
¼ cup white wine   1 egg yolk
4 mushrooms, chopped   Dash lemon juice
2 tablespoons flour   1 teaspoon minced parsley
                  2 tablespoons browned bread crumbs *

1. In a small saucepan melt half the butter and in it cook onion for 2 minutes.
2. Add scallops and white wine, bring liquid to a simmer, cover saucepan tightly, and cook scallops over low heat for 2 minutes.
3. In another saucepan heat remaining butter and in it cook mushrooms for 5 minutes.
4. Stir in flour.
5. Drain liquid from scallops into measuring cup. It should measure ¾ cup. If not add hot water or clam juice. Add to flour mixture, stirring vigorously, and cook, stirring, until sauce is thickened.
6. Add salt and pepper, cover, and cook over simmering water for 10 minutes.
7. Stir in cream, beaten with egg yolk.
8. Add lemon juice, parsley, and scallops and mix.
9. Divide mixture into 2 buttered ramekins or shells.
10. Sprinkle with crumbs and bake in a preheated 350° F. oven for 15 minutes.
* *Brown Crumbs* by sauteeing crumbs in a small frying pan in a little hot butter, stirring constantly, until golden.
Note: One-half pound fillet of sole or other white fish may be used in place of the scallops. After cooking, the fish should be flaked.

CHICKEN AND EGG CASSEROLE   Serves 2.

1 cup diced cooked chicken   ½ teaspoon salt
2 hard-cooked eggs, sliced   1 teaspoon minced onion
½ cup Basic Sauce   ¼ cup chicken stock or milk
                    ½ cup biscuit mix

1. Arrange chicken and egg slices in alternate layers in a 1 quart casserole
2. Combine Basic Sauce, salt, onion, and chicken stock or milk and pour over chicken and eggs.
3. Make biscuit dough according to package directions. Roll out ½ inch thick and cut into rounds with a floured biscuit cutter.
4. Arrange biscuits on top of casserole, about 1 inch apart.
5. Bake in a preheated 425° F. oven for 15 minutes.

CREAMED FISH OR SEAFOOD IN CASSEROLE

1 cup cooked, flaked fish or mixed   ¼ teaspoon salt
  chopped shrimp and crabmeat   Dash pepper
½ tablespoon minced onion   ¾ cup Cream Sauce
2 tablespoons butter   4 tablespoons bread crumbs
1 tablespoon sherry   2 tablespoons shredded cheese

1. In saucepan cook fish or seafood and onion in butter for 3 minutes.
2. Sprinkle with sherry, salt, and pepper, and stir in cream sauce.
3. Pile mixture into shells or ramekins and sprinkle with the bread crumbs mixed with cheese.
4. Bake in a preheated 400° F. oven for 12 to 15 minutes, or until topping is brown and sauce is bubbling.

SHRIMP IN BEER SAUCE
Serves 2.

Beer, America's favorite beverage, becomes the basic liquid in this sauce, made in the same way as a Basic Sauce, then flavored with tomatos. Combined with America's favorite shellfish, shrimp, it becomes a memorable dish. Men love it!

¾ cup beer or ale
1 tablespoon chopped onion
1 spray parsley
1 lemon wedge
½ bay leaf
½ teaspoon salt

1 pound raw shrimp,
   shelled and deveined
1 tablespoon butter
1 tablespoon flour
½ cup tomato sauce
2 dashes Tabasco

Pinch sugar

1. Bring beer to a boil with onion, parsley, lemon wedge, bay leaf and salt.
2. Add shrimp. Bring liquid again to boil, reduce heat and simmer for 5 minutes.
3. Strain shrimp liquid into cup.
4. In saucepan melt butter and stir in flour.
5. Add shrimp liquid, stirring, vigorously, and cook, stirring, until sauce is smooth and thickened.
6. Add tomato sauce, Tabasco, and sugar and bring to a boil.
7. Add shrimp and cook until shrimp are heated through.
8. Serve with cooked rice.

BROILING

OVEN BROILING

Tender cuts of meat, such as porterhouse and sirloin steaks, lamb chops, ham slice, young poultry, fish steaks and fillets, and burgers are all suited to this method of cooking.

1. Remove broiler rack and rub with fat or oil.
2. For easy cleaning, line pan beneath rack with aluminum foil.
3. Preheat broiler.
4. Place food on broiler rack and broil 2 to 3 inches below heat, or as specified in recipe, for half the cooking time.
5. Turn food with spatula or tongs and continue to cook for remaining time.
6. Sprinkle with salt and pepper before serving.

BROILING TIME, depends on the thickness of the meat. The following chart of cooking times are general.

Food	Total Cooking Time 2 to 3 inches from heat
Chops or steak, 1 inch thick	8 minutes
Chicken halves or parts	20 to 30 minutes
Fresh or smoked ham, ½ inch thick	15 minutes
Fish steaks	8 to 10 minutes
Fish fillets	5 to 8 minutes
Whole fish, split	8 to 10 minutes
Whole fish such as sea bass, weakfish, flounder	10 to 15 minutes.

PAN BROILING

When a good oven broiler is not available, pan-broiling can be a most satisfactory way of cooking meat and chops. For it you need a heavy bottomed skillet—like one of those old-fashioned iron skillets your mother used to have. Heat it over direct heat to smoking hot. Rub it with a little fat from the meat stuck on a fork, then put in the meat. Sear for about 1 minute on one side; turn and sear the other. Continue to cook for same length of time as for oven broiling, half on one side and half on the other.

HE-MAN BURGERS
A really good hamburger is mighty fine eating and makes a quick, always enjoyable meal, served with a salad of crisp Western Iceberg lettuce combined with a big red onion, sliced, and a simple dressing of garlic, oil and wine vinegar. Doubleday & Company recently published an entire book on hamburgers, called *365 Ways to Cook Hamburgers*, by Doyne Nickerson.

HEAVENLY HAMBURGER   *Serves 2.*
1. Buy 1 pound round without fat or a piece of rump or top sirloin and have it ground to order.
2. Divide in half and mold gently into patties about 1½ inch thick. Pat together, do not press.
3. Broil to sear outside for 1 minute, turn and sear the other side.
4. Sprinkle with salt and coarsely ground pepper and broil for 2 minutes. Turn and again sprinkle with salt and pepper and broil for 2 minutes longer. It should be crusty on the outside, tender and rare or medium rare on the inside.
5. Place on warm serving plate on a slice of toast, if desired, and top with a pat of butter, a dash each of Worcestershire sauce, Tabasco, and lemon juice, and sprinkle with chopped parsley.

BROILED HALIBUT DINNER
If your wedding presents included a broiling plank, now is the time to put it to use; otherwise use a large shallow baking dish that can be taken to the table.

PLANKED HALIBUT   *Serves 2.*

2 ½-pound halibut steaks, fresh or frozen | 1 cup mashed potatoes
2 tablespoons melted butter | 2 small tomatoes
Salt and pepper | Pimiento Butter or Parsley Lemon Butter

1. If halibut is frozen, let thaw in refrigerator or at room temperature.
2. Place fish on an oiled wooden plank or large shallow baking dish.
3. Brush fish with melted butter and sprinkle with salt and pepper.
4. Broil about 3 inches from heat for 8 to 10 minutes.
5. Turn steaks, brush again with butter, and sprinkle with salt and pepper.
6. Spoon potatoes around border of plank and arrange tomatoes at one end.
7. Continue to broil for 10 to 12 minutes longer, or until potato is browned and fish flakes easily when tested with a fork.
8. Serve on the plank or baking dish with favorite butter sauce.

PIMIENTO BUTTER SAUCE

Melt 2 tablespoons butter. Stir in 1 chopped pimiento and 2 teaspoons lemon juice.

PARSLEY LEMON BUTTER

Melt 2 tablespoons butter and stir in 1 tablespoon minced parsley and 2 teaspoons lemon juice.

DEEP FAT FRYING

. . . where foods are completely submerged in hot shortening or cooking oil, is not a popular method of cooking today, except in Southern states. It is worth the effort for such foods as batter fried shrimp or golden fried onion rings, which cannot be duplicated by any other method. To deep fry small quantities of food, no special equipment is necessary except a deep-fat frying thermometer. An ordinary heavy-bottomed skillet, about 2-inches deep, makes a suitable utensil in which to heat the shortening or oil and does not require such a quantity of fat as a saucepan. An electric skillet may also be used.

FRYING BATTER

1 egg, separated
½ cup beer or ale
Dash Tabasco
½ cup plus 2 tablespoons sifted all-purpose flour

½ teaspoon salt
½ teaspoon paprika
1 tablespoon melted butter

1. Beat egg yolk and beer with dash of Tabasco until well blended.
2. Combine flour, salt, and paprika and gradually stir into beer-egg mixture. Continue to stir until batter is smooth.
3. Stir in melted butter
4. Beat egg white until fluffy and stiff and fold into batter.

TEMPURA

In Japan all manner of foods are dipped in batter and deep fried. The most popular of them all in this country are the Butterfly Shrimp. Fry a few whole, cooked green beans and some slices of cooked sweet potato and serve with the shrimp. Serve with soy sauce, and hot mustard, or with a special *Tempura* Sauce. Beer is the natural beverage to serve with *Tempera*.

BUTTERFLY SHRIMP

Use deveined shrimp or remove shells from raw shrimp, leaving tail intact. With a sharp knife, slit shrimp deeply down back without cutting them all the way through and discard black vein which runs down back. Wash shrimp and spread them open on a towel. Cover with another towel until ready to fry. Dip in fritter batter and fry a few at a time in hot deep fat. Drain on absorbent paper and serve hot with favorite sauce.

TEMPURA SAUCE

Combine ½ cup beer or ale, 2 tablespoons soy sauce, ¼ teaspoon sugar, and ½ to 1 teaspoon horseradish.

The recipe for Lamb Kidneys with Rosemary may be found on page 251. The Parsley Rice Ring is on page 247 and the Citrus Maraschino Mold is on page 257.

BATTER FRIED ONION RINGS   Serves 2.

Slice a medium onion ¼ inch thick and separate slices into rings. Make Frying Batter. Put enough shortening or cooking oil into a small deep skillet to measure 1 inch in depth and heat to 370° F. Dip onion rings, a few at a time, into frying batter. Lift out with a two-tined fork and transfer carefully to the hot oil or shortening. Fry until golden brown, from 2 to 3 minutes. Lift out of fat with fork and place on absorbent paper to drain. Sprinkle with salt and serve, while hot, with hamburgers, steaks, or chops.

BATTER FRIED VEGETABLES

Other vegetables lend themselves to deep fat frying and make a delicious first course to a meal, served with wedges of lemon. In Italy, this is called *Fritto Misto*, meaning "mixed fry."

Prepare vegetables: Separate cauliflower flowerets and broccoli stalks and cook for 5 minutes in boiling, salted water; drain well and dry on paper towel. Slice eggplant or summer squash and cut into thin julienne strips. Dip vegetables into batter and fry as above. Although not a vegetable, wedges of Gruyere cheese are wonderfully good dipped in batter and fried as above.

BATTER FRIED FISH

Dip small whole fish, oysters, scallops, or finger-length strips of fish fillets into frying batter and fry as above.

OVEN FRYING

OVEN FRIED FISH   Serves 2.

2 small dressed fish	⅓ cup fine dry bread crumbs
⅓ cup milk	1 teaspoon paprika
1 teaspoon salt	Dash cayenne

2 tablespoons melted butter, margarine, or bacon drippings

1. Wipe fish with a damp paper towel.
2. In a flat dish combine milk and salt.
3. On piece of waxed paper, mix bread crumbs, paprika, and cayenne.
4. Dip fish in milk and roll in crumbs.
5. Place fish in well-greased baking dish.
6. Pour melted fat over fish.
7. Bake in a preheated 500° F. oven on shelf near top of oven for 10 to 12 minutes, or until fish flakes easily when tested with a fork.
8. Serve on warm serving plates garnished with lemon wedge. Buttered parsley potatoes and asparagus make excellent vegetable accompaniments.

This appetizing dish is Creamed Eggs in a Corned Beef Crust. You can read how to make it on page 252.

SKILLET FRYING

The most practical and economical method of cooking meat, poultry, and fish for the young homemaker cooking for two, is top of the stove, skillet cooking called sauteeing—or frying in a small quantity of hot shortening. Many dishes may be started by this method and later finished in the oven.

SKILLET FRIED CHICKEN   *Serves 2.*

¼ cup all-purpose flour   4 pieces frying chicken
1 teaspoon salt   ¼ cup shortening, part butter or margarine

1. Mix flour and salt.
2. Roll chicken pieces in the seasoned flour.
3. In skillet, melt shortening over medium heat. Cook floured chicken in the hot shortening until browned, turning frequently with tongs, so that the pieces become golden all over.
4. Reduce heat to low, cover, and cook for about 30 minutes, or until chicken is tender when tested with a fork.
5. If desired, sprinkle with 1 tablespoon chopped parsley, chives, or dill, or dust with paprika before serving.

Note: If you wish chicken to be crisp, uncover during last 10 minutes of cooking.

SKILLET CHICKEN WITH MUSHROOMS

Follow directions for Skillet-Fried Chicken. After chicken has cooked for 15 minutes, add 1 small onion, minced, ½ green pepper, finely chopped, and ½ cup sliced fresh mushrooms. Cover and continue to cook until chicken is tender. Remove chicken to hot platter, spoon vegetables over chicken, and sprinkle with minced parsley.

SKILLET CHICKEN PAPRIKASH

Follow recipe for Skillet-Fried Chicken. When chicken has cooked for 15 minutes, add 1 small onion, finely chopped, 1 teaspoon paprika, and ¼ cup chicken stock or white wine. Turn chicken pieces so that all are flavored with the paprika. Cover and continue to cook until chicken is tender. Arrange chicken on hot platter and stir into pan juices ½ cup cream, sweet or sour. Stir until cream is hot and pour sauce over chicken.

SKILLET CHICKEN MEXICANA

Follow recipe for Skillet-Fried Chicken. When chicken has cooked for 15 minutes, add ¼ cup diced pimiento, 1 clove garlic, minced, and 1 small onion, sliced. Cover and continue to cook until chicken and vegetables are tender.

SKILLET CHICKEN WITH ALMONDS

Follow directions for Skillet-Fried Chicken. When chicken has cooked for 15 minutes, add ½ cup blanched, sliced almonds. Cover and continue to cook until chicken is tender. Remove chicken and almonds to hot platter. To pan add 1 tablespoon butter and 1 teaspoon lemon juice. Swirl pan until butter is melted and pour pan juices over chicken.

SKILLET CHICKEN WITH CURRY

Follow directions for Skillet-Fried Chicken. When chicken has cooked for 15 minutes, add 1 small onion, minced, 1 clove garlic, minced, and 1 teaspoon curry powder. Turn chicken pieces so that all are flavored with curry. Add ¼ cup chicken stock or white wine. Cover and continue to cook until chicken is tender. Arrange chicken on hot platter and stir into pan juices, ½ cup cream. Stir until cream is hot and pour sauce over chicken.

SKILLET CHICKEN CACCIATORE

Follow recipe for Skillet-Fried Chicken. When chicken pieces are well browned on all sides, add 1 ripe tomato, cut into eight sections, or ½ cup canned tomatoes, 1 onion, sliced, 1 green pepper, sliced, 1 clove garlic, minced, ½ bay leaf, 1 spray parsley, and ¼ cup chicken stock, tomato juice, or white wine. Cover and cook for 15 minutes. Add 4 mushrooms, and 1 teaspoon lemon juice. Cover and continue to cook for 15 minutes, or until chicken is tender. Remove parsley and bay leaf before serving.

HERBED CHICKEN

3 tablespoons butter or margarine	4 pieces frying chicken
3 tablespoons all-purpose flour	2 tablespoons chopped onion
1 teaspoon salt	¼ cup chopped canned mushrooms
⅛ teaspoon pepper	2 tablespoons mushroom liquid
⅛ teaspoon rosemary	1 tablespoon lemon juice
⅛ teaspoon thyme	½ teaspoon sugar
1 tablespoon chopped parsley	½ cup canned tomatoes

1. In skillet melt butter or margarine.
2. Combine flour, salt, pepper, herbs, and parsley.
3. Dip chicken pieces in seasoned flour and brown well in the hot shortening on all sides. (Reserve leftover flour mixture).
4. Add onion and mushrooms and cook until onion is tender.
5. Stir in reserved flour.
6. Add mushroom liquid, lemon juice, sugar, and tomatoes and bring sauce to a boil.
7. Reduce heat, cover, and cook for about 30 minutes, or until chicken is tender.

SOUTHERN FRIED CHICKEN, PAN GRAVY

1 frying chicken, cut into serving pieces

1 egg, beaten

6 tablespoons all-purpose flour

½ teaspoon salt

⅛ teaspoon pepper

¼ cup shortening

1. Dip chicken pieces in beaten egg and roll in flour seasoned with salt and pepper.
2. Saute in hot shortening until well browned, turning pieces frequently to brown them evenly on all sides.
3. Cover and cook over low heat for 30 minutes, or until tender.
4. Serve with Pan Cream Gravy.

PAN CREAM GRAVY

Remove chicken pieces from skillet to serving platter and keep warm. There should be 2 tablespoons shortening remaining in skillet. If not, add enough to make 2 tablespoons. Stir in 2 tablespoons flour and sprinkle with 1/4 teaspoon salt and a dash of pepper. Gradually stir in 1 cup Carnation evaporated milk and cook, stirring, until sauce thickens. Cook over low heat for 3 minutes longer and pour over chicken. Sprinkle with chopped parsley.

FROM SKILLET TO OVEN

GINGER CHICKEN

Follow recipe for Skillet-Fried Chicken. When pieces are brown transfer to an oven-proof casserole, which can be brought to table. In small saucepan combine 1/4 cup sherry, 1 tablespoon soy sauce, 2 tablespoons butter, 1 tablespoon lemon juice and 2 tablespoons finely chopped preserved or candied ginger. Bring to a boil, pour over chicken, cover, and bake in a preheated 350° F. oven for 1 hour, turning pieces once during the cooking.

OVEN-FRIED CHICKEN

Follow recipe for Skillet-Fried Chicken. When pieces are brown, transfer to a small oven-proof casserole, which can be brought to table. Dot pieces with 1 tablespoon butter and bake in a preheated 350° F. oven for 1 hour, turning pieces occasionally.

OVEN-BARBECUED CHICKEN

Follow recipe for Skillet-Fried Chicken. When pieces are brown, transfer to a small oven-proof casserole, which can be brought to table. In small saucepan heat 2 tablespoons butter. Add 1/2 cup chili sauce, 1/4 cup water, 1 tablespoon lemon juice, 1 tablespoon minced onion, 1/2 tablespoon Worcestershire sauce, 1 tablespoon brown sugar, 1/4 teaspoon paprika and 1/4 teaspoon salt. Bring mixture to a boil and pour over chicken in casserole. Cover and bake in a preheated 350° F. oven for 1 hour.

CHICKEN IN WINE SAUCE

Follow recipe for Skillet-Fried Chicken. When pieces are brown, transfer to small oven-proof casserole, which can be brought to table. In small sauce pan heat 2 tablespoons butter. Add 1 small clove garlic, minced, 1/4 teaspoon each salt and pepper, 1/4 teaspoon thyme, 1 tablespoon grated or minced onion, and 1/4 cup white wine. Bring to a boil. Pour over chicken, cover, and bake in a preheated 350° F. oven for 1 hour.

CHICKEN BAKED IN CREAM   *Serves 2.*

2 tablespoons flour
½ teaspoon salt
¼ teaspoon pepper
1 teaspoon paprika
1 teaspoon celery salt
1 teaspoon curry
½ teaspoon oregano

1 small frying chicken,
  cut into portions
2 tablespoons butter
¾ cup cream
¼ cup sour cream
2 tablespoons chopped parsley

1. In paper bag combine flour, salt, pepper, paprika, celery salt, curry and oregano.
2. Drop chicken parts into bag and shake gently until pieces are coated with the seasoned flour.
3. In skillet heat butter and in it saute the chicken pieces until golden brown on all sides. Transfer to a small oven casserole.
4. Add cream, cover, and cook in a preheated 350° F. oven for 35 minutes.
5. Mix a little of the hot sauce with the sour cream and stir into sauce in casserole. Bake for 10 minutes longer.
6. Sprinkle with parsley and serve.

CHICKEN MARENGO   *Serves 2.*

¼ cup flour
½ teaspoon salt
¼ teaspoon pepper
½ teaspoon dried tarragon
1 small frying chicken,
  cut into portions
2 tablespoons butter

1 tablespoon cooking oil
¼ cup dry white wine
¼ cup chicken stock
1 cup canned tomatoes
1 clove garlic, minced
4 mushrooms, sliced
2 tablespoons chopped parsley

1. In a paper bag combine flour, salt, pepper, and tarragon.
2. Drop chicken parts into bag and shake gently until pieces are coated with the seasoned flour.
3. In skillet heat butter and oil and in it saute the floured chicken pieces until golden brown on all sides. Transfer to small oven casserole.
4. To oil and butter remaining in skillet, stir in remaining flour mixture from bag.
5. Gradually stir in wine and chicken stock and cook, stirring, until sauce is smooth and thickened.
6. Pour sauce over chicken. Add remaining ingredients.
7. Cover and cook in a preheated 350° F. oven for 50 minutes.

CHICKEN WITH MIXED HERBS AND WINE

Follow recipe for Skillet-Fried Chicken. When pieces are brown, transfer to small oven-proof casserole, which can be brought to table. In small saucepan combine 2 tablespoons butter, ¼ cup white wine, 1 small clove garlic, minced, 1 tablespoon minced onion, ¼ teaspoon salt, dash pepper, and a good pinch each thyme, marjoram, oregano, and rosemary. Bring to a boil. Pour over chicken, cover, and bake in a preheated 350° F. oven for 1 hour, turning pieces once during the cooking.

SKILLET FRIED MEAT

CHINESE PEPPER STEAK

½ pound round steak,
   cut 1 inch thick
2 tablespoons shortening
1 small clove garlic, minced
¼ teaspoon salt
dash pepper
2 tablespoons soy sauce

¼ teaspoon sugar
½ cup canned bean sprouts
½ cup canned tomatoes
1 green pepper, cut into strips
1 teaspoon cornstarch
1 tablespoon cold water
2 green onions, sliced

1. Slice steak as thinly as possible into short strips.
2. In skillet heat shortening and in it saute beef slices until lightly browned on both sides. Add garlic, salt, and pepper and saute for 1 minute longer, stirring.
3. Stir in soy sauce and sugar, cover, and cook over high heat for 5 minutes.
4. Add bean sprouts, tomatoes and green pepper. Cover and cook for 5 minutes longer.
5. Dissolve cornstarch in cold water and stir into sauce. Cook, stirring until sauce is thickened.
6. Sprinkle with green onions and serve with cooked rice.

Note: The vegetables should be crisp and not cooked until tender.

EASY BEEF STROGANOFF   *Serves 2.*

Saute ½ small onion, minced, in 1 tablespoon butter until onion is tender. Add ½ teaspoon paprika, ¼ cup canned beef gravy, and 1 teaspoon tomato paste. Stir in ½ cup warm sour cream. Season to taste with salt and pepper and heat over simmering water. Saute 4 thin slices beef tenderloin in 1 tablespoon butter for 1 minute on each side. Transfer to serving platter and pour hot sauce over. Serve with parsley noodles.

MEAT BALLS   *Serves 2.*

1 tablespoon minced onion	1 egg
1 tablespoon shortening	½ teaspoon salt
½ cup bread crumbs	dash pepper
⅓ cup milk	1 tablespoon all-purpose flour
½ pound ground meat, beef and part veal	½ cup cream

1. In skillet saute onion in shortening until golden.
2. Soak bread crumbs in milk, add meat, egg, onion, salt and pepper and mix thoroughly but lightly.
3. Shape mixture into small balls, roll in flour, and saute in skillet until brown all over and cooked.
4. Transfer meat to serving dish and keep warm.
5. Combine the 1 tablespoon flour with the cream and gradually stir into pan juices. Simmer for 3 minutes, stirring frequently. Pour over meat and serve hot.

VEAL CUTLETS   *Serves 2.*

2 veal cutlets, ⅓ inch thick	flour
1 egg	¼ teaspoon salt
1 tablespoon water	dash pepper

2 tablespoons butter or shortening

1. Dip cutlets into egg beaten with the water, then into flour seasoned with salt and pepper.
2. Saute cutlets on both sides in hot butter or shortening until browned on both sides.
3. Add a couple of tablespoons of water, cover, and cook over low heat for 30 minutes, or until tender.

VEAL CUTLETS HUNGARIAN STYLE

When cutlets are browned on both sides, sprinkle with 1 teaspoon paprika. Add ½ cup chicken stock, or half chicken stock and half white wine. Cover and simmer for 30 minutes, or until tender. Arrange meat on hot platter and stir into pan juices ½ cup warm sour cream. Heat and pour sauce over veal. Serve with cooked noodles.

VEAL CUTLETS PROVENCALE

When cutlets are browned on both sides, add 1 small clove garlic, minced, 1 ripe tomato, peeled and chopped, or ½ cup canned tomatoes, ¼ cup chicken stock or tomato juice. Cover and simmer for 30 minutes, or until tender. Sprinkle with chopped parsley before serving.

BREADED VEAL SCALLOPS
Serves 2.

4 thinly pounded veal scallops
flour
salt and pepper

1 egg
1 tablespoon water
½ cup fresh bread crumbs

¼ cup butter or margarine

1. Dip scallops into flour seasoned with salt and pepper. Dip in egg beaten with the water, then in bread crumbs. Press meat lightly with the flat side of a knife to make the crumbs stick.
2. Saute scallops slowly in hot butter or margarine for about 3 minutes on each side, or until golden brown.
3. Arrange on serving platter and garnish with lemon slices.

VEAL SCALLOPS WITH MUSHROOMS
When scallops are cooked, arrange on serving platter. To skillet in which they were cooked, melt 1 tablespoon butter and in it cook 1 tablespoon minced onion, and ½ cup sliced mushrooms until vegetables are lightly browned. Add 3 tablespoons chicken stock (or part stock and part sherry). Bring liquid to a simmer and cook for 2 minutes. Add pinch of dry tarragon and 1 tablespoon minced parsley. Pour sauce over meat and serve hot.

VEAL BIRDS
Serves 2.

4 4-inch squares thinly sliced
  veal or beef
Choice of stuffing (see below)
2 tablespoons all-purpose flour
2 tablespoons butter or margarine
1 onion, sliced
1 small carrot, sliced

¼ teaspoon salt
dash pepper
⅛ teaspoon thyme
½ bay leaf
½ cup canned tomatoes, chopped
½ cup stock or wine
1 tablespoon chopped parsley

1. On each square of meat, arrange desired filling, roll up meat like a small jelly roll, and tie with string.
2. Dip rolls in flour and saute in butter or margarine in skillet until browned on all sides.
3. Add remaining ingredients, except parsley, cover, and simmer for 45 minutes.
4. Place rolls on serving dish and strain gravy over them.
5. Sprinkle with chopped parsley.

Note: If desired, 2 tablespoons cream may be stirred into the pan gravy.

PIQUANT STUFFING
Place on each square of meat 1 slice onion, 1 thin lengthwise strip of carrot and 1 thin lengthwise strip dill pickle.

BREAD STUFFING

Saute 2 mushrooms, chopped, and ½ tablespoon chopped onion in 2 tablespoons shortening until lightly browned. Stir into 1 cup fresh bread crumbs. Season with chopped parsley and a pinch each of dried thyme and marjoram, ¼ teaspoon salt and a good dash pepper.

VEGETABLE STUFFING

Place on each square of meat 1 slice onion, 1 sliver garlic, and 1 teaspoon chopped parsley.

VEAL MARENGO   *Serves 2.*

¾ pound veal, cubed	¾ cup chicken stock
½ teaspoon salt	¼ cup white wine
⅛ teaspoon pepper	½ cup canned tomatoes
2 tablespoons shortening	1 tablespoon chopped parsley
1 onion, chopped	1 tablespoon chopped celery
1 small clove garlic, minced	½ bay leaf
2 tablespoons flour	6 small onions, peeled

1. Sprinkle meat with salt and pepper and brown in shortening over high heat. turning cubes to brown on all sides.
2. Lower heat to medium and add chopped onion and garlic and cook until vegetables are lightly browned.
3. Stir in flour and cook until flour is lightly browned.
4. Gradually stir in chicken stock and wine and bring to a boil.
5. Add tomatoes, parsley, celery, and bay leaf.
6. Cover and cook over low heat for 1 hour.
7. Add onions, cover, and continue to cook for 30 minutes longer.

SKILLET FRIED FISH

SKILLET SCAMPI   *Serves 2.*

4 tablespoons butter	⅛ teaspoon pepper
¾ pound uncooked shrimp, shelled and deveined	1 clove garlic, minced
	1 tablespoon lemon juice
¼ teaspoon salt	2 tablespoons chopped parsley

1. Melt butter in skillet and in it saute shrimp for about 5 minutes, or until cooked and pink in color, shaking pan over high heat to turn shrimp and cook them on all sides.
2. Sprinkle with salt and pepper and transfer to serving plate.
3. To butter remaining in skillet, add garlic, lemon juice, and parsley. Stir and cook for 30 seconds, and pour contents of skillet over shrimp.

FISH PROVENCALE   *Serves 2.*

1 tablespoon butter   dash pepper
1 very small onion, minced   ½ cup canned tomatoes, chopped
½ clove garlic, minced   ¼ cup white wine
½ can sliced mushrooms, drained   ½ pound frozen haddock fillets
pinch thyme   1 tablespoon chopped parsley
¼ teaspoon salt   1 tablespoon soft butter
1 tablespoon flour

1. In skillet melt butter and in it saute onion and garlic over medium heat for 3 minutes.
2. Add mushrooms, thyme, salt, pepper, tomatoes, and white wine.
3. Place frozen fillets in center of skillet and bring liquid to a boil.
4. Sprinkle with parsley, cover tightly, and simmer for 20 minutes.
5. Uncover and break fish into small pieces with a fork.
6. Mix soft butter and flour to a smooth paste and stir into liquid in skillet, bit by bit. Cook, stirring, 3 minutes longer.
7. Serve hot on toast or with cooked rice.

POACHING

This is a method of cooking food in a hot liquid which is kept just below the boiling point. Poaching is usually done on top of the stove, but may be done in the oven. Eggs are poached in water, milk, or tomato juice. Fish is usually poached in a seasoned liquid called a *court bouillon*. This is a mixture of fish stock and white wine, but bottled clam juice makes an excellent substitute for fish stock.

FILLETS IN DUGLERE SAUCE   *Serves 2.*

4 small fillets of flounder   ½ cup canned tomatoes, drained and chopped
1 tablespoon butter   1 tablespoon minced parsley
¼ cup clam juice   1 tablespoon minced onion
¼ cup white wine or water   Salt and pepper to taste

1. Roll fillets and tie with thread.
2. In small skillet melt butter and arrange fillets in pan.
3. Add clam juice, white wine or water, tomatoes, parsley, and onion and bring to a boil.
4. Cook over very low heat for 10 to 12 minutes, or until fillets are cooked, turning them once with a spatula so they will cook on all sides.
5. Remove fillets to warm serving platter. Discard thread.
6. Season sauce with salt and pepper and cook over high heat, stirring for 2 minutes.
7. Pour sauce over fillets and garnish with parsley or water cress.

FISH IN MARINE SAUCE   *Serves 2.*

2 tablespoons butter   ½ cup clam juice (or half clam
1 tablespoon flour   juice and half white wine)
½ cup hot milk   1 teaspoon minced onion
4 small fish fillets   1 egg yolk
                    2 tablespoons minced parsley

1. In saucepan melt half the butter and stir in flour. Add hot milk, stirring vigorously. Cook, stirring, until sauce is thick. Keep hot over simmering water.
2. Roll fillets and tie with coarse thread.
3. In small skillet melt remaining butter and place rolled fillets in it.
4. Add clam juice and minced onion, bring liquid to a boil, and cook over very low heat for 10 minutes, turning fillets once so they will cook on all sides.
5. Place fillets on warm serving dish and discard thread.
6. Stir liquid from skillet gradually into egg yolk, then stir egg yolk mixture into the hot sauce. Cook sauce, stirring, for 2 minutes.
7. Stir in parsley and pour sauce over fish.

ROASTING

There are two methods of roasting meat and each has its devotees. The first is known as the SEARING METHOD by which the roast is cooked in a very hot 450° F. oven, for 15 to 20 minutes, or until surface is well browned, and the CONSTANT HEAT METHOD, where the roast is allowed to cook at low temperature throughout.

GENERAL ROASTING CHART FOR SEARING METHOD

Meat	*Total Roasting Time*
Beef (rare)	20 minutes per pound
Beef (medium)	25 minutes per pound
Beef (well done)	30 minutes per pound
Lamb (medium)	18 to 20 minutes per pound
Lamb (well done)	25 minutes per pound
Veal	25 minutes per pound
Pork	30 minutes per pound
Chicken, Duck, or Turkey	25 minutes per pound

GENERAL ROASTING CHART FOR CONSTANT 325° F. TEMP.

Beef (rare)	25 minutes per pound
Beef (medium)	30 minutes per pound
Beef (well done)	35 minutes per pound
Lamb (medium)	25 minutes per pound
Lamb (well done)	35 minutes per pound
Veal	35 minutes per pound
Pork	45 minutes per pound
Chickens and Ducks	30 minutes per pound
Turkey (7 to 10 pounds)	30 minutes per pound
Turkey (over 10 pounds)	20 minutes per pound

PREPARING A ROAST FOR THE OVEN FOR EITHER METHOD

Place a wire rack or trivet in a shallow roasting pan and place meat on it, fat side up. Sprinkle generously with salt and pepper and dust with flour, letting a little of the flour fall onto bottom of the pan. The flour will brown and blend with the drippings as the meat cooks to give you a dark rich gravy.

PAN GRAVY

There are two kinds of pan gravy. Both are made from the natural juices from the roast plus a little additional liquid, but one is thickened with flour. If this latter method is used, care should be taken never to make the gravy too thick.

UNTHICKENED

Pour off all the extra fat in pan. Place roasting pan on top of stove and add ½ cup beef stock, chicken stock, or water. Cook, stirring in all the brown bits on the bottom and sides of the roasting pan. Add 1 tablespoon butter or margarine and stir just until the butter is melted. Do not boil after adding the butter. Strain into a sauce boat.

THICKENED

Pour off all but 2 tablespoons of the fat in the roasting pan. Place roasting pan on top of the stove. Add 1½ tablespoons flour and cook, stirring in all brown bits from bottom and sides of pan, until flour becomes a rich brown. Gradually stir in 1 cup boiling water, stock, or hot milk. Season with salt and pepper and cook, stirring constantly, for 5 minutes. Strain into a sauce boat.

ROAST DUCKLING, APRICOT STUFFING

Serves 2.

1 duckling, 4 to 5 pounds   Salt, Pepper, Paprika

Apricot Stuffing

1. Thaw duckling; remove giblets and neck. Wash, drain and pat dry. Score skin with a sharp knife over entire duckling at intervals of one inch.
2. Season duckling generously with salt, pepper and paprika.
3. Stuff with Apricot Rice Stuffing. Fasten neck skin to back with skewer. Loop a cord around leg ends and bring together; tie.
4. Place duckling breast side up in shallow roasting pan on rack and roast in a preheated 325° F. oven for 2½ to 3 hours. Duckling is well-done when thickest portions are fork-tender. Serve with Apricot Sauce.

APRICOT RICE STUFFING

For 1 duckling.

1⅓ cups packaged pre-cooked rice
¼ cup butter or margarine
1¾ cups diced celery and leaves
¼ cup chopped onion.

2 tablespoons chopped parsley
1 teaspoon salt
1½ cups giblet broth or bouillon
½ teaspoon allspice

1 cup chopped cooked dried apricots

1. Saute rice in butter or margarine for 3 minutes.
2. Add celery, onion, parsley, and salt.
3. Add giblet broth or bouillon and bring to a boil. Remove from heat, cover, and let stand until slightly cool.
4. Stir in allspice and apricots and spoon stuffing lightly into duckling.

APRICOT SAUCE

1¼ cups dried cooked apricots
½ cup drained crushed pineapple
¼ cup syrup from pineapple
¼ cup brown sugar

2 tablespoons honey
1 tablespoon vinegar
1 teaspoon ginger
¼ teaspoon salt

1 clove garlic

1. Puree apricots in food mill or electric blender.
2. Combine all ingredients, bring to a boil, and simmer for 2 to 3 minutes. Remove garlic. Serve warm with Roast Duckling.

DUCKLING A L'ORANGE

Serves 2.

1 duckling, 4 to 5 pounds
1 orange
½ cup white wine

1 lump sugar
1 teaspoon vinegar
¾ cup brown gravy

Juice of ½ lemon

1. Do not stuff the duck, but prepare, truss, and roast as in previous recipe.
2. While duckling is roasting, remove the thin orange rind from the orange, being careful not to include any of the bitter white pulp beneath the rind. Use a vegetable peeler for this. With scissors or sharp knife, cut the orange rind into very thin strips, not more than 1 inch long. Put rind in a saucepan, cover with water, and bring to a boil. Drain off water and set rind aside. Juice the orange and set juice aside.
3. When duckling is cooked, place it on a warm serving platter.
4. Pour off excess fat from pan and place pan over direct heat.
5. Add wine, sugar, and vinegar and cook for a few minutes, stirring in all brown bits from bottom and sides of pan.
6. Stir in brown gravy, orange and lemon juice, and correct seasoning with salt. Add orange rind and serve with Roast Duckling.

POTATOES, WHITE

BOILED POTATOES

Select potatoes of uniform size. Peel. If large, cut into uniform pieces. Drop potatoes into a saucepan containing enough boiling salted water to cover and continue to boil until potatoes are tender when pierced by a fork—about 20 minutes for medium-size potatoes. Drain thoroughly and then hold pan containing potatoes over stove for a few minutes, shaking pan to remove excess moisture and dry potatoes out. Add a good chunk of butter and sprinkle with chopped parsley, chives, or dill.

VERY SMALL NEW POTATOES may be well washed, cooked in their jackets and served without peeling, with butter and chopped parsley or chives.

FLUFFY MASHED POTATOES

Boil potatoes until very tender. Drain and dry thoroughly. Put potatoes, a few at a time, through a potato ricer into a mixing bowl. Season with salt and pepper. Add a chunk of soft butter and beat in enough hot milk or cream to make potatoes very creamy and fluffy.

BAKED POTATOES

Scrub uniform-sized potatoes and bake in a hot oven (425° F.) for 40 to 60 minutes, or until potatoes can be pinched. When half cooked, prick potatoes in several places with a fork to allow steam to escape.

PARISIENNE POTATOES

Select small new potatoes or cut large potatoes into balls with a melon ball cutter. Cook balls in boiling salted water until almost tender. Drain thoroughly on paper towels and saute in a skillet in hot shortening until browned on all sides.

DUCHESSE POTATOES   *Serves 2.*

1 cup hot seasoned mashed potatoes   1 egg yolk

1. Mix potatoes and egg and beat briskly until mixture is fluffy.

To use as a garnish: Put potatoes into a pastry bag fitted with a large fluted tube and press out a ruffled border around platter or plank.
For individual servings: Use pastry bag or spoon to make attractive mounds on a baking sheet. Brown under broiler and transfer carefully with spatula from baking sheet to serving platter.

POTATO CAKES

Form Potatoes Duchesse into flat cakes. Coat with flour and saute in hot shortening until brown on both sides. If desired, stir into potato mixture finely chopped green onion tops, chives, parsley, or dill.

YAMS

Yams should be cooked in their jackets whenever possible. Bake them in a hot oven (425° F.) for 45 to 50 minutes, or cook in boiling salted water for 30 to 35 minutes. Drain the boiled yams, peel, and cut in half. Mash, if desired, and beat in butter and hot milk or orange juice.

JAM YAMS   *Serves 2.*
Cook 2 medium Louisiana yams in boiling salted water until tender. Drain, peel, and cut in half. Serve topped with one of the following glazes.
Currant Almond Glaze: Combine 2 tablespoons each currant jelly and blanched almonds. Bring to a boil, stirring, over low heat.
Orange Glaze: Combine 2 tablespoons orange marmalade and 2 orange slices. Bring to a boil, stirring, over low heat.
Grape Glaze: Combine 2 tablespoons grape jelly and 2 lemon slices. Bring to a boil, stirring, over low heat.
Pineapple Glaze: Combine 2 tablespoons pineapple preserves and 1 tablespoon lemon juice. Bring to a boil, stirring, over low heat.
Apple Glaze: Combine 3 tablespoons apple jelly and 1/4 teaspoon clove. Bring to a boil, stirring, over low heat.

VEGETABLES

Nothing can match the flavor of fresh vegetables in season, simply cooked and seasoned with salt, pepper, and butter. Try to include one fresh vegetable at every meal—fresh peas, asparagus, spring carrots, string beans, new beets, young cabbage, spinach, broccoli, ripe tomatoes, summer and winter squash, fall turnips etcetera. And in winter, experiment with the wonderful root vegetables always available. Some unusual ones found in vegetable markets are exceptionally inexpensive and flavorful. If you see a root vegetable that you don't recognize, ask your green grocer to identify it and look it up in your general cookbook. Such winter vegetables as Jerusalem artichokes, oyster plant, celery root (celeriac), parsnips and rutabagas make mighty fine eating and, since you are cooking only for two, won't take you long to prepare.

Canned and frozen vegetables certainly have their place in today's living and are easy to store and quick to prepare. The tiny little French canned peas (*petits pois*) are especially delicious, frozen baby lima beans, frozen chopped spinach, frozen artichoke hearts and Brussels sprouts are all flavorful. A 10-ounce box of frozen vegetables is just right for two. Cook them according to package directions, but add your own special touch: A few chopped almonds or cashew nuts are delicious with sprouts; try a sliced water chestnut in the spinach or string beans, or a touch of nutmeg and a squeeze of lemon juice. Chopped parsley, herbs, and melted butter are always good.

SAUTEED MUSHROOMS   *Serves 2.*

¼ pound fresh mushrooms   1½ tablespoons butter
Salt and pepper to taste

1. Wash mushrooms, but do not peel, and trim stems. Slice lengthwise, including remaining stem.
2. In skillet melt butter. Add mushrooms and cook slowly for about 8 minutes, stirring frequently. Sprinkle with salt and pepper. Sprinkle with chopped parsley, if desired.

PAN-FRIED EGGPLANT   *Serves 2.*

1 small eggplant   1 egg
Salt and pepper   ¼ cup water
Flour   ¼ cup cooking oil

1. Wash eggplant, but do not peel. Slice ¼ inch thick.
2. Sprinkle slices with salt and pepper and dust with flour.
3. Beat egg and water and pour into a flat dish.
4. Dip eggplant slices in beaten egg and dip again in flour.
5. Saute quickly in hot cooking oil until golden brown on both sides.

STUFFED TOMATOES   Serves 2.

2 ripe tomatoes   2 tablespoons butter
½ small clove garlic, minced   ½ teaspoon salt
2 tablespoons minced onion   2 dashes pepper
2 tablespoons chopped celery   ¾ cup fresh bread crumbs
                    1 tablespoon chopped parsley

1. Hollow out tomatoes, being careful not to break through skins, leaving cases ¼ inch thick. Chop tomato removed and set aside.
2. Saute garlic, onion, and celery in butter over low heat until onion is transparent.
3. Add chopped tomato, sprinkle with salt and pepper, and cook, stirring occasionally, until vegetables are tender.
4. Stir in bread crumbs and parsley and fill tomato cases with the mixture.
5. Place stuffed tomatoes in a small greased baking dish and bake in a preheated 350° F. oven for 10 to 15 minutes.

STUFFED EGGPLANT OR SUMMER SQUASH

Follow recipe above using 1 small eggplant or summer squash, halved lengthwise. If desired add some ground leftover meat or chicken and season with a favorite herb such as tarragon, dill or basil.

CREAMED ONIONS

Cook 8 to 10 small silver skin onions in boiling water to cover for 15 to 20 minutes, or until barely tender. Drain and remove skins. Return to saucepan and add ½ cup Cream Sauce. Keep hot until ready to serve. Sprinkle with paprika or chopped parsley.

BRUSSELS SPROUTS AND CELERY POACHED IN WINE

1 package (10 oz.) frozen California   ¼ teaspoon celery salt
    Brussels Sprouts   Pinch nutmeg
½ cup chopped celery   Dash pepper
1 tablespoon butter or margarine   1 chicken bouillon cube
1 tablespoon flour   ½ cup water
                    ¼ cup heavy cream

1. Cook Brussels sprouts according to package directions. Drain.
2. Cook celery in butter in saucepan over low heat, stirring frequently.
3. Stir in flour, seasonings, and bouillon cube. Slowly stir in water and cook, stirring, until bouillon cube dissolves and sauce thickens. Stir in cream.
4. Add Brussels sprouts and heat thoroughly.

BAKED ACORN SQUASH

1 acorn squash	⅛ teaspoon pepper
¼ teaspoon salt	1 teaspoon brown sugar or honey

1 tablespoon butter

1. Cut squash in half lengthwise and scrape out seeds.
2. Place in small baking pan and sprinkle with salt and pepper.
3. Put brown sugar or honey in center cavity and dot with butter.
4. Cover with aluminum foil and pour a little hot water into bottom of pan.
5. Bake in a preheated 375° F. oven for 40 minutes, or until squash is very tender when tested with a fork.

SALADS

THE TOSSED SALAD

To make a tossed salad, use a variety of greens, not only for texture, but for color—curly endive, escarole, romaine, field salad, water cress, Bibb lettuce—and toss lightly with a good French dressing. Wash greens and dry thoroughly by shaking in a towel or salad basket. Tear greens into bite-size bits into a salad bowl rubbed with a cut clove of garlic. Pour dressing over the greens just before serving and toss lightly, but thoroughly. Other vegetables may be added as desired, such as sliced scallions, cucumber, tomatoes, radishes, green pepper, or carrots. Salad may be flavored with chopped fresh herbs.

BASIC FRENCH DRESSING   *Makes 1 cup*

1 teaspoon salt	¼ teaspoon pepper
1 teaspoon dry mustard	¼ cup vinegar or lemon juice

¾ cup salad oil

1. In a small bowl mix salt, mustard, and pepper.
2. Stir in vinegar or lemon juice.
3. With a fork beat in salad oil gradually until ingredients are thoroughly blended. Store in refrigerator. This will dress four or five tossed salads for 2 people. Shake or beat again with a fork before using.

Note: For a garlic flavor, let half a clove of garlic soak in the dressing overnight. Finely chopped parsley, chives, or other herbs may be added.

COLE SLAW   *Serves 2.*

¼ medium head cabbage	1 tablespoon chopped parsley
1 tablespoon minced onion	¼ cup sour cream
1 tablespoon minced green pepper	2 tablespoons mayonnaise
1 tablespoon shredded raw carrot	1 tablespoon wine vinegar

Salt and pepper to taste

1. Shred cabbage as finely as possible into a bowl and toss with other vegetables.
2. Combine sour cream, mayonnaise, and vinegar. Add to salad.
3. Season with salt and pepper to taste and toss well.
4. Chill before serving.

Note: ½ teaspoon celery seeds, mustard seeds, or caraway seeds may be added.

POTATO SALAD   *Serves 2.*

8 small new potatoes
1 medium onion, minced
½ cucumber, peeled and diced
¼ cup diced celery
2 tablespoons minced green pepper

1 tablespoon minced parsley
¼ cup Basic French Dressing
1 teaspoon lemon juice
¼ cup mayonnaise
Salt and pepper to taste

1. Scrub potatoes and cook in boiling salted water for 20 minutes, or until tender.
2. Drain, cool slightly, peel and slice thinly into salad bowl.
3. Add other vegetables and mix lightly.
4. Combine French dressing, lemon juice, and mayonnaise and pour over the vegetable mixture while potatoes are still warm.
5. Correct seasoning with salt and pepper. Mix well.
6. Chill until ready to serve.

Note: Fresh herbs, such as chopped tarragon, dill, or sweet basil may be added —about 1 teaspoon.

CAESAR SALAD   *Serves 2.*

Salt
1 cut clove garlic
¼ teaspoon dry mustard
½ tablespoon lemon juice
Dash Tabasco
1½ tablespoons olive oil

1 small bunch romaine,
    washed and dried
1 tablespoon grated Parmesan cheese
6 anchovy fillets
1 soft cooked egg
    (3 minutes)

¼ cup bread cubes, browned in hot olive oil

1. Sprinkle bottom of wooden salad bowl with salt and rub with garlic.
2. Add mustard, lemon juice, and Tabasco and stir with wooden spoon until salt is dissolved.
3. Add olive oil and stir until well blended.
4. Tear romaine leaves into bite-size pieces and add to salad bowl.
5. Sprinkle with cheese, add anchovies, and break egg over salad.
6. Sprinkle with browned bread cubes and mix gently but thoroughly with wooden salad fork and spoon.

ORANGE SPINACH SALAD ORIENTAL

Serves 2.

1 cup raw spinach leaves, washed
   and drained
4 button mushrooms, fresh or canned,
   sliced
2 water chestnuts, diced
1 Florida orange, peeled and diced
2 tablespoons salad oil

1 teaspoon vinegar
1 tablespoon Florida orange
   juice
1 teaspoon soy sauce
Dash Tabasco
Salt
Pinch dry mustard

1. Tear spinach leaves coarsely into salad bowl.
2. Add mushrooms, water chestnuts, and diced oranges.
3. Combine oil, vinegar, orange juice, soy sauce, Tabasco, salt and dry mustard.
   Pour over salad and toss.

SPINACH EGG SALAD   *Serves 2.*

2 handfuls fresh spinach leaves
  (about ¼ pound)
Salt
Cut clove of garlic
⅛ teaspoon dry mustard
Dash Tabasco

½ tablespoon lemon juice
1½ tablespoons salad oil
Freshly ground pepper
Tomato wedges
1 hard-cooked egg, quartered

1. Wash spinach well, drain, and cut into bite-size portions.
2. Sprinkle bottom of salad bowl with a little salt and rub with garlic.
3. Add to bowl the mustard, Tabasco, lemon juice, salad oil, and pepper.
4. Stir dressing ingredients with a fork until well blended.
5. Add spinach and toss until leaves are coated.
6. Garnish bowl with tomato and hard-cooked egg.

Cooked vegetables—broccoli, beets, and cauliflower—are as tempting served cold in salads as they are hot, especially when combined or surrounded by generous amounts of crisp western iceberg lettuce.

BEET CITRUS SALAD ON SHREDDED LETTUCE

½ head western iceberg lettuce
1 cup sliced cooked beets
3 green onions, chopped

⅓ cup mayonnaise or French Dressing
1 orange peeled and thinly sliced
Parsley for garnish

1. Core lettuce; wash in cold water and drain well.
2. Line serving dishes with outer lettuce leaves; shred remaining lettuce and arrange in center of plates.
3. Toss beets, green onions, and dressing lightly and arrange on top of lettuce.
4. Garnish with orange slices and parsley sprays and serve with additional dressing if desired.

AVOCADO SEAFOOD SALAD   *Serves 2.*

1 medium avocado
1 cup flaked lobster meat or Alaska
  King Crab Meat
2 green onions, minced
⅓ cup mayonnaise
1 tablespoon minced parsley

2 tablespoons minced gherkins
  or dill pickle
⅛ teaspoon dry mustard
1 teaspoon lemon juice or
  tarragon vinegar
Salt and pepper to taste

1. Cut avocado in half lengthwise and remove peel and seed.
2. Combine remaining ingredients with salt and pepper to taste.
3. Fill avocado halves with the seafood mixture. If desired, garnish each serving with water cress and stuffed olives.

LETTUCE VEGETABLE SALAD   *Serves 2.*

1 head western iceberg lettuce
1 pound fresh or 1 package
    (10 oz.) frozen broccoli,
    cooked, drained, and chilled

1 medium tomato, quartered
Cucumber slices
⅓ cup Basic
    French Dressing

1. Core lettuce; wash head in cold water and drain well. Separate outer lettuce leaves and use to line a serving plate or individual salad plates.
2. Arrange broccoli, tomato wedges, and cucumber slices on the lettuce. Chill until serving time.
3. Serve dressing separately.

CUCUMBERS VINAIGRETTE   *Serves 2.*

1 small cucumber, peeled
2 tablespoons chopped onion
2 tablespoons chopped parsley

Salt and pepper
2 tablespoons vinegar
2 tablespoons water

2 tablespoons salad oil

1. Slice cucumbers thinly into serving dish.
2. Sprinkle with onion and parsley, salt and pepper.
3. Combine vinegar, water, and salad oil and pour over cucumber.
4. Chill for at least 1 hour before serving.

ARRANGED SALAD WITH LOUIS DRESSING

Line individual salad plates with western iceberg lettuce. Arrange hard-cooked egg slices in center and surround by tomato slices or wedges, cooked sliced carrots, cooked string beans, lobster meat or crab meat or practically any salad ingredient you wish—avocado and cucumber slices are nice. Sprinkle salad with a little salt and serve with Louis Dressing. The photograph shows what pretty things can be done with different vegetables.

LOUIS DRESSING

½ cup mayonnaise
2 tablespoons chili sauce
1 hard-cooked egg, finely chopped

1 tablespoon chopped ripe olives
1 teaspoon minced chives
1 teaspoon lemon juice

1. Combine all ingredients and chill until serving time.

Note: Store remaining dressing in refrigerator and serve as a dip with fresh raw vegetables—scallions, carrot curls, cauliflower flowerets, cucumber sticks, radishes.

FRUIT DESSERTS

There is no more appropriate dessert for two than fruit, fresh or cooked. It's refreshing, economical, and delicious. Serve fresh fruit or berries in season. Try sliced fresh peaches, sprinkled with a little sugar and orange juice; any kind of berries with sugar and cream; peaches, strawberries, or canned pears covered with a raspberry puree, quickly made by pressing a box of defrosted raspberries through a fine sieve. Sprinkle sweetened fresh or cooked fruits with a favorite liqueur or with a little brandy or rum. A fruit melange is simply a combination of various fruits.

PEARADISE COMPOTE

Canned Bartlett pear halves, are mixed with dark sweet cherries, pineapple chunks, apricot halves, and figs. Just before serving a mixture of cherry juice and pear syrup from the cans is poured over the fruit. Use 1 part cherry juice to 2 parts pear syrup. Make up your own combination of cooked and fresh fruit and include at least one serving in your daily menus. Leftover fruit compotes make a nutritious first course for breakfast.

DESSERT PEARS WITH CARAMEL SAUCE

Serve chilled canned Bartlett pear halves with caramel sauce and a sprinkling of chopped nuts. To make the sauce, combine ½ cup evaporated milk, 1 cup brown sugar, and 1 teaspoon butter. Bring to a boil and cook over low heat for 3 minutes. Serve hot or cold.

Cake is a natural accompaniment to fruit desserts. An unusual fruit-and-cake dessert with an exotic flavor is pictured here. Pineapple chunks combined with a rum-flavored ginger syrup are generously ladled over chiffon or sponge cake. Add a final touch of sweet or sour cream.

TROPICAL DELIGHT   *Serves 2.*

1 8-¾-ounce can pineapple tidbits   2 tablespoons Jamaica rum
1 tablespoon brown sugar   ½ cup whipping cream or
2 tablespoons slivered preserved ginger*   dairy sour cream
                    Sponge or chiffon cake

1. Drain pineapple and mix with brown sugar, ginger, and rum.
2. Cover and let stand several hours or overnight in refrigerator.
3. Whip sweet cream until thick enough to mound.
4. For each serving put a wedge of cake on a dessert plate. Top with a generous scoop of pineapple ginger rum mixture.
5. Spoon on as much sweet or sour cream as desired.
* Or use candied ginger, but the preserved type with a little of the syrup included gives better flavor.

FRUIT AND ICE CREAM

And what more pleasing dessert combination can you think of than fruit a la mode, for two, four, six, or a hundred. A quart of ice cream can serve six, but you need a pint for just you two. This fruit cup is made with vanilla ice cream, but don't forget strawberry or pistachio, or extra cool mint, and those wonderful fruit flavored sherbets—they're all delicious with fruit.

FRUIT CUP A LA MODE   *Serves 2.*

1 tablespoon lemon juice   1 orange, sectioned
2 tablespoons orange juice   ¼ cup green grape halves
1 tablespoon sugar   ¼ cup blueberries
½ cup diced cantaloupe   1 banana

1 pint vanilla ice cream

1. Combine fruit juices and sugar; stir until sugar is dissolved.
2. Combine melon, orange sections, grapes, and blueberries.
3. Pour sweetened fruit juices over fruit and chill.
4. Just before serving, slice and fold in banana.
5. Spoon into serving dishes and top with ice cream.

Time to Entertain

THERE COMES A TIME in every honeymoon couple's life when it's time to entertain at the dinner table. Pity the poor husband whose wife loudly and proudly proclaims that "she simply can't cook a thing!," for a good cook and a gracious hostess can be the greatest asset a man has, not only in his personal life but in his business career.

What kind of a cook and hostess are you going to be? Are you going to be nervous, apologizing for the dishes you put upon your table, or are you going to be relaxed, entertaining, and fun at your own parties? The answer springs partly from your philosophy of life and partly from your ability to plan, cook, and serve a good meal, which is seemingly effortless.

You must truly want to entertain your friends and enjoy having them in your home, then you must be able to plan a menu which leaves you free to spend the greater part of the time in the living room with your guests. Simplicity is the keynote and the meal should be composed of dishes which can be made in advance or ones that can cook largley undisturbed until it is time to put the finishing touches to them and bring them to the table.

Let's suppose you have invited your husband's parents to dinner Saturday night. Think out every last detail—every pot and pan you are going to need, every spoon and dish you are going to put on the table. Prepare as much as possible in advance. Have your appetizer and dessert ready in the refrigerator. A soup, if you plan to have a soup course, ready to heat over simmering water. Your salad in the salad bowl, but not tossed with the dressing, and a casserole ready to go into the oven. Of course, you will have selected dishes which you have made before and those which already have had your husband's seal of approval.

If you have thought through every detail, prepared the food carefully, and have set a pretty table, you will be radiant with a new inner confidence; conversation will sparkle, your guests will leave their plates empty, and the time you spent on the dinner will seem like pleasure.

APPETIZERS

If you plan to begin your dinner with an appetizer at table, do not serve rich or elaborate canapes with preprandial drinks or cocktails. Instead, simply place at convenient spots around the room, a bowl of toasted nuts, another of assorted olives, or a bowl of chilled radishes accompanied by a tiny dish of coarse salt for dunking. Or have an arrangement of raw vegetables centrally located beside a pretty bowl filled with a sour cream or cheese dip and let your guests help themselves.

If you do not wish to begin your meal with an appetizer, this is the time to serve a lovely first course in the living room. Don't rush it. Wait until everyone is enjoying their drink and conversation is lively before bringing out a beautiful arrangement on one of your prettiest platters. If you wish you may place small plates, forks, and cocktail napkins on the coffee table, not only for convenience, but as advance notice to your guests that an appetizer is going to be served.

A few suggestions for first courses which are suitable to serve either at the table or in the living room prior to dinner are:

DEVILED EGGS
Cut hard-cooked eggs in half, press yolks through a fine sieve, and flavor with salt, mustard, and Tabasco. Mash to a smooth paste with a little mayonnaise. Spoon back into the whites, or press out through a large fluted tube.

PIMIENTO AND ANCHOVY
Arrange canned pimientos on a bed of shredded lettuce like the petals of a poinsettia radiating from a center filled with drained capers. Garnish with anchovy fillets. The dish should be served with cruets of olive oil and vinegar.

PROSCIUTTO AND MELON
Arrange paper-thin slices of prosciutto ham (available at Italian delicatessens) over peeled wedges of ripe melon.

A chilled glass of tomato juice, half a grapefruit, or a lovely fruit cocktail are all simple but excellent choices for a first course. If possible, serve them on a bed of crushed ice and garnish with a spray of mint or a rose geranium leaf. And, of course, a shrimp cocktail has universal appeal as a table appetizer.

SHRIMP IN COURT BOUILLON   *Serves 4.*
1 quart water   Juice of ½ lemon
1 carrot, sliced   1 teaspoon salt
1 small onion, sliced   ½ teaspoon pepper
                    1 pound jumbo shrimp

1. Put water into a saucepan with the carrot, onion, lemon juice, salt, and pepper. Bring water to a boil.
2. Add shrimp and, if necessary, more water to cover shrimp. Turn heat down so water just simmers. Cover saucepan and let shrimp cook for just 5 minutes.
3. Drain shrimp and, as soon as they are cool enough to handle, remove shells. Slit open the backs with a sharp knife and remove the intestinal vein which runs down the back.
4. Put into a bowl, cover, and chill until serving time.

COCKTAIL SAUCE

2 tablespoons prepared horseradish　　　3 tablespoons chili sauce
¾ cup tomato ketchup　　　　　　　　　2 tablespoons lemon juice
Salt and Tabasco to taste

1. Mix all ingredients and chill.

An elegant appetizer that belies the fact it is easy to make is Salmon Mousse. Keep chilled until serving time and serve with thinly sliced buttered pumpernickel bread.

SALMON MOUSSE
Serves 4 to 6.

2 envelopes plain gelatin　　　　　　　1 teaspoon lemon juice
2 tablespoons cold water　　　　　　　 Few drops Tabasco
1 chicken bouillon cube　　　　　　　　¼ teaspoon salt or to taste
1 cup boiling water　　　　　　　　　　½ cup mayonnaise
1 1-pound can salmon　　　　　　　　　½ cup cream, whipped

1. Soften 1 envelope of the gelatin in cold water for 5 minutes.
2. Dissolve bouillon cube in boiling water, add to gelatin, and stir until gelatin is thoroughly dissolved. Pour into bottom of a 1-quart mold and chill until set.
3. Drain liquid from salmon into measuring cup and add water to make a total of ½ cup liquid. Soften remaining envelope of gelatin in this mixture for 5 minutes, then set cup into pan containing simmering water and stir until gelatin is thoroughly dissolved.
4. Flake salmon into a bowl and beat in lemon juice, Tabasco, and salt. Continue to beat while gradually adding the dissolved gelatin. Use your electric beater for this and mix until salmon is smooth and fluffy.
5. Stir in mayonnaise and finally fold in the whipped cream.
6. Pack the mousse into the aspic-coated pan and chill for 2 hours, or until ready to serve.
7. To serve: Run a knife around the inside edge of mold. Dip mold in and out of water, just hot to the hand, three times and invert mold over serving platter. Mold should lift cleanly away. Garnish with lettuce leaves and hard-cooked egg.

DIPS
. . . are made in seconds in an electric blender. Serve them with potato chips, crackers, or an assortment of fresh vegetables. There are many more recipes where these came from, *The Blender Cookbook,* published by Doubleday.

BASIC CHEESE DIP
Makes 1 pint.

¼ cup water or milk
8 ounces cottage cheese
6 ounces cream cheese

2 ounces blue cheese
1 small clove garlic
Few drops Tabasco

1. Into container of the electric blender put the water or milk and the cottage cheese. Cover container and blend on high speed for 20 seconds.
2. Add remaining ingredients, cover, and blend on high speed for 10 seconds, or until mixture is smooth. If vortex ceases to form in a heavy mixture such as a dip or spread, remove cover and carefully break surface with a rubber spatula (the thin bottle-scraper kind), pulling mixture from sides of container into center. This will introduce air and the vortex will be re-created. Be careful not to dip the spatula too deeply into the revolving blades.

CHEDDAR BEER DIP
Makes 3 cups.

8 ounces cream cheese
¾ cup beer
8 ounces Cheddar cheese, cubed

1 clove garlic
12 small gherkins
1 teaspoon poppy seeds

1. Into container of the electric blender put cream cheese and ½ cup of the beer. Cover and blend on high speed for 8 seconds.
2. Add remaining beer, Cheddar cheese, and garlic. Cover and blend for 20 seconds.
3. Add gherkins and poppy seeds. Cover and blend for 2 seconds only.

AVOCADO DIP
Makes 1 pint.

2 avocados, peeled, seeded, and sliced
2 tablespoons lemon juice
4 tablespoons salad oil
1 clove garlic

1 tablespoon cut chives or green onion tops
1 teaspoon salt
1 teaspoon dill weed
Dash hot pepper sauce

1. Into container of the electric blender put all ingredients.
2. Cover container and blend on high speed until smooth, stopping to stir down if necessary. Chill until ready to serve.

This colorful dish is called Brussels Sprouts in a Cranberry Rice Ring. The recipe is on page 245.

SOUPS

. . . are another good way to begin a sit-down dinner. In this day and age, very few meals provide for both a table appetizer and a soup, but one or the other should be offered, even if the soup selection is nothing more difficult than a well-seasoned consomme, chicken or beef, or a jellied madrilene. But no matter how simple and casual the meal, there is one rigid rule: Serve a hot soup very hot and a cold soup well chilled. If possible, ladle hot soups at table from a steaming tureen and serve a cold soup in sparkling glass bowls surrounded by crushed ice.

CHICKEN BROTH, PLAIN OR WITH RICE
Heat and serve with finely chopped parsley or chives or a lemon wedge. Or 2 minutes before serving add a little shredded lettuce or spinach, or a few small sprays of water cress.

EGG DROP SOUP   *Serves 4.*
Bring 3 cups chicken broth to a rapid boil. Beat 2 eggs until well blended and gradually add to the boiling broth, while stirring rapidly. The eggs will form delicate threads. Serve with a sprig of water cress in each cup.

GREEK LEMON SOUP   *Serves 4.*
Bring 3 cups chicken broth to a rapid boil. In a small bowl beat 2 eggs with the juice of ½ lemon. Remove broth from heat. Gradually beat about ½ cup of the hot soup into the egg-lemon mixture. Then add this mixture to the rest of the soup, stirring, vigorously. Do not return soup to the heat. Pour into hot bouillon cups and serve immediately.

BEEF CONSOMME
Heat and just before serving add a little sherry, Port, or Madeira. Or 2 minutes before serving add cooked diced carrots, asparagus tips, a spoonful of cooked peas, some sliced, sauteed mushrooms. Garnish with a sprig of parsley, water cress, or mint. The addition of a couple of tablespoons of light rum, makes hot beef consomme with added gelatin taste mighty like an expensive turtle soup. Try it!

CONSOMME BELLEVUE
Combine half chicken broth and half clam juice. Heat and serve with a garnish of chopped parsley or chives.

MADRILENE
Serve well chilled with a topping of sour cream and red caviar, or with finely minced onion, parsley, lemon juice, salt, and pepper.

The recipe for this Seafood Loaf may be found on page 252.

CLAM CONSOMME   *Serves 4.*

Into container of the electric blender put 2 cups clam juice, 1 fresh tomato, quartered, ½ small onion, sliced, 1 thin slice lemon, ½ teaspoon celery salt, and a dash of pepper. Cover and blend on high speed for 20 seconds. Heat and simmer for 3 minutes.

CHICKEN CURRY SOUP   *Serves 6 to 8.*

¼ cup butter
¼ cup flour
1½ teaspoons salt
1 teaspoon curry powder
1 quart reliquefied instant non-fat
   dry milk crystals (made according
   to package directions)

1 cup or 1 6-ounce can cooked,
   diced chicken
1 cup chicken broth.
¼ cup chopped toasted almonds
1 tablespoon cut chives
1 tablespoon lemon juice
¼ teaspoon crushed rosemary

1. Melt butter in saucepan, stir in flour, salt, and curry and cook, stirring over low heat, until mixture is well blended.
2. Gradually stir in the non-fat milk and cook, stirring, until sauce is smooth and thickened. Cover and cook over low heat for 3 minutes. Cool.
3. Combine remaining ingredients in container of the electric blender. Cover and blend on high speed until smooth. Add to milk mixture and chill thoroughly.

CASSEROLES

. . . are perfect dishes around which to plan a company dinner. They make little demands on the cook once they are prepared, and can remain in the oven without harm for a considerable time beyond the scheduled moment of serving.

CHICKEN DIVAN   *Serves 4.*

There's a marvelous combination of flavors in this dish which may be prepared well ahead of time or even the night before. Serve it in the same dish in which it is baked, or transfer to a serving dish. The photograph on the opposite page shows you how good this looks.

¼ cup salad oil
6 chicken breasts
2½ cups chicken stock or bouillon
4 tablespoons butter
¼ cup flour

¼ teaspoon salt
½ cup heavy cream
½ teaspoon Tabasco
1½ pounds fresh broccoli
½ cup freshly grated Parmesan cheese

1. In skillet heat oil and in it saute chicken breasts until golden on both sides. Add ½ cup of the chicken stock, cover, and cook over low heat for 20 minutes, or until chicken is tender. Set aside.
2. In small saucepan melt butter. Stir in flour and salt and cook, stirring, until mixture is smooth. Gradually stir in remaining chicken stock or bouillon and cook, stirring, until sauce is smooth and thickened. Remove from heat and stir in cream and Tabasco.
3. Soak broccoli in cold water for 10 minutes. Drain. Discard large leaves and tough parts of stalks. Cut deep gashes in bottom of thick stalks. Put in saucepan in 1 inch boiling water. Cover tightly and cook for 10 to 12 minutes. Drain.
4. Place broccoli and chicken in a buttered 2-quart casserole. Pour sauce over and sprinkle with cheese.
5. To serve: Cover and bake in a preheated 350° F. oven for 30 minutes.

CHICKEN-SHRIMP-RICE CASSEROLE   *Serves 4.*

1 pound chicken breasts
1 tablespoon salt
1¼ cups chicken broth
½ pound shrimp
3-ounce package chive
   cream cheese
½ cup light cream

1 tablespoon cornstarch
Dash pepper
2 cups cooked rice
1 tablespoon minced parsley
2 tablespoons minced pimiento
2 tablespoons blanched,
   halved almonds

1. Cook chicken breasts in water to cover with half the salt until tender, about 30 minutes. Drain, reserving 1¼ cups of the broth. Remove skin and bones and cut meat into thin slices.
2. Simmer shrimp in water to cover with remaining salt for 5 minutes. Drain, shell, and devein. Cut large shrimp in half lengthwise.
3. Soften cream cheese, gradually stir in cream, and beat until smooth.
4. Blend cornstarch and chicken broth and stir into cheese mixture. Add pepper and cook over moderate heat until thickened, stirring constantly.
5. Spread half the rice in bottom of a buttered 1½ quart casserole. Arrange half the chicken, shrimp, parsley, pimiento, and almonds over rice and pour half the sauce over this layer.
6. Repeat layers. If desired, cover, and chill.
7. To serve: Bake casserole, covered, in a preheated 350° F. oven for 40 minutes. Remove cover during last 10 minutes of baking.

PREPARE-IN-ADVANCE DISHES

VEAL PARMIGIANA   *Serves 6.*

Careful attention to last minute details make this dish a success. The meat can be cooked, the sauce made, the cheese sliced, all ready to assemble a few minutes before serving time.

¾ teaspoon salt
⅛ teaspoon pepper
1 cup finely crushed corn flakes
½ cup grated Parmesan cheese
2 eggs, lightly beaten
⅓ cup butter

6 veal cutlets, ⅓ inch thick
2 8-ounce cans tomato sauce
1 teaspoon oregano
¼ teaspoon onion salt
½ teaspoon sugar
6 slices Mozzarella cheese

1. Combine salt, pepper, corn flake crumbs, and Parmesan cheese.
2. Dip each cutlet into egg, then into crumbs, then egg, and crumbs again.
3. In skillet melt butter and in it brown cutlets on both sides. Add a few tablespoons water, cover, and cook over low heat for 30 minutes. Keep covered and warm.

4. In saucepan combine tomato sauce, oregano, onion salt and sugar. Heat and, if necessary, keep hot over simmering water, or reheat at serving time.
5. To serve: Arrange meat in an oven-proof serving dish. Pour the hot sauce around the meat and top each piece of meat with a slice of cheese. Bake in a preheated 400° F. oven for about 3 minutes, or until cheese is slightly melted. Garnish with parsley and serve immediately.

GOLDEN RICE BEEFBURGER CASSEROLE   *Serves 6.*

2 tablespoons butter or margarine	⅔ cup tomato sauce
¾ cup chopped celery	1 tablespoon barbecue sauce
¾ cup chopped onions	1 4-ounce can sliced mushrooms
½ cup chopped green pepper	1 teaspoon salt
1 pound ground beef round	¼ teaspoon pepper

Golden Rice

1. In skillet melt butter and in it saute the celery, onion, and green pepper until vegetables are tender, but not browned. Remove from heat.
2. Add meat and remaining ingredients; mix well.
3. Turn into a 2-quart casserole or baking dish and top with Golden Rice. If desired, cover, and chill.
4. To serve: Bake, covered, in a preheated 400° F. oven for 30 to 40 minutes.

GOLDEN RICE

In saucepan bring 2½ cups beef consomme or broth to a boil. Add 1 cup raw rice, cover saucepan tightly, and cook over very low heat for 20 minutes, or until rice is tender. Stir in 2 tablespoons minced parsley, 2 tablespoons diced pimiento, 1 tablespoon prepared mustard, ½ teaspoon salt, and a dash of pepper.

CANTONESE CHICKEN   *Serves 4.*

This dish may be made and reheated before serving. Serve it on a bed of cooked white or brown rice, or serve the rice separately.

1 broiler-fryer, about 2½ pounds, ready-to-cook, cut up	1 can (1 lb. 4 oz.) sliced pineapple
⅓ cup cornstarch	1 cup celery, 1-inch slices
2 teaspoons paprika	2 tablespoons brown sugar
¼ cup cooking oil	2 tablespoons soy sauce

2 tomatoes, sliced

1. Shake chicken, 2 or 3 pieces at a time, in a paper bag containing cornstarch and paprika to coat evenly. Save leftover cornstarch mixture.
2. In skillet brown chicken slowly in the cooking oil, turning when necessary with kitchen tongs. When lightly browned, 15 to 20 minutes, reduce heat, cover skillet tightly, and cook for 10 to 15 minutes longer.
3. Drain pineapple, saving liquid. Add pineapple slices and celery slipping them under the chicken. Cover and cook 5 minutes.
4. Combine 1 tablespoon of the reserved cornstarch mixture with brown sugar, soy sauce, and ¼ cup pineapple liquid. Pour over chicken and blend with pan juices. Cover and cook for 5 minutes longer.
5. To serve: Reheat for 5 minutes and serve atop cooked rice or serve rice separately. Garnish with alternate slices of tomato and pineapple.

RICE

... is an excellent substitute for potatoes for company meals. It can be cooked in advance and keeps hot and fluffy over steaming water.

FLUFFY RICE   *Makes 4 cups cooked rice, serves 4 to 6.*
2½ cups water or other liquid   1 cup raw converted rice
1 teaspoons salt   2 tablespoons butter

1. In a heavy saucepan bring water and salt to a rapid boil.
2. Add rice, cover saucepan tightly, and turn heat to very low. Let rice cook, undisturbed, for 20 minutes. By this time the rice should be tender and all the liquid absorbed. If not, remove cover and raise heat and cook until liquid is evaporated.
3. Turn rice into a sieve or collander, fluff with a fork, and set collander over a pot of simmering water. Bury the nugget of butter in the center of the rice, cover lightly with a towel, and forget until serving time.

RICE PILAFF   *Serves 4 to 6.*
½ cup butter (1 stick)   1 clove garlic, minced (optional)
2 tablespoons minced onion   1 cup raw rice
1 13½ oz. can chicken broth or 1¾ cups bouillon

1. In heavy saucepan melt butter and in it saute onion and garlic for 3 minutes, or until onion is tender.
2. Add rice and cook, stirring, until rice is lightly browned.
3. Add broth or bouillon and bring to a rapid boil.
4. Cover saucepan tightly, reduce heat, and cook, undisturbed, for 25 to 30 minutes. Remove cover, fluff rice with a fork, and keep over very low heat for a few minutes, until ready to serve.

BRUSSELS SPROUTS IN CRANBERRY RICE RING
3 cups fresh cranberries   ½ cup boiling water
1 cup sugar   5 cups hot cooked rice (1¼ cups raw)

1. Cook cranberries with sugar and boiling water in covered saucepan for about 5 minutes, or until cranberries pop.
2. Mix cranberries and rice and pack into a greased 8-inch mold, pressing firmly. Let stand for 5 minutes, then unmold ring onto serving platter.
3. Fill center with Buttered Brussels Sprouts as in photograph on page 237.

BUTTERED BRUSSELS SPROUTS
4 packages (10-oz. each) frozen   3 tablespoons butter or
  California Brussels sprouts   margarine
                    Salt and pepper to taste

1. Cook Brussels sprouts according to package directions. Drain, toss lightly with butter and salt and pepper.

PARSLEY RICE RING

Cook 2 cups rice according to package directions using chicken broth for the liquid. When tender, stir in ¼ cup butter and ½ cup finely chopped parsley. Pack with spoon into lightly oiled 5½ cup ring mold. Let stand 10 minutes; unmold on serving plate. Fill center with sauced vegetables, fish, meat or poultry as in photograph on page 203.

DISHES FROM FOREIGN LANDS

Curried dishes are always popular. Go easy with the curry powder unless you know your guests enjoy a really hot curry. All curry dishes should be served with chutney and, if desired, other condiments such as toasted coconut, chopped peanuts, minced raw onion and green pepper, chopped hard-cooked egg, etcetera. The photograph shows . . .

CURRIED CHICKEN LIVERS   *Serves 4.*

1 pound fresh or thawed chicken livers   1 teaspoon salt
4 tablespoons butter or margarine   ¼ teaspoon pepper
¼ cup minced onion   1 tablespoon curry powder
⅔ cup beer or ale

1. Cut chicken livers in halves.
2. Melt butter in skillet or chafing dish. Add livers and onion and saute for 5 to 8 minutes, stirring frequently, until livers are cooked.
3. Add salt, pepper, and curry powder, and saute for 2 minutes longer.
4. Gradually stir in beer and bring to a boil.
5. Cook over low heat for 2 minutes longer, or cover and reheat before serving. Serve with Fluffy Rice.

CALCUTTA CURRY   *Serves 4 to 6.*

¼ cup salad oil   1 cup seedless raisins
2 large onions, chopped   1 cup water
1½ cups chopped celery   4 cups diced cooked lamb
2 tablespoons curry powder   1½ cups chicken bouillon
1½ cups chopped green apples

1. In saucepan heat oil and in it cook onions, celery, and curry powder until vegetables are tender.
2. Add raisins, water, lamb, and 1 cup of the bouillon. Cover and cook over low heat for 35 minutes.
3. Add apples and remaining bouillon. Mix well, cover, and cook over low heat for 10 minutes, or until apples are tender.
4. Reheat before serving. Serve with Fluffy Rice.

INDIAN FISH DINNER

Save this dish for friends who like exotic food. Serve with cooked rice, chutney, and pickled lime slices.

BENGAL POACHED HADDOCK   *Serves 6.*

1 quart buttermilk	1 tablespoon cumin seeds
1 tablespoon lemon juice	¼ cup chopped green pepper
1½ teaspoons salt	2 teaspoons turmeric
¾ teaspoon Tabasco	3 pounds haddock

¼ cup butter

1. In large skillet combine buttermilk, lemon juice, salt and Tabasco. Bring to a boil and simmer for 10 minutes. Add cumin seeds and green pepper.
2. Sprinkle turmeric over fish fillets and rub in gently. Add fish to liquid in skillet and simmer for 10 to 12 minutes.
3. If necessary, reheat and, just before serving, melt butter, letting it brown slightly. Stir into liquid in skillet.

Serve fish and liquid over hot Fluffy Rice.

OSSO BUCO
Serves 4 to 6.

. . . from the city of Milan, Italy, is surprisingly easy to make and will win you plaudits as a cook of excellence. Like most stews, it improves by being made in advance and reheated before serving. Serve with beer or ale.

2 whole veal shanks
½ cup flour
2 teaspoons salt
¼ teaspoon pepper
¼ cup olive oil
1 onion, finely chopped
1 bay leaf
Pinch of rosemary

Pinch of sage
1 small carrot, grated
2 stalks celery, diced
1 bottle or can (12 ounces) beer or ale
1 can (1 pound 3 ounces) tomatoes
1 clove minced garlic
2 tablespoons minced parsley
1 teaspoon grated lemon rind

Few drops Tabasco

1. Ask your butcher to select the meaty part of 2 foreleg shin-bones of young veal and saw each into 3 pieces about 3 inches thick with their surrounding layer of meat, each forming a kind of circular steak with marrow in the center of the bone.
2. Roll meat in flour mixed with half the salt and the pepper. Brown them in a heavy pot with the olive oil, turning to brown on all sides. Then set bones upright to hold in the marrow.
3. Add onion, bay leaf, rosemary, sage, carrot, and celery. Cover and cook over low heat for 10 minutes.
4. Add beer and tomatoes and bring to a simmer. Cover and cook very slowly for 1½ hours.
5. Reheat and 2 minutes before serving add the garlic, parsley, lemon rind and Tabasco.

OTHER COMPANY DISHES

RINGS, PIES, LOAVES

. . . are economical but attractive dishes to set before guests. They may all be made well in advance.

TABASCO BEEF RING
Serves 4 to 6.

2 pounds ground beef
1 cup prepared stuffing mix
¼ cup milk

2 eggs
1 medium onion, minced
2 teaspoons salt

1¼ teaspoons Tabasco

1. Combine all ingredients. Pack into a greased 9-inch ring mold and bake in a preheated 350° F. oven for 35 to 40 minutes.
2. Carefully remove meat from mold to serving platter and fill center with fluffy mashed potatoes. Garnish with cooked vegetables.

APPLE-BEEF MEAT RING   *Serves 8.*

¾ cup chopped onion   ½ teaspoon basil
¼ cup butter or margarine   1 teaspoon salt
1 egg, beaten   2 cups canned apple sauce
1 cup seasoned dry bread crumbs   2 pounds ground chuck
½ teaspoon oregano   ¼ cup sherry

Green Bean Succotash

1. Saute onion in butter until delicately browned.
2. Combine egg, seasoned crumbs, oregano, basil, salt, and apple sauce. Add meat and onion and mix thoroughly.
3. Pack mixture into a greased 9-inch ring mold.
4. Bake in a preheated 375° F. oven for 30 minutes.
5. Spoon sherry over meat and bake for 30 minutes longer.
6. To serve: Have green bean succotash hot over simmering water. Remove meat from ring to platter and pour Succotash in center as in photograph on page 170.

GREEN BEAN SUCCOTASH

Cook 1 package (9 ounce) quick frozen Frenched green beans and 1 package (10 ounce) quick frozen whole kernel corn. Drain. Add ¼ cup butter, 1 tablespoon sugar, ½ teaspoon salt and a dash pepper. Mix well.

SHEPHERD'S PIE   *Serves 6.*

¾ cup grated Cheddar cheese   2 tablespoons salad oil
3 cups cooked mashed potatoes   2 cups well-seasoned gravy
2 packages (10 ounces each) frozen   ¾ cup drained cooked small onions
   California Brussels sprouts   1 cup drained cooked sliced carrots
2 cups diced cooked lamb   ¼ cup canned pimiento strips
1 tablespoon flour   Salt and pepper to taste.

1. Combine cheese and potatoes.
2. Cook Brussels sprouts according to package directions.
3. Coat lamb with flour and brown lightly in the salad oil. Add gravy, sprouts, onions, carrots, pimiento, and salt and pepper and heat, stirring, until well mixed.
4. Turn mixture into a buttered 2½-quart casserole and top with a ring of potatoes. Cover with aluminum foil until ready to bake.
5. Bake in a preheated 350° F. oven for 30 minutes, or until hot and potatoes are lightly browned.

GLAZED MEAT LOAF
Serves 6.

1½ pounds ground beef
¾ cup ginger snap cooky crumbs
½ cup minced onion
2 eggs

⅔ cup (small can) undiluted
  evaporated milk
1½ teaspoons salt
½ teaspoon cinnamon

Peach Glaze

1. Combine beef, crumbs, onion, eggs, milk and seasoning. Turn into a greased 1½-quart loaf pan. Bake in a preheated 350° F. oven for 1 hour. Drain off drippings and cook for 5 minutes longer.
2. Carefully unmold and spread Peach Glaze over top. Garnish with sliced peaches and parsley.

PEACH GLAZE
Mix ½ cup peach preserves and ¼ cup water in saucepan. Cook and heat over low heat until thick and smooth.

LAMB KIDNEYS WITH ROSEMARY
Serves 6 to 8.

1 cup butter
½ pound mushrooms, sliced
1 large onion, sliced
1 clove garlic minced
¼ teaspoon salt
⅛ teaspoon pepper

12 lamb kidneys, split and
  trimmed
1 tablespoon crushed
  rosemary
3 tablespoons lemon juice
Parsley Rice Ring

1. In large skillet melt butter. Add mushrooms and cook for 5 minutes, or until mushrooms are tender. Remove from skillet and keep warm.
2. To hot butter remaining in skillet, add onion, garlic, salt and pepper. Cook over low heat until onion is lightly browned. Remove onion and keep warm.
3. Add kidneys to hot skillet and sprinkle with rosemary. Cook over high heat for 7 to 9 minutes, or until kidneys are tender but still pink in center, turning frequently.
4. Return mushrooms and onion to skillet, sprinkle with lemon juice and cook for 5 minutes longer.
5. Arrange kidneys, mushrooms and onion in center of Parsley Rice Ring as in photograph on page 203.
in photograph on page 203.
Serve the butter sauce from skillet separately.

CREAMED EGGS IN CORNED BEEF CRUST   *Serves 4 to 6.*

1 can (12 ounces) corned beef
1 slice white bread, crumbed
1 egg, lightly beaten
6 hard-cooked eggs, sliced

1 can (10¾ ounces) mushroom soup
¼ cup milk or cream
1 can (3 ounces) whole mushrooms
1 teaspoon Worcestershire sauce

1. Flake corned beef with a fork. Add bread crumbs and egg and mix well. Press mixture into bottom and on sides of an 8-inch pie plate.
2. Combine soup, milk or cream, mushrooms and Worcestershire sauce and heat over simmering water.
3. 15 minutes before serving, bake "pie crust" in a preheated 350° F. oven for 15 minutes. Reserve a few egg slices for garnish and add remaining eggs to the hot mushrooms and sauce.
4. Remove pie from oven, pour hot creamed eggs and mushrooms into it, and garnish with reserved egg slices and parsley. Serve immediately.
   See photograph on page 204.

SEAFOOD LOAF   *Serves 6 to 8.*

4 eggs
½ cup sliced stuffed olives
2 tablespoons grated onion
2 cups (2 cans 6½ to 7 ounces each)
   drained flaked tuna
1 cup soft bread crumbs

1 tablespoon salt
3 quarts boiling water
2 cups elbow macaroni
   (8 ounces)
2½ cups 3-Minute Cheese Sauce
¼ cup melted butter

1. Beat eggs lightly. Add olives, onion, tuna and bread crumbs.
2. Add salt to rapidly boiling water. Gradually add macaroni so that the water continues to boil. Cook uncovered, stirring occasionally for 12 to 15 minutes, or until macaroni is tender. Drain.
3. Combine egg mixture, macaroni, cheese sauce and butter.
4. Line bottom of 9 x 5 x 3 inch pan with aluminum foil. Butter foil well. Turn mixture into pan and bake in a preheated 350° F. oven for 1 hour 15 minutes. Serve warm or cold.
   See photograph on page 238.

3-MINUTE CHEESE SAUCE

Simmer 1⅔ cups (large can) undiluted evaporated milk with ½ teaspoon salt, 1 teaspoon dry mustard and 1 tablespoon prepared horseradish to just below boiling for 2 minutes. Add 2 cups (about 8 ounces) grated processed American cheese. Stir over low heat until cheese melts, about 1 minute longer.

SALMON MACARONI MOUSSE
Serves 6 to 8.

1 cup elbow macaroni
3 cups milk
½ cup (1 stick) butter
  or margarine
1 1-pound can salmon
6 eggs

1 4-ounce can pimiento, drained
  and chopped
2 tablespoons chopped green onions
2 cups soft bread crumbs
2 teaspoons salt
Dash cayenne pepper

1 cup grated American cheese

1. Cook macaroni according to package directions. Drain and rinse.
2. In a small saucepan combine milk, butter, and the liquid from the can of salmon. Heat until mixture is hot and butter is melted.
3. Beat eggs until light and beat in hot butter-milk mixture. Add pimiento, macaroni, onion, bread crumbs, salt and cayenne.
4. Flake salmon, add, and mix lightly.
5. Line a large loaf pan (11½ x 4½ x 2¾ inches) with aluminum foil; oil foil. Turn salmon mixture into the prepared pan and sprinkle with grated cheese.
6. Bake in a preheated 350° F. oven for 50 to 60 minutes. Turn out onto serving platter.
7. Serve hot or cold, with a mushroom or lemon sauce.

BARBECUED CHICKEN WITH PINEAPPLE
Serves 4.

And one recipe for the man-of-the-house, who likes to officiate at the grill.

2 broiling chickens
1 lemon
Salt, pepper, paprika
½ cup salad oil or melted butter

½ cup dry white wine
Fresh or dried herbs
1 (8½ ounce) can pineapple slices
Butter, curry powder

1. Have chickens split, and quartered if large. Brush all over with cut lemon. Sprinkle with salt, pepper, and paprika.
2. Mix oil and wine.
3. Snip in 1 to 3 teaspoons fresh chives, parsley, thyme, rosemary, or tarragon (use ½ as much dried ones). Pour over chicken and let stand several hours, turning occasionally.
4. Starting with cut side, barbecue slowly over charcoal or very low heat in oven broiler until browned and tender, 35 to 45 minutes. Turn and brush with marinade often.
5. Just before serving, brush pineapple with butter and sprinkle with curry powder. Grill or saute until tinged with brown. Serve hot with the chickens.

CREAMED DISHES

. . . can be made in advance. Keep them hot over simmering water. Here is one that is fit for a king.

SHRIMP A LA KING   *Serves 6.*

1½ pounds shrimp   3 cups milk
¼ cup butter or margarine   1 pimiento, cut into strips
½ green pepper, cut into strips   1 teaspoon Worcestershire sauce
¼ pound mushrooms, sliced   1 tablespoon sherry or to taste.
¼ cup flour   Salt and pepper to taste

1. Shell and devein shrimp. Cook in boiling salted water to cover for 3 minutes, until shrimp are pink. Drain.
2. In saucepan melt butter and in it cook green pepper and mushrooms until vegetables are tender. Remove from heat. Add flour and stir until smooth. Return to heat. Gradually stir in milk and cook stirring until sauce is smooth and thick. Remove from heat and stir in pimiento, Worcestershire sauce, sherry, salt and pepper, and shrimp.
3. To serve, reheat and cook over simmering water for 5 minutes.

There are other recipes for creamed dishes on page 191.

SALAD AND CHEESE

"If you can toss a salad without spilling it out of the bowl, you'll have a happy marriage," is an old French proverb. The French serve their salad as a separate course after the entree, and usually with cheese such as Brie, Port du Salut, or Bleu. Or the cheese is served after the salad with a bowl of fresh fruit. Their dressing for the lettuce is three or four parts olive oil to one part vinegar, salt, freshly ground pepper, and a sprinkling of fresh or dried tarragon.

LETTUCE WITH TARRAGON FRENCH DRESSING   *Serves 6.*

1 medium head western iceberg lettuce   ½ teaspoon salt
1 clove garlic, split   ¼ teaspoon freshly ground
¼ cup olive or salad oil   pepper
1 tablespoon wine vinegar   1 to 2 teaspoons fresh tarragon
                                            or ½ teaspoon dried tarragon

1. Core lettuce; wash in cold water and drain well. Place in plastic bag and refrigerate.
2. Rub wooden salad bowl with garlic. Add oil, vinegar, salt, pepper, and tarragon to bowl and let stand for one hour or longer at room temperature.
3. To serve: tear lettuce into bowl and toss to coat with dressing.

MOLDED SALADS

You'll want to use your pretty gift molds for salads as well as for desserts. This one is attractively garnished with cucumber slices, radish roses and tender stalks of celery.

COTTAGE CHEESE VINAIGRETTE MOLD Serves 4 to 6.

1 envelope plain gelatin	¼ cup green pepper strips
1 cup milk	¼ cup thin radish slices
⅔ cup French dressing	¼ cup shredded raw carrot
1 12-ounce carton cottage cheese	¼ cup minced cucumber
¼ cup chopped celery	2 tablespoons minced onion

1. Soften gelatin in ¼ cup of the cold milk. Heat remaining milk to lukewarm. Dissolve gelatin over hot water in saucepan, add to warm milk and stir until gelatin is thoroughly dissolved. Stir in French dressing and cottage cheese.
2. Cool mixture until it starts to thicken. Fold in vegetables and pour into an oiled 1-quart ring mold. Chill until firm.
3. Unmold on crisp lettuce and garnish attractively. Serve plain or with salad dressing.

COMPANY DESSERTS

. . . . as easy as applesauce

Someone once remarked that the most valuable ingredient in a dish is imagination. That's why the cherry in the center of the grapefruit, the chopped parsley over buttered vegetables, the sprigs of dark green watercress in a salad, are important. They are the touch of color and glamor that makes the food look more interesting, more inviting, and more appetizing.

These little touches call forth the creative talent with which so many women are handsomely endowed, and it is this creative satisfaction which makes the preparation of food for the table one of the real pleasures in life. Even slices of plain white bread take on an air when arranged in an attractive formation on a pretty plate. The simplest casserole, salad, or dessert becomes important when you add a little imagination.

Take apple sauce, for instance.

Apple sauce in cans or jars is found on most pantry shelves, with good reason. Everybody likes it. It's a good everyday family dessert, a flavorful topping for puddings and cakes, and, with a little flourish, becomes an exciting finale to a company meal.

Place a big bowl of icy cold apple sauce on the table. Now circle the big bowl with a series of smaller ones, each containing a different topping, and invite everyone to choose his own—and not just one topping—but several.

Here are some suggestions for toppings:

Salted almonds

Toasted coconut

Candied cherries

Candied mixed peels

Fresh berries

Chopped dried apricots or dates

Mixed light and dark raisins

Crumbled peppermint candy

Whipped or sour cream

Chocolate bits

Marshmallow cream

Currant jelly

SUNSHINE APPLE SAUCE

Blend canned apple sauce with orange juice and sugar to taste. Spoon into goblets or dessert dishes and insert a few lady fingers along the side. Top with whipped or sour cream and sprinkle with grated orange rind.

LIME APPLE TARTS

Make tart shells from a pastry mix and bake until lightly browned. Flavor canned apple sauce with lime juice and sugar to taste and tint it a delicate shade of green with a few drops of green food coloring. Spoon sauce into the tart shells and garnish each with a slice of banana.

NO-BAKE ORANGE CHEESE CAKE   *Serves 8.*

1 package (3¼ ounces)
   vanilla pudding mix

2 envelopes plain gelatin

2 cups orange juice

1 cup sugar

2 eggs yolks, lightly beaten

1 cup creamed cottage cheese

½ cup instant nonfat dry milk crystals

½ cup ice water

2 tablespoons lemon juice

2 egg whites, stiffly beaten

Crumb Mixture

1. In saucepan combine pudding mix, gelatin, orange juice, half the sugar, and egg yolks. Cook over low heat, stirring constantly, until mixture thickens. Cool thoroughly.
2. Beat cottage cheese until creamy. Beat in pudding mixture.
3. Combine instant crystals and ice water in bowl and beat until soft peaks form, from 3 to 4 minutes (use electric beater). Gradually beat in remaining sugar. Fold the whipped instant crystals and the egg whites into pudding mixture.
4. Pour into spring-form pan lined with crumbs and chill for about 3 hours, or until set.
5. To serve: Remove sides of spring form pan and garnish cake with additional crumbs, if desired, and with orange sections and maraschino cherry slices. See photograph on page 271.

CRUMB MIXTURE

Blend ½ cup fine graham cracker crumbs with 1 tablespoon sugar and 1 tablespoon melted butter. Line bottom of 8-inch spring-form pan with waxed paper or aluminum foil. Press crumbs over bottom of pan.

ELECTRIC BLENDER CHEESECAKE

Crumb Crust
2 eggs
½ cup sugar

2 teaspoons vanilla
1½ cups sour cream
1 pound soft cream cheese

2 tablespoons melted butter

1. Line an 8-inch layer cake pan with seasoned crumbs.
2. Into container of the electric blender put eggs, sugar, vanilla, and sour cream. Cover and blend on high speed for 15 seconds. With motor on, gradually add the cheese and melted butter.
3. Pour into prepared pan and bake in a preheated 325° F. oven for 30 to 40 minutes, or until set in center. The filling will be soft, but it will firm as the cake cools. Chill before serving.

CRUMB CRUST

16 graham cracker squares
½ cup sugar

½ teaspoon cinnamon
¼ cup melted butter

1. Break 5 graham crackers at a time into blender container. Cover and blend on high speed for 5 seconds. Empty crumbs into bowl and repeat until all crackers are crumbed. Add sugar, cinnamon, and melted butter. Mix and press crumbs into buttered pie plate or layer cake pan.

CITRUS MARASCHINO MOLD   *Serves 6.*

3 envelopes plain gelatin
½ cup cold water
¾ cup strained orange juice
20 red maraschino cherries, quartered
1 can (11 ounces) mandarin oranges, drained

½ cup small seedless grapes
⅓ cup sugar
⅓ cup grapefruit juice
⅓ cup lemon juice
⅓ cup orange juice
¼ cup lime juice
Additional cherries and grapes

1. Soften 1 envelope of the gelatin in cold water. Add strained orange juice and stir over low heat until gelatin is dissolved. Cool. Pour half into a 6¾ inch plain charlotte mold. Chill until set. Reserve remaining orange gelatin at room temperature.
2. Lightly mark gelatin layer into quarters with toothpick. Arrange cherries in two opposite quarters, mandarin oranges in third and grapes in fourth. Carefully pour remaining orange gelatin over fruit and chill untill set.
3. Meanwhile combine remaining gelatin with sugar and fruit juices. Stir over low heat until gelatin is dissolved. Chill until nearly set. Turn into mixing bowl and beat with electric beater until tripled in volume and very pale in color. Spoon into mold and chill for at least 2 hours.
4. To serve: Unmold and garnish with whole cherries and grapes as in photograph on page 203.

PEARS HELENE   *Serves 6.*

6 small fresh pears   ¼ teaspoon green food coloring
1½ cups sugar   Few drops mint extract
1½ cups water   1 quart vanilla ice cream
                         Chocolate Sauce

1. Peel pears, cut in half lengthwise, and core.
2. Combine sugar, water, and green color in saucepan. Bring to a boil, stirring until sugar is dissolved. Add pears and cook gently for 5 to 8 minutes.
   Transfer fruit to refrigerator dish. Stir mint extract into syrup and pour
   over pears. Chill.
3. To serve: drain pears and arrange 2 halves with ice cream in each large
   serving dish. Pour warm or chilled chocolate sauce over ice cream and fruit.

CHOCOLATE SAUCE   *Makes 1½ cups*

In saucepan heat ½ cup each light corn syrup and sugar with 2 tablespoons
water and a dash of salt, stirring constantly until sugar is dissolved. Bring to a
boil and boil for 3 minutes. Remove from heat. Add 2 squares (2 ounces) semi-
sweet chocolate and stir until melted. Stir in ½ cup light cream, 1 tablespoon
butter, and 1 teaspoon vanilla and beat with a rotary beater until sauce is
smooth.

ALMOND CHERRIES JUBILEE   *Serves 6.*

If you received a handsome chafing dish for a wedding present, now is the time
to put it to good use. Make the cherry almond sauce right at the table to spoon
over cold ice cream. Or make it in advance if you wish and keep it hot in a casserole set over a candle warmer.

½ cup slivered almonds   1½ teaspoons cornstarch
2 tablespoons butter   ¼ teaspoon almond extract
1 1-pound can bing or red pitted   2 tablespoons kirsch or brandy
   dessert cherries   1 quart vanilla ice cream

1. Saute almonds in butter until a light golden color. Set aside.
2. Drain juice from cherries into chafing dish or saucepan and stir in cornstarch. Bring to a boil, stirring, and cook until sauce is thickened and clear.
3. Add cherries and almonds and heat.
4. Stir in almond extract.
5. Pour kirsch or cognac over cherries and ignite. Let flame burn out, then
   spoon the hot cherries and almonds over vanilla ice cream.

ORANGE PUMPKIN PIE
Serves 6

1 cup sugar

1½ teaspoons cinnamon

½ teaspoon ginger

½ teaspoon salt

1 tablespoon grated orange rind

2 eggs

1½ cups canned pumpkin

1⅔ cups (large can) undiluted evaporated milk

9-inch unbaked pie shell

1. Combine sugar, spices, salt, and orange rind. Stir in eggs, pumpkin, and evaporated milk.
2. Pour into pie shell. Bake in a preheated 425° F. oven for 15 minutes; reduce oven temperature to 350° F. and continue to bake for 40 minutes longer. Cool.

   To serve: Top with Orange Whipped Topping and garnish with orange half-slices, if desired.

ORANGE WHIPPED TOPPING
Makes 2 cups

Chill ⅔ cup (small can) undiluted evaporated milk in refrigerator tray until soft ice crystals form around edges of tray (15 to 20 minutes). Whip until stiff (about 1 minute). Add 2 tablespoons lemon juice; whip until very stiff (about 2 minutes longer). Beat in ¼ cup sugar and 1 teaspoon grated orange rind.

FRESH CRANBERRY TARTS
Makes 8 tarts.

1 package instant pie crust mix

1 package (3½ ounces) vanilla pudding filling

½ teaspoon almond extract

½ cup sugar

½ cup water

1 cup fresh cranberries

1 teaspoon grated orange rind

1. Prepare pie crust, following package directions. Shape into 8 tart shells. Bake.
2. Prepare vanilla pudding, following package directions. Add almond extract. Cook, then chill.
3. Boil sugar and water together for 5 minutes. Add cranberries and boil, without stirring, until all the skins pop open, about 5 minutes. Add orange rind. Cool.
4. Just before serving, spoon pudding into tart shells. Top with cranberry mixture. See photograph on page 170.

   Serve with whipped cream if desired.

HOMEMADE ICE CREAM

When a guest remarks, "how delicious, you made it yourself!", don't let on how easy it is to make ice cream in a refrigerator tray!

VANILLA GELATO   *Serves 8.*

2 envelopes plain gelatin	1 quart whole milk
1/2 cup cold water	1 cup sugar
2 cups instant nofat dry milk crystals	2 teaspoons vanilla

1. Add gelatin to cold water and let soften for 5 minutes.
2. Stir instant crystals into whole milk, then stir in softened gelatin and sugar. Cook over low heat, stirring constantly, until gelatin is thoroughly dissolved. Cool. Stir in vanilla.
3. Turn into refrigerator trays and freeze until firm.
4. Remove from tray and beat until smooth.
   To serve as in photograph opposite, pipe the gelato through a large fluted pastry tube into pretty glasses.

RASPBERRY MARBLE GELATO

Sieve 2 packages (10 ounces each) defrosted red raspberries. Ripple through or serve over the gelato.

FRENCH CHOCOLATE ICE CREAM   *Serve 6*

1/4 cup sugar	3 egg yolks
1/2 cup water	1 1/2 cups heavy cream, whipped
1 6-ounce package semisweet chocolate pieces	

1. In a small saucepan combine sugar and water. Bring to a boil and boil rapidly for 3 minutes.
2. Into container of an electric blender put chocolate pieces and the hot syrup. Cover and blend on high speed for 6 seconds or until smooth.
3. Add egg yolks, cover, and blend for 5 seconds, stopping to stir down if necessary.
4. Fold chocolate mixture into whipped cream, spoon into refrigerator tray and freeze for 2 to 3 hours, or until frozen. This ice cream remains creamy without stirring.

PINEAPPLE MAGIC   *Serves 4.*

Into container of the electric blender put 2 cans frozen pineapple chunks. Cover and blend on high speed to the consistency of a smooth creamy sherbet, stopping to stir down if necessary. Serve immediately, garnished with a sprig of mint.

CRANBERRY ICE CREAM   *Serves 6.*

¼ cup butter, at room temperature

¾ cup sugar

1 teaspoon grated lemon rind

2 eggs, at room temperature

1 can (7 ounces) whole cranberry sauce

½ cup ice water

½ cup instant nonfat dry milk
      crystals

1 tablespoon lemon juice

1. In an electric beater, cream butter, sugar, and lemon rind until mixture is light and fluffy. Add eggs, one at a time, beating well after each addition. Beat at high speed for 5 minutes.
2. Stir in cranberry sauce.
3. In bowl, mix ice water and instant crystals. Whip for 3 to 4 minutes, or until soft peaks form. Add lemon juice and continue whipping until stiff peaks form. Fold into cranberry mixture and freeze until firm.

FROZEN RASPBERRY CREAM   *Serves 4.*

⅔ cup (1 small can) evaporated milk

1 thin slice lemon

1 package frozen raspberries, cut into 16 pieces

1. Put all ingredients into container of an electric blender. Cover and blend on high speed for 30 seconds, or until mixture is smooth. Pour into ice cube tray and freeze until firm.

The Bride and Groom at Home

ORMAL PARTIES are practically out-moded. The modern trend is toward
informal gatherings, where host and hostess have as much fun as anybody else. Afternoon tea or coffee parties, buffet suppers, after-dinner
come-for-dessert-and-coffee parties are all increasing in popularity as economical, relaxing ways of enjoying your friends. But for newlyweds, faced with the
problem of how to entertain many in their new home, the easiest way to say
hello to everyone at once is by means of a cocktail party. In the long run,
chances are it's the least expensive way to extend hospitality to that overwhelming list of "guests we want to invite."

THE COCKTAIL PARTY

The simplest way to invite people is by telephone and, in terms of etiquette,
is perfectly correct. It gives you an immediate tally of the number of guests to
expect without waiting for a mailed reply. However, if you prefer, you can send
attractive cocktail party invitations and disregard the RSVP in your advanced
planning. You'll need to have more refreshments than you are likely to use,
anyhow and, one good thing about alcoholic beverages—they keep!

No special decorations are needed for a cocktail party. Just have a few fresh
flowers in the right places and some big containers of green leaves or some
potted plants. And do be sure to put many extra ash trays around in every
conceivable place. Small cocktail napkins should be in good supply, too. These
can be placed at strategic spots around the room.

If you have no home bar, set up a sturdy table in a spot away from the most
heavily trafficked area of the room, but leave plenty of surrounding room for

access to the table. Set up the bar with everything you anticipate needing, including a bottle opener and such garnishes as cocktail onions, tiny olives, lemon peel, and sliced fruit. If you don't have enough glasses, your friends will be more than glad to supplement your supply or, for a very large affair, you may want to enlist the aid of a party rental service. This is well worth the small rental charge, for the glasses are picked up the next day—unwashed!

Be sure to have plenty of liquor, ginger ale, club soda, and tonic on hand, and you should make arrangements for supplementary ice as you will, undoubtedly, need more than your refrigerator can make at one time.

Not everybody at a cocktail party drinks cocktails. You'll find that many of your guests will prefer scotch and soda, bourbon and water or, in warm weather, a gin or vodka and tonic; others will want their drinks "on the rocks." Martinis, Manhattans, and Old-Fashioneds seem to be the most popular cocktails, in the strict sense of the word, and the Bloody Mary has definitely come to stay. In addition to the makings of these cocktails and the longer drinks, it's a good idea to have one bottle of sherry or Dubonnet for those who prefer a fortified wine to the harder liquor, and a good host is always prepared with pitchers of cold tomato juice or orange juice, coke and other soft drinks for his abstemious friends.

Unless you plan to have the cocktail party food catered, keep it simple. You can have plenty of "nibble" food placed around the room with supplementary supplies in the kitchen. This leaves you free to circulate among your guests with only an occasional glance to see if a plate or platter needs refilling or refreshening. Don't burden yourself with having to constantly pass platters of cold canapes or rush to the kitchen to take hot ones from the oven. Bowls of salted nuts, pretzels, potato chips, popcorn, mixed olives, small pickles, crisp vegetables are more than sufficient. Remember, your guests came to see you and wish you well—not to get a free meal. If you wish, and if you have room, you can set out several attractive platters of an assortment of really good cheese and crackers.

Remember, too, your guests came to see your husband as well as you so, unless you plan to hire a professional bartender, do enlist the cooperation of your best friends. Ask a few of the men to each do "bar service" for a certain period of time. Chances are they will enjoy the opportunity to officiate without having to be the host at the party. It's much harder to be a good host than a good bartender!

Show your friendly bartenders where additional supplies are kept and advise them not to overload the drinks with liquor. Another suggestion is to use plenty of ice and serve every drink really cold. This is especially important in making a good martini. Most martini-drinkers will tolerate a variable in the accustomed quantity of vermouth, but will never forgive you for serving one that is lukewarm. Enjoy yourself, for if you are having a good time, your guests will also!

THE VERY DRY MARTINI

Fill a pitcher with ice cubes. Pour gin and dry or French vermouth over the cubes in the proportion of one part vermouth to six of gin. Stir until the pitcher frosts, then pour into martini glasses. Serve with a twist of lemon peel or a cocktail olive. If a tiny pickled onion is used, the cocktail becomes a Gibson.

THE DRY MANHATTAN

This is made in the same way as the martini above, except you use four or five parts rye or bourbon to one part of Italian vermouth. Some people like a dash of Angostura bitters, but don't add this unless a guest requests it. Serve very cold with a twist of lemon peel or a maraschino cherry.

THE OLD FASHIONED

These drinks are made individually. In an old-fashioned glass put ½ cube of sugar, 1 teaspoon water and a dash of Angostura bitters. Mash and muddle the sugar until it is dissolved. Add 2 ice cubes, half a slice of lemon and orange and, if desired, a cherry and a stick of pineapple. Pour a jigger of rye, scotch, or bourbon over the ice.

THE BLOODY MARY

Have the tomato juice mixture in pitchers in the refrigerator. To 1 quart tomato juice add the juice of 2 lemons, 1 tablespoon Worcestershire sauce, 1 teaspoon Tabasco, salt, freshly ground black pepper, and celery salt to taste. For each drink, pour a jigger of vodka and ½ cup tomato juice mixture into a cocktail shaker over crushed ice and shake vigorously. Strain into a goblet or old-fashioned glass.

Many young couples find it more economical to offer a really good punch to the exclusion of cocktails and other mixed drinks. There is no reason in the world why you should not do this if you wish. When you issue the invitations, simply specify "party," rather than cocktail party. Make the punch table as gay and pretty as possible; have it the focal point of the room and keep the bowl full of a well-iced punch.

CHAMPAGNE TEA PUNCH   *25 servings*

1 quart freshly brewed tea
1 cup sugar
2 cups (1 pint) Cognac
½ cup light rum

1 can frozen pineapple chunks
  with liquid
2 bottles dry champagne, chilled
Mint leaves

Fresh peeled fruit, cubed, and melon balls for garnish

1. Cool tea to room temperature. Add sugar and stir until sugar is dissolved.
2. Add Cognac, rum, and pineapple chunks and chill thoroughly.
3. When ready to serve, pour the tea mixture into a punch bowl over a large chunk of ice, add champagne, and garnish with fresh fruit and mint leaves.

JAMAICA PUNCH   25 *servings*

¼ pound lump sugar   1 quart gin
Oranges   2 cups (1 pint) Jamaica rum
1 quart clear, strong tea   1 Teaspoon Angostura bitters
2 cups lemon juice   1 quart chilled ginger ale

Garnishes

1. Rub sugar lumps on rinds of oranges until they become saturated with the oil from the rind.
2. Put sugar in a punch bowl. Add cool tea and mix until sugar is dissolved.
3. Add lemon juice, gin, rum and bitters and refrigerate.
4. When ready to serve, place a large block of ice in the punch bowl, add ginger ale, and garnish with mint, cherries, and orange slices.

TEA AND COFFEE PARTIES

More suited to a gathering of women than men, the tea party, essentially an intimate affair, can be expanded into a gracious and economical way of entertaining a sizeable group. But whether the group is large or small, this is the time to polish your silver and to bring forth your best, most delicate china, your prettiest table linens.

THE INTIMATE TEA PARTY

When entertaining only a few guests for tea, the tea tray with the entire tea service is brought into the living room and placed on a table or is wheeled in on the tea cart. The tea service should include a pot of freshly brewed, strong tea, a second pot of boiling hot water, the cream pitcher, sugar, and tea strainer. You will also need a small plate of very thin lemon slices for those who prefer this to milk or cream. The sugar is more convenient served in lump form, so there should be sugar tongs. The cups and saucers, with matching plates are placed on the table conveniently around the tray.

Food, as simple as very thin bread and butter or marmalade sandwiches or crisp delicate cookies are all that are needed to serve with tea. You can, if you wish, serve an assortment of crustless sandwiches, cut into different shapes, and a platter of assorted dainty cakes. Small hot baking powder biscuits with jam or honey are also delicious.

You, the hostess, pour the tea at an intimate affair and each person goes to you to collect her cup and to select the food accompaniments. Or, one of the guests may decide to serve the others, a nice custom, especially if you have a guest of honor or an older woman included in the company. It is perfectly correct for you to ask one of the guests to, "please pass this to Mrs. Helscher."

There need be nothing dull, old-fashioned, or stereotyped about the modern tea party. Serve a glass of dry sherry along with the tea, if you wish, or lace the tea with a good dollop of Jamaica rum.

THE INTIMATE COFFEE PARTY

Some young people prefer coffee to tea and lean more toward the continental coffee break in the afternoon than to the English pot of tea. Again the coffee service, complete, is brought or wheeled into the living room and again the hostess pours.

Coffee lends itself more to the service of a rich pastry or a lavishly frosted cake than to dainty sandwiches and cookies, and the more spirited accompaniment is a small glass of brandy or your favorite liqueur.

THE LARGE TEA PARTY

Both tea and coffee should be served at a more formal tea, and a large variety of small, dainty sandwiches, cookies and tea cakes are offered to the guests. Salted nuts and candies may also be added to the tea menu.

A long table should be set up at one end of a room, closest to the kitchen, and covered with a lovely linen cloth. Set a bowl of pretty flowers in the center of the table. At one end of the table the tea service will be placed, and the coffee service will be set at the opposite end. Cups and saucers should be placed conveniently around the tea and coffee trays, and plates should be stacked on the table with a dainty napkin on each, so that guests may help themselves to the array of cakes and sandwiches.

At formal teas it is customary to ask good friends if they will pour the tea and the coffee, leaving you free to circulate among your guests and be the charming hostess. The "pouring" is considered an honor. Guests return to the table to have their cup replenished as they wish it.

TEA FARE

CUCUMBER SANDWICHES

Butter thin slices of bread and cut into rounds with a biscuit cutter. Top each with a thin slice of cucumber, spread with mayonnaise, and cover with another round of bread.

SAVORY TEA SANDWICHES

Mix soft butter with anchovy paste or deviled ham, or with lemon juice and finely minced water cress. Butter thin slices of bread with the savory butter, and put two slices together. Trim crusts and cut into finger-size shapes.

WATER CRESS OR ASPARAGUS ROLLS

Roll trimmed bread with a rolling pin to flatten. Spread with mayonnaise mixed with a little mustard. Place a tender stalk of cooked asparagus, trimmed to length, or a spray of water cress on each slice and roll up. Fasten with a toothpick and place rolls in a pan. Cover with a damp towel and chill for 3 hours. Remove toothpicks before serving.

CRAB MEAT SANDWICHES

Flake and chop 1 can King Alaska Crab Meat. Beat in ½ cup butter, 1 teaspoon lemon juice, and salt and pepper to taste. Spread between thinly sliced bread, trim, and cut into squares.

AVOCADO AND CHIVE SANDWICHES

Peel and remove seed from a ripe avocado. Mash with a silver fork and mix in 2 tablespoons chopped chives, 2 teaspoons lemon juice, and salt and pepper to taste. Spread thin slices of whole wheat bread with the mixture. Cover with a thin slice of white bread, trim, and cut into rectangles.

CHICKEN HAM SANDWICHES

Mix ½ cup cooked ground chicken with 2 tablespoons ground boiled ham. Stir in 2 tablespoons finely chopped almonds and 1 tablespoon crushed pineapple. Add enough mayonnaise to moisten and mix to spreading consistency. Spread lightly buttered bread with the mixture. Cover with another slice, trim, and cut into fingers.

TEA BISCUITS

Use standard recipe for biscuits. Roll dough ¼ inch thick and cut into small rounds. Spread half the rounds with softened butter and cover with remaining rounds. Bake in a preheated 450° F. oven for 10 to 12 minutes.

BUTTERMILK TEA BISCUITS   *Makes 2 dozen.*

Use standard recipe for biscuits, substituting buttermilk for regular milk. Roll dough ½ inch thick. Cut out biscuits 1½ inches in diameter with floured cutter. Brush tops lightly with milk. Bake in preheated 450° F. oven for 10 to 15 minutes, or until biscuits are golden. Serve with Lemon Curd as in photograph on page 169.

LEMON CURD   *Makes about 3 cups.*

4 eggs	¼ cup soft butter
Pinch of salt	½ cup lemon juice
2 cups sugar	2 tablespoons grated lemon rind

1. Beat eggs. Add salt. Stir in sugar, butter, lemon juice and rind.
2. Cook over simmering water for 30 minutes or until thick and smooth, stirring occasionally. Cool. Store in refrigerator.

FRUIT BISCUITS

Use standard recipe for biscuits, adding ½ cup chopped raisins or dates to the flour-shortening mixture before adding the milk.

BUFFET PARTIES

Serving a meal buffet-style is usually the most practical and enjoyable way to serve guests numbering more than half a dozen. It is by no means restricted to dinner parties, but can be applied as successfully to party breakfasts, lunches and suppers.

The one key rule is, *don't extend yourself beyond your physical limits in either menu or number of guests.* Fit your buffet to your house, your kitchen and serving facilities, and your pocket book. Plan a menu which both you and your guests can manage with ease, and don't invite more people than you can accommodate either at individual tables or at card tables set up around the room. Don't expect guests to eat from their laps: Balancing a plate precariously requires so much concentration that both conversation and the enjoyment of food are bound to suffer.

As in the giving of any successful party, careful planning to every detail of preparation, decoration, table accessories, and service are important. The end of the party must run as smoothly and neatly as the beginning.

Set up your buffet table in the most convenient place in the room, the closer to the kitchen the better, but leave plenty of room for the guests to move freely. The food, silver, and napkins should be arranged in the order they are needed, and every serving piece should be placed beside each dish on the table; the carving set beside the baked ham or roast.

Fine silver, china, linens, and beautiful serving dishes are all at home on the buffet table. Equally at home are such accessories as wooden bowls and trays, raffia baskets, and colorful pottery. Just don't mix them. Coordinate your accessories, centerpiece, and colors as you would your new spring or fall suit. Use plenty of electric buffet servers, candle warmers, hot plates, or alcohol burners to keep hot foods hot, and cold foods are always more appetizing and attractive if they are set into a container of crushed ice.

If you are serving wine or beer or another beverage with the meal, you may set this up, with appropriate glasses, on a side table apart from the buffet table or at the extreme end of the buffet table, if it is large enough to accommodate the beverage without crowding.

Don't forget the salt and pepper shakers, and there should be a pitcher of ice water available for those who might like a sip between courses.

Dessert should not be on the table with the main part of the meal. It can be set up on a separate table or on the main buffet, after the main course is finished, but not until every last dish of food, every plate and serving piece have been cleared away. Your guests don't mind waiting, so take time to tidy up, dump ash trays, stack dishes. And, of course, you will have planned a special place to store the used dishes!

THE BUFFET HAM   *Serves 12.*

There's nothing quite as handsome as a beautifully glazed ham on the buffet table. It's practical, too, for it goes a long way, yet there are endless dishes that can be made from the leftover meat. Even the bone adds flavor to a pot of bean or lentil soup.

1 14-pound pre-cooked ham	¼ cup sweet pickle liquid
1 cup firmly-packed brown sugar	Lemon slices and cloves
¼ cup prepared mustard	Fresh cucumber pickle slices

1. Score fat on the ham with a sharp knife. Put ham in a shallow roasting pan and bake in a preheated 325° F. oven for 2 hours.
2. Drain drippings from roasting pan.
3. Combine brown sugar, mustard and pickle liquid in saucepan. Cook and stir over low heat until smooth. Spread over ham. Bake ham for ½ to 1 hour longer, basting occasionally, until browned and glazed.
4. Serve hot or warm garnished with lemon and cucumber pickle slices studded with cloves.

BRUSSELS SPROUTS SOUTHERN STYLE   *Serves 12.*

4 packages (10 ounces each) frozen California Brussels sprouts	2 cups cooked small onions
½ cup melted butter	1 teaspoon celery salt
	½ teaspoon salt

½ teaspoon pepper

1. Cook Brussels sprouts according to package directions. Drain and combine with remaining ingredients.
2. Mix well and cook over low heat, stirring occasionally, for 5 minutes.

PINEAPPLE PECAN LOUISIANA YAMS   *Serves 12.*

4 cans (1 pound each) Louisiana yams	1 teaspoon salt
2 cans (9 ounces each) crushed pineapple	½ teaspoon ginger
1 cup chopped pecans	Pecan halves for garnish

1. Cook yams over low heat to serving temperature. Drain and mash.
2. Mix yams with undrained pineapple, chopped pecans, salt and ginger and keep hot over simmering water until ready to serve.
3. Serve hot garnished with pecan halves.

This luscious dessert is called No Bake Orange Cheesecake. The recipe is on page 256.

Flemish Lamb Stew is another perfect buffet dish. Beer is a good beverage to serve, for the stew has beer as an ingredient.

LAMB A LA FLAMANDE
Serves 6.

2 pounds lamb shoulder, cut in
   1½ inch cubes
2 tablespoons flour
1½ teaspoons salt
¼ teaspoon pepper
¼ cup salad oil
2 medium onions, sliced

1 cup sliced green onions,
   or scallions
1 clove garlic
1 bottle (12 ounces) beer or ale
1 tablespoon chopped parsley
1 bay leaf
¼ teaspoon thyme

1 package (10 ounces) frozen cut beans, thawed

1. Dredge lamb with flour mixed with salt and pepper.
2. In heavy saucepan or casserole brown the meat well in the salad oil over high heat.
3. Reduce heat to low. Add onions, scallions, and garlic, and cook until onions take on a little color. Add beer, parsley, bay leaf, and thyme. Cover tightly and simmer for 1½ hours, or until meat is tender.
4. Add beans and cook for 10 minutes longer.
5. Serve with cooked buttered noodles.

HOT CORNED BEEF TEMPTERS
Makes 6 dozen.

2 cans (12 ounces each) corned beef,
   unchilled
1 medium onion, finely chopped
1 tablespoon minced parsley
½ cup butter, melted
1 cup all-purpose flour
1 teaspoon dry mustard

1 teaspoon salt
1 cup milk
1 can (1 pound) sauerkraut,
   drained
2 eggs
¼ cup water
Fine dry bread crumbs

1. Flake corned beef and mix with onion. Cook with parsley in butter for 5 minutes. Stir in flour, mustard, and salt. Gradually add milk and cook, stirring constantly, until thickened.
2. Chop kraut finely and add to meat mixture. Mix thoroughly and cool.
3. Shape into ½-inch balls. Chill.
4. Beat eggs with water. Dip balls into egg mixture and roll in bread crumbs.
5. Fry in hot deep fat (375° F.) for about 2 minutes, or until golden.

Note: These may be fried in advance and reheated in a 325° F. oven. Spread them on cookie sheets, lined with paper toweling to drain.
To serve: Pile them in an attractive bowl and spear with amusing cocktail picks.

The photograph shows you just how tempting these Hot Corned Beef Tempters really are.

Top-of-the-stove or oven casseroles are the best possible choice for the buffet table, and many rich stews, sautees, or ragouts of international fame are not only popular but can set the stage for the buffet colors and decorations. *Paella* is an outstanding casserole dish from Spain.

PAELLA VALENCIANA   *Serves 6.*

½ pound pork shoulder,
  cut into 2-inch cubes
3-pound broiler-fryer chicken,
  cut into serving pieces
¼ cup olive or salad oil
2 teaspoons salt
2 cloves garlic, halved
1½ cups uncooked rice
1 large onion, chopped
½ teaspoon saffron
2¼ cups chicken stock
1 1-pound can whole tomatoes,
  quartered

¼ teaspoon pepper
¼ teaspoon crushed tarragon
¼ teaspoon crushed oregano
¾ cup halved pimiento olives
½ pound uncooked shrimp,
  shelled and cleaned
6 Cherrystone clams
6 mussels
1 package (10 ounces) frozen
  asparagus spears
1 package (10 ounces) frozen
  artichoke hearts

1. In a Dutch oven or heavy saucepan brown pork and chicken in hot oil. Sprinkle with half the salt. Add garlic, cover and cook over low heat for 30 minutes or until meat is tender.
2. Remove meat and discard garlic.
3. Add rice and onion to drippings in pan and cook, stirring, until golden.
4. Stir saffron into a little boiling water to bring out flavor and add to chicken stock, tomatoes, remaining salt, the seasonings, and olives. Add to rice and bring to a boil.
5. Cover pan tightly, and cook over low heat for 20 minutes.
6. Gently mix in shrimp. Add clams, making sure they touch sides of pan. Top with meat, asparagus, and artichokes. Cover and cook for 10 to 15 minutes longer.

THE SMORGASBORD

Scandinavian foods, served buffet-style, are known in Sweden as *smorgasbord*, in Denmark, as *smorrebrod*, in Norway, *smorgaas,* and in Finland, *voileipoyta.* But, by any name, it's one of the most hospitable yet easily served party meals imaginable. All foods for the meal are displayed on the table at one time, including the traditional beer as a beverage, eliminating many trips to the kitchen for the host and hostess. Meat balls and shrimp are two of the favorite hot dishes on the smorgasbord, and all kinds of cold meat, fish, and salads have their rightful place on the bountiful table.

SHRIMP IN BEER   *Serves 8.*

3 pounds raw jumbo shrimp,
  fresh or frozen
2 12-ounce bottles or cans
  beer or ale
1 clove garlic
1 tablespoon salt
1 teaspoon thyme

2 bay leaves
2 tablespoons celery seeds
2 tablespoons chopped
  parsley or dill
¼ teaspoon Tabasco
Juice of ½ lemon
Melted butter

1. Wash shrimp. Remove legs but not the shells. Split down back and remove black vein from each.
2. Put beer and seasonings in large saucepan. Bring mixture to a boil. Add shrimp. Return to boil, reduce heat, and simmer not more than 5 minutes.
4. Serve hot with melted butter or cold with a tangy salad dressing.

SWEDISH MEATBALLS   *About 4 dozen small meatballs.*

¾ pound ground beef
½ pound ground veal
1 egg, lightly beaten
½ cup bottled or canned beer or ale
1½ cups soft bread crumbs

2 tablespoons minced onion
4 tablespoons butter
1 teaspoon salt
⅛ teaspoon pepper
¼ teaspoon nutmeg

⅛ teaspoon allspice

1. Have meat ground twice.
2. Combine egg and beer and pour over crumbs. Let stand 10 minutes.
3. Simmer onion in 1 tablespoon of the butter until tender, but not brown.
4. Combine meat, softened bread crumbs, onion and seasonings and mix well. Shape into 1-inch balls and roll in flour.
5. In skillet melt remaining butter and in it brown meatballs on all sides, shaking pan frequently to keep balls round.
6. To make gravy: Remove meatballs from skillet and keep warm. Pour off all but 2 tablespoons of the fat. Stir in 2 tablespoons flour and cook over low heat until flour is browned. Gradually stir in 1 cup milk (or part milk and part cream), and cook, stirring constantly, until gravy thickens and comes to a boil. Flavor to taste with salt, pepper, and nutmeg.

SWEDISH VEGETABLE SALAD   *Serves 8.*

2 cups finely shredded cabbage
2 cups finely shredded carrot
2 cups thin cucumber strips

1½ cups thinly sliced radishes
Salad greens
¾ cup French dressing

1. Crisp vegetables in bowls of salted ice water. When firm and crisp drain well.
2. Arrange vegetables in mounds on greens in deep salad bowl to make a pleasant contrast of colors. Chill well.
3. Pour French dressing over salad just before serving.

DANISH MEAT SALAD   *Serves 8.*

3 cups cubed cooked beef or veal
¾ cup diced green pepper
5 large stuffed olives, sliced
10 pickled onions, chopped
⅛ teaspoon pepper
½ teaspoon salt or to taste

¼ teaspoon dry mustard
1 tablespoon minced fresh dill or
 1 teaspoon dill weed
½ cup mayonnaise
¼ cup beer or ale
1 tablespoon lemon juice

1. Combine meat, green pepper, olives and onions. Chill.
2. Make dressing by combining pepper, salt, mustard, and dill with mayonnaise. Stir in beer and lemon juice.
3. Mix dressing and meat mixture and toss lightly. Chill for at least 1 hour. Garnish with onions and olive slices.

NORWEGIAN FISH PUDDING   *Serves 8.*

1 pound raw fish fillet, cut into chunks
1 cup milk
2 tablespoons corn starch

2 eggs
¼ teaspoon nutmeg
½ cup milk

1 cup heavy cream

1. Into container of an electric blender put fish, the 1 cup milk, corn starch, eggs, and nutmeg. Cover and blend on high speed for 2 minutes. Remove cover and, with motor on, pour in about ½ cup milk, or enough to fill jar three-quarters full. Then pour in the cream. Turn off motor immediately.
2. Pour mixture into a buttered quart mold, set mold in pan containing about 1 inch warm water, and bake in a preheated 325° F. oven for 1 hour, or until pudding is set in center.
3. Serve in mold, or turn out and garnish with cooked shrimp. Serve with Sour-Cream-Dill sauce.

SOUR-CREAM DILL-SAUCE   *Makes 1 cup.*

Into container of an electric blender put 1 cup commercial sour cream and 1 small bunch fresh dill with stems, coarsely cut. Cover and blend on high speed for 20 seconds. Heat until lukewarm over hot water. Do not let boil. To serve cold, chill. The sauce will set in a few minutes. If desired, parsley clusters may be added along with the dill.

A PERFECT FINALE

A cup of strong fragrant coffee, a dessert of fresh fruit and tangy cheese—what could be a more fitting climax to any festive meal. Coffee, of course, has a natural affinity for brandy. Serve it in sparkling snifters, to be sipped slowly along with the hot coffee. An exciting dimension to an evening has been added.

AFTER-DINNER DEMITASSE, American Style
This is simply regular coffee brewed in your customary way, but half again as strong as you usually make it.
To make 8 demitasse servings, use the following ratio of coffee to water:
3 measuring cups of fresh, cold water
6 Standard Coffee Measures of coffee, or 12 level measuring tablespoons.

Cream is never used in demitasse coffee, but sugar is. If you prefer lump sugar, make it the tiny dot size, and for a bit of color and extra flavor, add a small twist of lemon peel.

AFTER DINNER CHEESE
Any of the blue-veined cheeses, soft ripening, semi-soft, or firm cheeses go well with fruit. Try to find a store in your vicinity which specializes in fine cheese—not necessarily imported, for there are some fine aged American cheeses, and discover a whole new world of good eating.

DESSERT AND COFFEE

In recent years, a most delightful way to entertain has gained rapidly in popularity. It's the "Come for Dessert and Coffee," invitation. Perhaps the refreshments are to be served preceding or climaxing an evening of bridge, or an evening devoted to conversation and music or, perhaps, color slides or a movie of your honeymoon. No matter what, under the warming influence of a fragrant cup of coffee and the bride's very special dessert, conversation sparkles, good cheer bubbles, and the evening is bound to be a success.

The coffee-dessert idea is an economical way to enjoy the company of your friends; it's a charming custom which can be repeated frequently without having the food budget burst at the seams. It gives time for a family meal without pressure and you, your husband, and your guests can enjoy the post-prandial refreshments in a relaxed atmosphere.

The formula for a successful dessert-and-coffee party is superb coffee, double strength, hot and abundant, and a luscious homemade dessert. There's no end to the wide variety of pastries, tortes, souffles, Bavarians, and cakes that fall into the category of special desserts. If you prefer to be strictly continental, you might present a selection of excellent cheese, premium fruits, and Italian coffee. Instant Italian coffee can be excellent and often better than most homemakers can brew from the ground bean. The secret is to make it by the potful and let it steep for a few minutes before serving. For best results be sure to use the correct measurements of coffee and water recommended on the jar.

CAKES

High on the list of most popular desserts are cakes with scrumptious frosting. Here, from General Foods Kitchens, are six rules for cake baking that every bride should know.

1. Choose a recipe that has been tried and proven by experts.
2. Use only the finest ingredients, the freshest eggs, butter and milk and cake flour for the finest cakes.
3. Measure ingredients exactly—just as specified in the recipe. Scoop dry ingredients lightly into a measuring cup until heaping full, then level off by drawing knife or spatula across the top. Always use a glass measuring cup for liquids.
4. Pan sizes are very important—all batters cannot be baked in all ways, so be sure to use size specified in recipe. Measurement usually is stamped on back of pan. For best results fill pans only half full. Shiny metal pans are a good choice since they heat quickly yet reflect the heat so that resulting cakes are delicately browned.
5. A well regulated oven is a good friend, and a necessary one. Higher or lower heat than recommended in the recipe can do strange and unappealing things to a cake.
6. When you have mastered your favorite cake recipe, cherish it, and use it again and again with different flavorings and frostings to get the variety you desire.

HAPPY DAY CAKE

2½ cups sifted cake flour
3 teaspoons double-acting
  baking powder
1 teaspoon salt
1½ cups sugar

½ cup shortening
  (at room temperature)
1 cup milk
1 teaspoon vanilla
2 eggs

1. Sift together flour, baking powder, salt, and sugar.
2. Stir shortening just to soften. Stir in dry ingredients.
3. Add ¾ cup of the milk and the vanilla and mix until all flour is dampened. Then beat 2 minutes at a medium speed of electric mixer or 300 vigorous strokes by hand. Add eggs and remaining milk and beat 1 minute longer in mixer or 150 strokes by hand.
4. Pour batter into two round 9-inch or three round 8-inch layer pans which have been lined on bottoms with paper.
5. Bake in a preheated 350° F. oven for 25 to 30 minutes, or until cake tests done when tested with a wooden pick.

CHOCOLATE AND CREAM LAYER CAKE

2⅓ cups sifted cake flour
1½ cups sugar
1 teaspoon soda
½ teaspoon double-acting
  baking powder
½ teaspoon salt
⅔ cup butter

1 cup buttermilk*
1 teaspoon vanilla
1 package (4 ounces) sweet cooking
  chocolate, melted and cooled
2 eggs, unbeaten
Sweet Chocolate Hungarian Frosting
1 cup heavy cream, whipped

1⅓ cups flaked coconut

* 1 cup minus 1 tablespoon regular milk soured with 1 tablespoon vinegar may be used in place of the buttermilk

1. Measure sifted flour into sifter; add sugar, soda, baking powder, and salt.
2. Stir butter just to soften. Sift in dry ingredients. Add ¾ cup of the buttermilk and the vanilla. Mix until all flour is dampened. Then beat 2 minutes at medium speed of electric mixer or 300 vigorous strokes by hand.
3. Add chocolate, eggs, and remaining ¼ cup buttermilk. Beat 1 minute longer with electric beater or 150 strokes by hand.
4. Pour batter into two 9-inch layer pans which have been lined on bottoms with paper. Bake in a preheated 350° F. oven for about 35 minutes, or until cake springs back when lightly pressed in center. Cool.
5. Spread half the frosting between the cake layers. Frost top of cake with remainder, spreading to within ½ inch of the edge. Spread whipped cream generously around sides and over ½ edge on top of cake. Sprinkle with flaked coconut.

SWEET CHOCOLATE HUNGARIAN FROSTING

1 package (4 ounces) sweet cooking chocolate
¾ cup (unsifted) confectioners' sugar
2 tablespoons hot water

1 egg yolk
2 tablespoons butter
½ teaspoon vanilla

1. Melt chocolate over hot water. Remove from heat. Add sugar, salt, and hot water. Blend well.
2. Add egg yolk and beat well.
3. Add butter, 1 tablespoon at a time, beating throughly after each. Stir in vanilla.

FLUFFY PEPPERMINT FROSTING

Cream 6 tablespoons butter until soft. Add ¼ teaspoon salt. Add 1 pound (about 4 cups) sifted confectioners' sugar alternately with 2 unbeaten egg whites, beating well after each addition. Add about 1 tablespoon milk and ½ teaspoon peppermint extract and beat well. If desired tint a delicate green with food coloring. Makes enough to frost top and sides of two 9-inch layers.

STRAWBERRY BAKED ALASKA

Serves 12 to 16.

1 package (17 ounce) sponge
cake mix

1 cup (½ pint) whipping cream,
whipped

2 cups sliced strawberries or 1 package
(1 pound) frozen strawberries

2 tablespoons sugar (omit if frozen
berries are used)

1 quart vanilla ice cream

4 egg whites

¼ teaspoon salt

¼ teaspoon cream of tartar

¾ cup sugar

1. Prepare sponge cake mix as directed on package. Pour into ungreased sponge or angel food cake loaf pan (15½ x 4¼ x 4½ inches.) Bake in a preheated 350° F. oven for 30 to 35 minutes, or until cake tests done when tested with a wooden pick. Invert, cool thoroughly, and remove from pan.

2. Cut a ¾-inch slice from top of loaf. Cut center from cake, leaving sides and bottom about ½-inch thick.

3. Blend together whipped cream, strawberries and sugar (if fresh berries are used). Spread a layer of the cream in bottom of cavity. Fill cavity with alternate spoonfuls of ice cream and whipped cream mixture. Cover with cake top. Place on foil on baking sheet in freezer until completely frozen. Leave whole or cut in half, as desired.

4. Just before serving beat egg whites, salt, and cream of tartar until eggs hold soft peaks. Add sugar gradually and continue beating until mixture is stiff and glossy. Spread top and sides of loaf or loaves completely and thickly with the meringue.

5. Bake in a preheated 450° F. oven for about 5 minutes, or until meringue is lightly browned.

6. Garnish with strawberries, if desired. Serve immediately with Strawberry-Rhubarb sauce.

STRAWBERRY RHUBARB SAUCE

Makes 2½ to 3 cups.

2 cups diced rhubarb (½ pound) or
1 package (1 pound) frozen
rhubarb

1 tablespoon water (omit if frozen
rhubarb is used)

2 cups sliced strawberries or
1 package (1 pound) frozen
strawberries

1 cup sugar (reduce to ¼ cup
if frozen fruit is used)

1. Put rhubarb and water (if used) in covered saucepan and cook for about 5 minutes, or until rhubarb is tender.

2. Add strawberries and sugar and simmer just until berries are tender.

3. Chill thoroughly.

FAMILY TWO-EGG CAKE

1¾ cups sifted cake flour

2¼ teaspoons double-acting
baking powder

½ teaspoon salt

½ cup shortening

1 cup plus 2 tablespoons sugar

2 eggs, unbeaten

¾ cup milk

1 teaspoon vanilla

1. Sift together flour, baking powder, and salt.
2. Cream shortening. Gradually add sugar, and cream together until light and fluffy.
3. Add eggs, one at a time, beating well after each.
4. Add flour mixture, alternately with milk, beating after each addition until smooth. Stir in vanilla.
5. Pour batter into two round 8-inch layer pans which have been lined on bottom with paper.
6. Bake in a preheated 375° F. oven for 25 to 30 minutes, or until cake tested done when tested with a wooden pick.

FUDGE FROSTING

In a saucepan combine 3 cups sugar, 1 cup water, 2 tablespoons corn syrup, 2 tablespoons butter, and 4 squares (ounces) unsweetened chocolate. Stir until ingredients are mixed, cover, and bring to a boil. Uncover and cook without stirring to the soft-ball stage (234° F.) Remove from heat and let stand until cool. Add 1½ teaspoons vanilla and beat until frosting is thick enough to hold its shape. If frosting becomes too thick to spread, stir in a little cream; if too thin to spread, stir in about ½ cup sifted confectioners' sugar.

COCOA FROSTING

Blend ½ cup soft butter, ½ cup cocoa, ¼ teaspoon salt, and 1 teaspoon vanilla. Stir in 4 cups sifted confectioners' sugar alternately with 4 to 6 tablespoons hot milk and beat until frosting is smooth and creamy.

TORTES LOOK LUSCIOUS AND LAVISH

GRAHAM HIGH TORTE   *Serves 12.*

1⅔ cup graham cracker crumbs

1 cup chopped walnuts

1 teaspoon cinnamon

½ teaspoon salt

½ teaspoon ginger

¼ teaspoon allspice

½ teaspoon baking powder

½ cup butter or margarine

¼ cup sugar

4 eggs, separated

½ cup milk

1. Combine crumbs, nuts, spices, and baking powder.
2. Cream shortening and gradually add sugar, beating until light and fluffy. Add egg yolks and mix thoroughly.
3. Add dry ingredients alternately with the milk, beating well after each addition.
4. Beat egg whites until stiff, but not dry and fold into batter.
5. Spoon batter into four 8-inch layer pans, lined with greased waxed paper. Bake in a preheated 325° F. oven for 20 minutes. Cool, then remove from pans to finish cooling on wire racks.

FILLING

2 cups canned apple sauce
1½ pints heavy cream, whipped
3 tablespoons confectioners' sugar
Shaved sweet chocolate
Maraschino cherry

1. Place one cake layer on plate and spread with apple sauce. Place second layer on cake, spread with whipped cream. Spread second layer with apple sauce and top with remaining layer.
2. Decorate outside rim of cake with whipped cream using a pastry bag fitted with a small fluted tube. Make decoration in center of cake. Place cherry on top and sprinkle with shaved chocolate pieces. Refrigerate until serving time.

Here is a dessert that is fun to make as well as eat.

MERINGUE LOW TORTE   *Serves 10 to 12.*

5 egg whites
1 cup granulated sugar
⅔ cup graham cracker crumbs
⅓ cup chopped blanched almonds
½ cup shaved sweet cooking chocolate
4 cups canned apple sauce
2 1¾ ounce jars cinnamon drops
Vanilla ice cream

1. Beat egg whites until frothy. Gradually beat in sugar and continue to beat until meringue is stiff and glossy. Fold in crumbs, almonds and chocolate.
2. On large cookie sheet place a sheet of brown paper. Draw a large apple approximately 10″ in diameter with a stem. Spoon meringue mixture into outline and spread to the edges. Make stem.
3. Bake in a preheated 275° F. oven for 1 hour. Turn off oven and let meringue cool in the oven away from drafts.
4. Melt cinnamon candies with apple sauce until blended. Chill.
5. To serve: place meringue on large tray. Spoon apple sauce over surface and place large spoonfuls of vanilla ice cream over all.

PRUNE TORTE   *Serves 10.*

½ cup butter
½ cup light brown sugar
1 cup sifted flour
½ cup chopped nuts
4 egg whites
Pinch of salt

½ tablespoon lemon juice
¼ cup plus 2 tablespoons sugar
½ cup plumped, pitted, chopped prunes
1 cup heavy cream, whipped
10 plumped pitted prunes
3 maraschino cherries

Chopped nuts

1. Cream together butter and brown sugar. Add flour and mix thoroughly. Stir in nuts.
2. Pat dough into bottom of a 9-inch cake pan lined with heavy duty aluminum foil. Bake in a preheated 350° F. oven for 20 minutes.
3. Combine egg whites, salt, and lemon juice and beat until stiff. Gradually beat in sugar and beat until meringue is stiff and glossy. Fold in chopped prunes. Spread over dough in pan and bake in a 300° F. oven for 1 hour. Cool.
4. Spread top of torte with whipped cream and garnish with prunes, maraschino cherries, and chopped nuts.

COFFEE COCONUT PRUNE PIE   *Serves 6.*

1 cup chopped plumped prunes
⅓ cup prune juice
2 tablespoons grated orange rind
3 eggs
½ cup light brown sugar
¼ cup granulated sugar

⅓ teaspoon salt
1 envelope unflavored gelatin
1 cup sour cream
Coffee Coconut Pie Shell
½ cup heavy cream, whipped
6 plumped prune halves

Maraschino cherries

1. In saucepan combine chopped prunes, prune juice, and orange rind.
2. Beat eggs with the sugars, salt, gelatin, and sour cream and add to prunes. Cook over medium heat about 10 minutes, stirring constantly, until thickened. Do not let mixture boil. Cool slightly.
3. Pour into Coffee Coconut Pie Shell and chill until firm.
4. To serve: Garnish with whipped cream, prune halves, and cherries.

COFFEE COCONUT PIE SHELL

Combine 1 3½-ounce can flaked coconut and 1 cup very strong coffee. Let stand for 30 minutes. Drain and spread coconut on paper toweling. Pat to absorb excess liquid. Spread a 9-inch pie plate with 2 tablespoons soft butter. Sprinkle in coconut and pat against bottom and sides of plate. Bake in a preheated 350° F. oven for about 10 minutes, or until coconut is tinged with brown.

CREAMS AND CUSTARDS

Creamy desserts, rich and luscious, smooth puddings, and frozen souffles all have their place in the entertainment dessert world.

ORANGE BLOSSOM BOWL   *Serves 8.*

1 pint heavy cream
2 tablespoons honey
1 Florida orange, sectioned*

6 tablespoons (½ 6-ounce can) frozen Florida orange juice concentrate, thawed, undiluted

1. In large bowl combine heavy cream and honey. With rotary beater or electric mixer, beat until consistency of whipped cream.
2. Fold in orange juice concentrate.
3. Split ladyfingers and line bottom and sides of a glass serving dish. Pour cream mixture into dish and chill for at least 4 hours before serving. Garnish with orange sections.

* To section oranges: Cut slice from top of orange, then cut off peel in strips from top to bottom, cutting deep enough to remove white membrane. Then cut slice from bottom. Go over fruit again, removing any remaining white membrane from outside to middle of core. Remove section by section, over bowl to retain juice from fruit.

WHIPPED PUDDING WITH STRAWBERRIES   *Serves 6 to 8.*

1 package (3¼ ounces) vanilla pudding and pie filling mix
1 tablespoon (1 envelope) gelatin
⅛ teaspoon nutmeg
1⅔ cups (large can) undiluted evaporated milk

1 cup water
2 tablespoons lemon juice
½ teaspoon vanilla
1 cup fresh strawberries, sliced
1 cup angel food cake squares

1. Combine pudding, gelatin, nutmeg, 1 cup of the undiluted evaporated milk, and the water in a saucepan. Cook and stir over medium heat until mixture comes to a boil. Cover and chill until pudding mounds from spoon.
2. Chill remaining ⅔ cup evaporated milk in refrigerator tray until soft ice crystals form around edges (10 to 15 minutes). Whip until stiff (about 1 minute). Add lemon juice and vanilla and continue to whip for about 2 minutes, or until very stiff.
3. Beat pudding until smooth. Fold in sliced strawberries and whipped milk.
4. Layer pudding and cake in a 1½ quart mold or bowl and chill for about 2 hours, or until firm.
5. Unmold and garnish with whole strawberries and whipped topping.

STRAWBERRY SOUFFLE
Serves 10 to 12.

4 teaspoons plain gelatin

¼ cup cold water

1 package (1 pound) quick-frozen strawberry halves, thawed

4 eggs, separated

2 tablespoons lemon juice

⅛ teaspoon salt

1 teaspoon almond extract

½ cup sugar

1 cup whipping cream

1. Sprinkle gelatin over cold water and let stand to soften.
2. Drain strawberries, measuring juice. Pour ¾ cup of the juice into top of double saucepan. Beat egg yolks slightly and stir into juice. Add gelatin. Place over simmering water and cook, stirring constantly, until gelatin is dissolved, about 5 minutes. Remove from heat. Stir in lemon juice, salt, and almond extract. Chill until mixture is the consistency of unbeaten egg whites.
3. Press strawberries through a fine sieve or blend in electric blender. Add to any remaining strawberry juice, then stir into gelatin mixture, blending well.
4. Beat egg whites until foamy. Gradually add sugar and continue beating until mixture will hold stiff peaks. Beat gelatin mixture with rotary beater until smooth. Carefully fold into beaten egg whites.
5. Whip the cream and fold into gelatin mixture.
6. Fasten a strip of waxed paper on the outside top edge of a 1½-quart souffle or other serving dish, making a collar. Pour in cream mixture. Chill for at least 4 hours, or until set.
7. To serve: Remove collar and garnish with dollops of whipped cream.

EGG NOG MOLD WITH PEACHES
Serves 8.

1½ cups prepared egg nog

1 envelope unflavored gelatin

¼ cup malted milk powder

1 teaspoon vanilla

2½ cups whipped instant nonfat dry milk crystals

2 packages (10 ounces each) frozen sliced peaches, thawed

1. Combine egg nog, gelatin, and malted milk powder in saucepan. Stir over low heat until gelatin dissolves. Chill until slightly thickened, about 30 minutes. Stir in vanilla.
2. Fold in whipped instant crystals and turn mixture into an 8-cup mold. Chill for about 2 hours, or until firm.
3. To serve: Unmold and garnish with some of the peaches. Serve with remaining peaches and their syrup.

TO WHIP INSTANT NONFAT MILK CRYSTALS
Makes about 2½ cups.

1. Mix ½ cup instant nonfat dry milk crystals with ½ cup ice water in bowl.
2. Whip until soft peaks form (3 to 4 minutes). Add 2 tablespoons lemon juice.
3. Continue whipping until stiff peaks form (3 to 4 minutes longer).
4. Gradually beat in ¼ cup sugar.

MOCHA BRAZIL NUT ICE CREAM   *Serves 8.*

1 envelope plain gelatin
¼ cup cold water
1 cup strong hot coffee
1 square unsweetened chocolate, melted
¾ cup light brown sugar

¼ teaspoon salt
1 teaspoon vanilla
1 tall can evaporated milk
1½ cups heavy cream
¾ cup chopped roasted Brazil nuts

1. Soften gelatin in cold water. Add to hot coffee and stir until gelatin is thoroughly dissolved. Slowly stir into the melted chocolate and stir until smooth.
2. Add brown sugar and salt and stir until sugar is dissolved. Cool.
3. Add vanilla, evaporated milk, and cream. Mix well.
4. Pour into refrigerator freezing trays and freeze to a stiff mush. Stir in Brazil nuts and freeze until firm.
5. If desired, garnish with unsalted Brazil nut chips.

STRAWBERRIES IN THE SNOW   *Serves 6.*

2 cups milk
1 tablespoon sugar
1 teaspoon vanilla
4 eggs, separated

Few grains salt
⅔ cup superfine sugar
1 pint fresh strawberries or 1 package frozen whole strawberries

1. In shallow saucepan combine milk and sugar. Stir over low heat until sugar dissolves and bring to scalding point. Add vanilla.
2. Beat egg whites to a froth. Add salt and beat until stiff. Add superfine sugar, a little at a time, beating constantly until meringue is stiff and glossy.
3. Shape meringue with a dessert spoon to resemble eggs and drop into scalded milk mixture. After 2 minutes cooking on one side, turn carefully and let cook for 2 minutes longer. Remove with perforated spoon to foil-lined tray.
4. Beat egg yolks with a little of the warm milk. Stir into remaining milk and cook, stirring, over low heat until mixture coats the spoon. Chill.
5. To serve: Spoon custard sauce into individual serving dishes. Top with meringue "eggs" and garnish with whole strawberries.

A delicious sauce over vanilla ice cream is a simple, yet sophisticated dessert which appeals to everyone. The following recipe for Grecian Orange Sauce makes approximately one quart of sauce, but it keeps for a long time in the refrigerator.

GRECIAN ORANGE SAUCE   *Makes 1 quart.*

6 Florida oranges
Water

3 cups sugar
¼ cup currant jelly

1. Wash oranges. Remove thin orange-colored rind with a vegetable peeler and cut into thin slivers. Put peel in saucepan with 2 cups water. Bring to a boil and boil for 15 minutes. Drain.
2. Cut away all white membrane from oranges and cut oranges into eighths over a bowl to save the juice. Measure juice and add water to make a total of 1 cup liquid.
3. In saucepan combine liquid with sugar and currant jelly. Stir, bring to a boil, and cook for 25 minutes. Add cooked peel and continue to cook to the soft ball stage (230° F. on candy thermometer), about 15 minutes.
4. Remove from heat and add orange eighths. Cover and store in refrigerator for at least 8 hours before serving.

HOLIDAY NOGS AND PUNCHES

The holiday season is a time for open house, for parties of all kinds from special breakfasts and brunches to holiday buffets, tree-trimming punch parties, or New Year's nog parties around a roaring fire. It's time to throw open homes and hearts to your friends.

COFFEE PUNCH
Makes 24 4-ounce servings.

6 tablespoons instant coffee
⅔ cup sugar
2 tablespoons sherry

3 quarts cold milk
Whipped cream
Nutmeg

1. In a bowl or electric beater bowl combine instant coffee, sugar, sherry, and 3 cups of the cold water. Beat with a rotary beater or at high speed for 30 seconds.
2. Pour into punch bowl along with remaining milk and mix well.
3. Top with a float of whipped cream and sprinkle with nutmeg.

MOCHA MILK PUNCH
Serves 6.

2 quarts reliquefied instant nonfat dry milk crystals (see package directions)
3 squares (1 ounce each) unsweetened chocolate

3 tablespoons instant coffee
¾ cup sugar
¼ teaspoon maple extract
1½ cups heavy cream, whipped
Cinnamon

1. Combine reliquefied instant crystals, chocolate, coffee, and sugar in large saucepan. Heat, stirring constantly, until chocolate is melted. Add maple extract and beat well. Stir in half the whipped cream.
2. Pour into punch bowl, top with remaining whipped cream, and sprinkle with cinnamon.

MILK PUNCH
In a large pitcher mix 1 quart cold milk and ¼ to ½ cup each of Jamaica rum and brandy. Stir and serve.

MULLED WINE
Serves 12.

In saucepan combine 1 quart Madeira, port or sherry, the peel of 1 lemon and 1 orange, 1 whole nutmeg, a 3 inch stick cinnamom and 6 whole cloves. Heat to serving temperature, but do not let boil. Strain out spices and serve in cups.

TOM AND JERRY
Serves 12.

12 eggs, separated
½ pound sugar
1 tablespoon ground allspice

1 tablespoon cinnamon
1 tablespoon clove
4 ounces Jamaica rum

Bourbon

1. Beat egg yolks until frothy, add sugar and continue to beat until mixture is thick and pale in color. Beat in spices and gradually stir in rum.
2. Beat egg whites until stiff and fold into yolk mixture. Store in a large bowl.
3. To serve: Put a ladleful of the egg mixture in a large mug, add 2 ounces bourbon, and fill mug with boiling water. Stir vigorously until the drink foams. If desired, dust with freshly ground nutmeg and float 1 teaspoon Cognac on top.

KENTUCKY EGG NOG
Serves 24.

12 eggs, separated
2 pounds sugar
1 quart bourbon

1 pint Jamaica rum
1 pint Cognac
1 pint milk

3 pints heavy cream

1. Beat egg yolks until frothy, add sugar and continue to beat until mixture is thick and pale in color.
2. Very slow pour in bourbon and rum, stirring constantly.
3. Stir in milk and cream, then the cognac.
4. Beat egg whites until stiff and fold into nog mixture.

HOT BUTTERED RUM
Pour a jigger of Jamaica rum into an old-fashioned glass. Add 2 teaspoons sugar and 2 teaspoons soft butter. Fill the glass with boiling water and stir well.

HOT GROG
Serves 1.
In highball glass combine 1 jigger Jamaica rum, 1 teaspoon sugar syrup, and 1 tablespoon lemon juice. Fill glass with boiling water or hot tea.

GLOGG
Serves 12.
Heat 1 quart Cognac until quite hot, but not boiling. Pour into silver bowl over ½ cup sugar, 1 dozen cloves, a 2-inch stick cinnamon, ½ cup raisins and ½ cup blanched almonds. Ignite Cognac and let flame burn out. Stir in 1 pint sherry and serve while still hot.

ENGLISH CHRISTMAS CUP   *Serves 42.*

4 cups instant nonfat dry milk
   crystals
2 cups chocolate syrup

3 quarts coffee
2 eggs, lightly beaten
2 tablespoons vanilla

1½ cups heavy cream, whipped

1. Stir instant crystals and chocolate syrup into coffee in saucepan. Heat to just below boiling.
2. Gradually stir about 1 cup hot mixture into beaten eggs, then stir into remaining hot mixture. Cook and stir for about 3 minutes, without letting mixture boil.
3. Remove from heat and stir in vanilla.
4. Fold in half the whipped cream.
5. Pour into punch bowl and top with remaining whipped cream as in photograph.

Your holiday party is complete when you bring in the old favorite, a luscious fruit cake.

NO-BAKE DATE-NUT FRUIT CAKE

48 marshmallows (¾ pound)
¾ cup undiluted evaporated milk
⅓ cup apple juice
4¾ cups crushed vanilla wafers

2½ cups crushed gingersnaps
1 cup chopped walnuts
1 cup candied lemon peel
1 cup chopped pitted dates

1 cup halved candied cherries

1. Cut marshmallows into quarters. Pour milk and apple juice over marshmallows and let stand 3 hours, stirring occasionally.
2. Combine crushed wafers, gingersnaps, walnuts, lemon peel, dates and cherries in a large bowl. Add marshmallow mixture and mix well.
3. Pack into a foil-lined 9 x 5 x 3 inch pan. Cover with foil and refrigerate several days before slicing. Serve with Fluffy Orange Sauce.

FLUFFY ORANGE SAUCE   *About 3 cups.*

Chill ½ cup undiluted evaporated milk in refrigerator tray until soft ice crystals form around edges of tray (about 10 minutes). While milk is chilling, beat 1 egg until foamy. Gradually beat in ½ cup sifted confectioners' sugar and continue to beat until mixture is thick and pale in color. Stir in 1 teaspoon vanilla, ½ teaspoon orange extract, 2 teaspoons grated orange rind, and ¼ teaspoon nutmeg. Whip chilled milk until stiff (about 1 minute). Add 1 teaspoon lemon juice and continue to whip for 1 to 2 minutes longer, or until very stiff. Gently fold beaten egg mixture into the whipped evaporated milk. Turn into serving bowl and sprinkle with chopped nuts or flaked coconut.

Index

297

Acknowledgements

We wish to express our appreciation to all the following who helped make this book possible.

The Cleanliness Bureau; American Carpet Institute; The International Silver Company; Melmac; Fostoria Glass Company; The Venetian Blind Institute; Bloomcraft Fabrics; Royal System Wall Furniture; Amtico Flooring; Potted Plant Association; Richardson/Nemschoff Furniture; Modern Bride magazine; The Window Shade Association; The Sterling Silversmiths Guild of America; Molasses; The National Dairy Council; Pacific Coast Canned Pear Service; American Brewers Foundation; The Halibut Association of North America; Carnation Company; Poultry and Egg National Board; Louisiana Yam Commission; The Florida Citrus Commission; Western Iceberg Lettuce; The Pineapple Growers Association; Tabasco; and the Spanish Green Olive Commission.

Color Photographs courtesy: The Processed Apples Institute, Inc., International Packers Limited; Carnation Company; Brussel Sprouts Marketing Program; National Macaroni Institute; International Tuna Fish Association; Spanish Green Olive Commission; Tea Council of the U.S.A.; Cherry Growers & Industries Foundation; American Lamb Council; Tom Weir, photographer; John Stewart, photographer; Avisco Rayon; Magee Carpet Company; Ernest Silva, photographer; The Corning Glass Works; and Sealy, Inc.